ROTHERHAM LIBRARY & INFORMATION SERVICES

This book must be returned by the date specified at the time of issue
as the DATE DUE FOR RETURN.
The loan may be extended (personally, by post or telephone) for a
further period if the book is not required by another reader, by quoting
the above number / author / title.

LIS7a

INCREDIBLE JOURNEYS

INCREDIBLE JOURNEYS

The stories behind 60 remarkable
adventures over land, sea and air

Thomas Cussans
foreword by Sir Chay Blyth

COLLINS & BROWN

First published in the United Kingdom in 2007 by
Collins & Brown
10 Southcombe Street
London
W14 0RA

An imprint of Anova Books Company Ltd.

Commissioning Editors: Victoria Alers-Hankey
  and Miriam Hyslop
Design Manager: Gemma Wilson
Project Manager: Chris Stone
Editorial Assistant: Tom Stainer
Designer: Tony Cohen
Senior Production Controller: Morna McPherson
Cartographer: Martin Brown

ISBN 978-1-84340-401-9

A CIP catalogue for this book is available from the British
Library.

9 8 7 6 5 4 3 2 1

Reproduction by Spectrum Colour Ltd, UK

Printed and bound by CT Printing, China

This book can be ordered direct from the publisher.
Contact the marketing department, but try your
bookshop first.

www.anovabooks.com

Contents

Foreword

Adventure is in our makeup. From Homer's Greek heroes and the Romans through the Vikings, Marco Polo, Columbus, Drake and Magellan, to the great empire builders and scientific explorers of the 17th, 18th and 19th centuries. Indeed, right up to the Wright brothers and the Himalayan expeditions of the first half of the 20th century and the exploration of space in our own time – adventure is in our DNA.

On land, on the sea and in the air someone somewhere has always striven to go further, go faster, go higher and go deeper than those who have gone before, forever pushing the boundaries of exploration, opening continents and widening the scope of human understanding. Such is the backdrop against which is played the great story of our life on earth. Tales of epic bravery and of suffering stoically borne; of triumphs and disasters; of gambles lost and won, and of friends together setting out at dawn but failing to return as the sun goes down.

Incredible Journeys is an excellent title for this collection of 'incredible' stories, each in its own way a testament to the indomitable nature of the human spirit, which as we see as we read on, is forged anew again and again in the face of seemly insurmountable odds. We learn about the aviation pioneers Wilbur and Orville Wright, Charles Lindbergh, and the quiet Australian Charles Kingsford-Smith who was the first man to fly the Pacific. We learn too about the great mountaineers, Edmund Hillary and Tensing Norgay and the man who climbed Everest without oxygen, the rugged Reinhold Messner. We can relive in the pages of this book, the exploits of adventurers like Thor Heyerdahl who skippered *Kon-Tiki* across the Pacific and into the history books; the great survivors – Jim Lovell and his crew apparently marooned in space in their crippled craft *Apollo 13* but coming safe home, and Ernest Shackleton rescued together with his crew as the Antarctic ice crushed his ship.

In these risk averse times when accountants and loss adjusters, not heroes and leaders, dictate our relationship with life – and death – this is a timely book. Few have known what it is to look into the abyss and fewer still have brought themselves to rest, if only for an instant, at that point of balance between life and death and return to tell their tale. This book is about them and I am proud to be included in their storied ranks.

And while you read, consider this. Here is detailed the adventures of the pioneers, the great explorers and adventurers, the great survivors and the great escapers whose incredible journeys to freedom should inspire us all, and yet the message is simple and universal: that without determination none of these great ventures would have succeeded.

For the incredible journeys in this book are not just about strength, the courage needed to face down physical dangers and technical skills, these are stories of journeys across some unrevealed inner landscape deep within each and every one of the people involved where fear and doubt time and time again cast whole enterprises into giant shadow. The common thread linking all is that each involved had the ability, to step always into the light. All were determined: Lindbergh to reach France, Hillary and Tensing to reach the summit of Everest, and the lads on the rugby tour to survive and come safe home.

Here are some adventures, some incredible journeys. Here is the greatness of the human spirit writ large. It is inspiring.

Sir Chay Blyth

Introduction

Great accomplishments often take a terrible toll, and the sixty incredible journeys documented in this book are no exception.

Whether it is an exploration that took place in the early 1900s or one that made the record books this year, the achievement does not come without struggle. After the sad death of expedition member Lawrence Oates, Antarctic explorer Robert Falcon Scott wrote on March 17, 1912, 'He has borne intense suffering for weeks without complaint'. Forty years later the challenges were just as extreme. Frenchman Alain Bombard, drifting across the Atlantic in a rubber dinghy – determined to prove that castaways could survive by catching fish and drinking seawater – had been reduced to a state of such despair he became convinced he would go mad. Intense fatigue caused Charles Lindbergh to hallucinate during his record-setting nonstop flight from New York to Paris in 1927, and Wiley Post, in 1933, was forced to tie a heavy tool to his hand to keep himself awake during his solo round-the-world flight.

For the first fifty years of the 20th century, it was still possible to make journeys of genuine exploration that were considered firsts, especially in aviation. And then, with the coming of the space race in the 1960s, the same was true of manned spaceflight. These were all inherently dangerous enterprises into the unknown.

After World War II a shift occurred. Challenges were now being initiated for the sheer sake of conquest. Edmund Hillary made it to the top of Everest in 1953 to fulfil a personal ambition. Later, whether sailing nonstop around the world single-handed or skateboarding across

The first man to fly solo around the world Wiley Post (far left), his navigator, Harold Gatty, and millionaire oil man F. C. Hall.

Board free Dave Cornthwaite skateboarded across Australia to raise money for charity. The 25-year-old Englishman skated from Perth to Brisbane – more than 5,800 km (3,600 miles).

Australia, the brave adventurers' goals became ever more personal.

But their trials didn't become easier. Ellen McArthur, who in 2005 set a new round-the-world single-handed sailing record, described the sleep deprivation she suffered as 'a form of torture'. More than twenty years earlier Reinhold Messner, the first man to climb Everest alone without oxygen, endured a state likened to 'death' during his ascent.

For these adventurers and others, such as Cal Rodgers, who in 1911 became the first man to fly across the United States, or Jim Shekhhdar, who in 2001 became the first man to row the Pacific single-handed, they set out with a purpose. The same cannot be said for another group of adventurers: those who in this book are called the Escapers. These were people that circumstances – usually war – forced into desperate struggles for survival. Two of these stories are particularly poignant because they concern children: Misha Defonseca, a six-year-old Jewish girl who set off to find her parents amid the barbarities of Nazi-occupied Eastern Europe, and Stephen Brookes, an English boy whose world was destroyed before his eyes when the Japanese invaded Burma. Theirs were perhaps the most incredible journeys, because they managed to survive at all.

It is impossible to produce a book such as this without being conscious of many other incredible journeys that were not included. For every story here, at least two others could have been featured. We salute all of the incredible men and women who have made these journeys across the world, over the tops of the highest mountains, to the far reaches of the universe, and into our hearts.

1

Air & Space

The first powered flight

A journey of 36 metres (120 ft) that lasted 12 seconds hardly suggests an epic feat. Yet this modest achievement marked perhaps the most momentous technical breakthrough in modern human history. It was the first sustained, controlled, powered flight by a heavier-than-air machine. And it happened due to the dogged determination of a pair of bicycle makers from Dayton, Ohio.

The first glider was flown in England, as early as 1809, by a man named Sir George Cayley. In 1842 another Englishman, William Henson, designed an 'aerial steam carriage'. Equally improbable machines followed in France, Russia, England and the United States. All were failures, aerodynamically flawed and powered by the only means of propulsion then available – steam.

The late 19th century, however, brought about two crucial breakthroughs. Starting in 1891, Otto Lilienthal, a German, built a series of gliders. Sadly, he was killed when one crashed in 1896. But by then he had not only made more than 1,000 flights, he had begun the first systematic investigation into the aerodynamic laws that govern flight. The other breakthrough was the invention of the internal combustion engine, which was lighter and more powerful than any steam equivalent.

In 1899 two American brothers, Wilbur and Orville Wright, began experiments in flight, first building a glider inspired by Lilienthal.

From bicycle makers to aviators

Sons of a Midwestern minister, neither had received more than a rudimentary education. They made their living first as printers and then as bicycle repairmen. Later they turned their attention to flying. They had two striking advantages: a willingness to take infinite pains and an instinctive understanding that any flying machine would be inherently unstable. Devising a practical means of controlling the plane was their crucial concern.

They owned a small bicycle company in Dayton, Ohio, which provided a solid, if modest, engineering background. To them bicycles suggested a parallel with

The Wright brothers Wilbur (left) and Orville – taciturn, suspicious and stubborn – made aviation history.

The most famous picture in aviation history On 17 December 1903, the Wright brothers' *Flyer* made the first powered flight at Kitty Hawk, North Carolina. Orville is at the controls, with Wilbur looking on. The brothers made four successful flights that day, the longest lasting 57 seconds.

flight. Precisely like an unpiloted airplane, a riderless bicycle will always crash. But given a rider with sufficient skills, it can easily be controlled. Was the same true of a flying machine?

In 1900, decamping for the first time to Kitty Hawk, North Carolina, chosen partly for its remoteness and partly for its reliably steady winds (which they rightly believed would generate extra lift for their machines), they conducted a series of trial glider flights. The results were discouraging.

Not only did the machines generate less lift than Lilienthal's calculations suggested, but Wilbur's attempts to control the gliders in flight were not working. To remain in the air, any flying machine has to move not just forward but also from side to side (yawing), up and down (pitching) and laterally (rolling). If the first two movements were relatively easy to achieve by means of an elevator and a rudder, the last was more problematic.

At the time, all would-be aviators assumed that a flying machine would have to be stable in flight. If the pilot wanted to change course, he would do so simply by moving the rudder while flying quite level, altering course much as a ship would. Wilbur, on the other hand, had realized that any such manoeuvre could be made only by banking, dipping one wing and raising the other. Just as a bicycle leans into a corner, so must a flying machine.

The Wright brothers hoped to achieve this by a process known as 'wing-warping' – physically distorting one wing via controlling wires to reduce the drag on it while raising the drag on the other wing. But it wasn't working. Wilbur and Orville returned to Dayton dispirited in the winter of 1901. Characteristically, they set out to solve the problem.

> ❛ Success four flights Thursday morning . . . average speed through air 31 miles longest 57 seconds inform Press home Christmas. ❜
>
> Telegram from Orville Wright to his sister, Katharine

Crucial breakthroughs

They made two discoveries. The first was that Lilienthal's apparently definitive data on aerodynamics were wrong. To test and correct the data, the brothers built a wind tunnel in which they tried a variety of wing shapes. They

Fliers or liars?

The muted reaction to the Wright brothers continued for five years. In part, this was due to their habitual secrecy. They were permanently alarmed at the thought others would steal their ideas and went to enormous lengths to protect them. But mostly the American press simply did not realize what the pair had done. By the autumn of 1905, their new plane, *Flyer III*, had made a flight of 39 minutes, covering 40 km (25 miles).

When Albert Santos-Dumont made the first flight in Europe in October 1906, it lasted 21 seconds and covered 217 metres (722 ft). Most assumed it was the first flight ever. Similar euphoria greeted the Anglo-French aviator Henri Farman in January 1908 when his *Voisin-Farman I* biplane wobbled around a 1-km (0.6-mile) course outside Paris in 1 minute, 28 seconds.

By contrast, the Wright brothers' claims (Wilbur is pictured above at the controls of a 1907 model *Flyer*) were greeted with disbelief. 'FLIERS OR LIARS?' one newspaper asked. But that summer their superiority was recognized when Wilbur sailed to France to demonstrate the *Flyer III*. The results were startling. 'Wright is a genius. He is the master of us all,' exclaimed French aviator Louis Blériot.

found that the most efficient shape – a hump toward the leading edge rather than in the middle – was critically different from Lilienthal's.

The second discovery was that wing-warping did work – if it was combined with the movement of the rudder. Hinging the rudder and coordinating it with the wing-warping did counteract the drag provided by the dipped wing. In 1902, flying their new glider at Kitty Hawk, they achieved a series of record distances. They had discovered the key to controlled flight.

Control, not power

That they were right was underlined by the failure of their most obvious rival, Samuel Langley, the most fêted scientist in America. In 1901 Langley had successfully flown a pilotless model of his radical petrol-engined flying machine. In the autumn of 1903, the real thing – the Great Aerodrome – was unveiled. It was to be launched by catapult from the roof of a specially built houseboat on the Potomac River.

It was flown twice, on both occasions plummeting directly into the water after suffering instant and catastrophic structural failures, its wings folding as though crushed by a giant. Langley's blunder was to assume that power was the key to flight. Unlike the Wrights, he seems never to have realised that structural integrity allied to control was what counted.

All that the Wrights now needed to make powered flight a reality was an engine. Their response was typical: they built one themselves. It produced no more than 12 horsepower. But with an airframe they knew would work, it was all they needed.

By early December 1903 they were back at Kitty Hawk with their new machine, optimistically named the

The Military Flyer In 1908 the US Army agreed to buy one of the Wright brothers' machines – provided it could do at least 65 km/h (40 mph) and carry one passenger. The result was the Wright Military Flyer, here flown by Orville during testing.

Flyer. On the 14th a first attempt with Wilbur at the controls ended with the machine nosedown in the sand.

On the 17th they tried again. This time Orville was the pilot. The flimsy machine trundled down its wooden guide rail. Before it reached the end, it rose into the air. It reached hardly more than 48 km/h (30 mph), and it never got more than 3 metres (10 ft) off the ground, but that it was flying was undeniable. That it was *being* flown was equally clear.

> ❛ Fifty-seven seconds? If it had been fifty-seven minutes then it might have made a news item. ❜
>
> The editor of Dayton's local paper, the *Journal*

By the end of the day, Wilbur and Orville had made three more flights. The fourth was the longest, lasting 57 seconds and covering 255 metres (852 ft).

This staggering achievement generated almost no interest. Many people flatly refused to believe the Wright brothers had flown at all. The telegram Orville sent home on the night of his and Wilbur's triumph met with almost universal derision on the part of the press. The editor of Dayton's local paper, the *Journal*, said, 'Fifty-seven seconds? If it had been fifty-seven minutes then it might have made a news item.'

The Channel conquered

LOUIS BLÉRIOT   **25 July 1909**

In time there was widespread astonishment at the extent of the Wright brothers' lead over European aviators. It was the Frenchman, Louis Blériot, however, who would become the next superstar of aviation. In July 1909 he became the first man to fly the English Channel. The Wrights may have already accomplished farther flights, but Blériot's had immense symbolic importance.

Aviation records tumbled following Wilbur Wright's triumphant demonstration of the *Flyer III* in France in 1908. Aircraft, principally the Wrights', were flying farther, faster and higher all the time. But no one had yet attempted a flight over a major body of water. However rapid the improvements to these first aircraft, they were still primitive. They had wooden frames braced by wires, stretched canvas wings and underpowered, overstressed engines.

The first fatality in powered flight occurred in September 1908 in Virginia, when a Wright *Flyer III*, piloted by Orville, suffered a propeller failure during a

Monsieur and Madame Blériot He may only have been a moderate aviator, but he made it to England. Louis Blériot, his wife and admiring crowds at Dover, 25 July 1909. In this picture his aeroplane shows few signs of the damage received upon landing.

demonstration flight for the US Army. Orville's passenger, Lt. Thomas Selfridge, was killed when the machine spun to the ground, and Orville was seriously hurt. Whatever the potential of aviation, the risks were obvious.

Northcliffe's challenge

But nothing, it seemed, could dampen the enthusiasm of flying's pioneers, particularly in France. Responding to this mounting excitement, newspaper magnate Lord Northcliffe, owner of the London *Daily Mail*, put up a £1,000 prize for the first man to fly the English Channel, 35 km (22 miles) wide at its narrowest point, between Dover and Calais.

It was clearly the next great challenge in flying. Northcliffe naturally hoped the prize would go to a Briton, while most imagined Wilbur Wright would win. Wright, more interested in selling his planes than in gratifying the whims of sensation-seeking newspapers, declined to take part. The gauntlet was picked up by three Frenchmen. They were Count Charles de Lambert, owner of two Wright Flyers; the dapper and insouciant Hubert Latham, one-time big game hunter; and Louis Blériot, whose fortune, made from selling car headlamps, was rapidly being exhausted by his passion for flying.

Over the Channel Louis Blériot in mid-Channel on his way to England and aviation immortality.

> Then I see the cliffs of Dover . . . I turn and now I am in difficulties, for the wind by the cliffs is much stronger and my speed is checked as I fight against it. My beautiful airplane responds.
>
> Louis Blériot

Following a crash, de Lambert withdrew. Latham and Blériot persisted, however. The excitement was intense, with huge crowds flocking to Calais and blanket press coverage on both sides of the Channel. The elegantly cosmopolitan Latham, flying the sleek, powerful 50-horsepower *Antoinette IV*, the future as it seemed of French aviation, was the favourite; the hangdog Blériot, far from a natural pilot and flying his barely tested, underpowered *Blériot XI*, was the outsider. Adding insult to injury, the accident-prone Blériot had badly burned his foot a few days earlier and could now only hobble around on crutches. His wife pleaded with him to abandon the flight.

Latham made the first attempt on 19 July. He managed only 11 km (7 miles) before his engine failed. He was picked up shortly afterwards, his machine placidly floating on a calm sea as he smoked a cigarette. On 25 July at 4:35 A.M., Blériot took off. The noise woke Latham, aghast that his rival had stolen a march on him. He dissolved into tears of impotent rage as Blériot crossed the French coast. (Latham in fact made a second attempt some days later: it, too, ended in engine failure.)

Flying blind

The weather was cloudy, the visibility poor. Within 10 minutes Blériot could see neither France nor England. There was also now no sign of the destroyer, *Escopette*, the French government had placed on hand to escort him.

Gamely, he plugged on, his frail craft making scarcely 64 km/h (40 mph) and flying at only 75 metres (250 ft). 'I am alone,' Blériot later reported. 'I can see nothing at all. For ten minutes, I am lost.' Tellingly, he had not so much as a compass on board. Navigation for Blériot was

True aviation pioneer

Louis Blériot (above) was an unlikely hero, looking more like a downcast village postman than a record-breaking aviator. Yet his determination to master this strange and obviously perilous new means of travel was never in doubt. By the early years of the 20th century, he was lavishing money on a variety of flying machines, most of which he tested – and crashed – himself.

If his cross-Channel flight was due as much to luck as to any innate piloting skills – even his most consistent supporters would never have placed him among the age's most natural fliers – his unshakeable conviction that aviation would transform the world was correct.

Aviation's first superstar A throng of supporters cheer the French aviator as he is driven from Victoria Station, London. Among the passengers in the car is Lord Northcliffe, who put up the £1,000 prize for the first man to fly the Channel.

a matter of pointing his machine in what he hoped was the right direction.

A curious sense of calm settled on the Frenchman. 'It is a strange position, to be alone, unguided, without a compass, in the air over the middle of the Channel.'

His fatalism was spectacularly rewarded. As the grey smudge of the English coast emerged, Blériot thought he was probably too far east. He was further encouraged to turn west by the sight of three ships steaming toward what he hoped was Dover. As he turned to follow them, the wind picked up, buffeting his machine and reducing his speed further. But his intuition was right. The imposing bulk of Dover Castle hove into view. 'A mad joy comes over me … I am over land!'

As he turned inland, he saw a French journalist, Charles Fontaine, waving a tricoleur and crying out, 'Bravo! Bravo!' Coming into land, his plane was caught in a sudden gust, causing it to spin around. 'At the risk of smashing everything, I cut the ignition at 20 metres. Now it was up to luck. The landing gear took it rather badly, the propeller was damaged, but my word, so what? I had crossed the Channel!' The flight had taken 36 minutes.

It was a measure of the genuine novelty of his exploit that customs in Dover, not knowing how to deal with the Frenchman, decided that his machine could officially be recorded only as a yacht, with Blériot its skipper.

> **At the risk of smashing everything, I cut the ignition at 20 metres. Now it was up to luck.**
> Louis Blériot

Gold medal aviator

His fame was instantaneous. Huge crowds turned out in London, even larger ones in Paris. The French Aéro-Club presented him with its gold medal. More than 100 orders flooded in for his machines. As important, a further surge of interest in aviation was sparked across the Continent. Less than a month later the world's first air show was held at Rheims in northern France. Thirty-eight fliers took part, Blériot among them.

Blériot's achievement was more than just a triumphant demonstration of the new reach of flight. It was a tangible sign that aviation was poised to revolutionize world transport. Flying was coming of age.

The first flight across the United States

CAL RODGERS   17 September–10 December 1911

Cal Rodgers – a heroic pioneer of American aviation – was a catastrophic pilot. In 1911 the 1.9-metre (6-ft 4-inch) Rodgers set out to win a $50,000 prize to become the first flier to cross the United States in less than 30 days. Numerous crashes and several broken bones later he made it. But it took him 84 days.

Calbraith (Cal) Rodgers came from one of the most distinguished military and naval families in America. But largely deaf from a childhood sickness, he was unable to take up a military career. Instead, his adult life was spent in pursuit of adventure – gold prospecting in Africa and racing cars and motor-bikes in America. In 1911, at the age of 31, he visited the Wright brothers' factory in Dayton. There, Cal had found his true métier: aviation.

On 5 June he started flying lessons. Within less than a fortnight he had bought his own Wright machine. By early August, awarded his pilot's licence, he took part in an air show at Chicago. It was here he decided to compete for a prize of $50,000, offered the previous year by William Randolph Hearst, to anyone who could cross America by plane in under 30 days.

Drink to success

By early September he had secured a sponsorship deal with the Armor Meat-Packing Company of Chicago, which was anxious to promote a new drink, Vin Fiz. Rodgers bought a second Wright machine, a Wright Model EX. It was painted with the name of the drink, as was a special train, also financed by the Armor Company, that would accompany Rodgers on his epic. On it were four mechanics and enough spare parts to rebuild the *Vin Fiz* twice over. They would be needed.

On 17 September, 41 days after winning his pilot's licence, Rodgers set off from Long Island. His prospects were grim. Orville Wright himself told Rodgers, 'There isn't a machine in existence that can be relied upon for 1,000 miles and here you want to go over 4,000. It will vibrate to death before you get to Chicago.'

The machine could fly for no more than two hours at a time. Its top speed was 96 km/h (60 mph), and it had no navigational instruments. Route-finding was a matter of identifying landmarks on the ground or following the train.

Catalogue of errors

The first day saw a promising 160 km (100 miles) covered. But the following morning, Rodgers crashed on takeoff, and the machine had to be largely rebuilt. He

Pursuit of the prize Rodgers on his aeroplane, *Vin Fiz*.

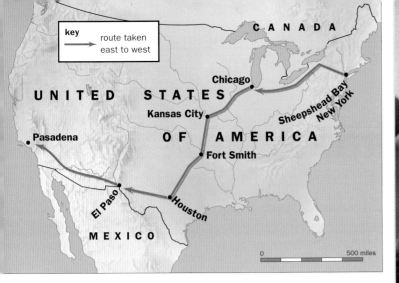

Cal Rodgers's 4,000-km (2,500-mile) flight across America in *Vin Fiz* was beset by accidents and technical faults.

would suffer three further crashes even before leaving New York state. But these were no more than the prelude to a litany of similar mishaps, at least five of them serious. When eventually he arrived in California, only the rudder and one wing strut were left from the machine in which he started. His engine had blown up twice.

Rodgers passed the 30-day limit with 1,600 km (1,000 miles) still to go. By 5 November, 49 days after starting, he had reached Pasadena, 43 km (27 miles) from the Pacific. It was decided that the machine needed a complete overhaul. On 12 November he began the last leg. With 19 km (12 miles) left, the engine twice failed, on the second occasion causing the most serious crash yet. Rodgers suffered a concussion, a broken ankle and ribs and severe burns.

Undaunted, his foot in plaster, his crutches strapped to the wings, on December 10 Rodgers flew the last 19 km (12 miles). When he symbolically wheeled his machine into the Pacific at Long Beach, there were 50,000 people waiting to greet him.

> ❝ There isn't a machine in existence that can be relied upon for 1,000 miles and here you want to go over 4,000. It will vibrate to death before you get to Chicago. ❞
>
> Orville Wright on Rodgers's prospects

Death of a legend

Rodgers's heroic refusal to abandon his flight – even after it was clear that the 30-day time limit could never be attained – made him a hero across America. People warmed to this iconic figure, cigar clamped firmly between his teeth even when in the air.

His repeated crashes – almost all his landings were heavy and necessitated repairs of one kind or another from his faithful team of mechanics – only added to his appeal. Rodgers was seen less as an epicly bungling amateur than as a genuinely intrepid aviator. In truth he was both.

He was killed in April 1912 at Long Beach, when he flew into a flock of seagulls during a demonstration flight. A bird became wedged in the machine's controls, and the plane crashed at the water's edge. It was less than a year since he had first flown.

The first flight from England to Australia

KEITH AND ROSS SMITH | 12 November–10 December 1919

World War I transformed aviation. In 1914 the world's aircraft were numbered in the hundreds; by 1918 almost 200,000 planes had been built. But the end of the war marked a collapse in the demand for military aircraft. Could the new technology be exploited commercially? A series of long-distance air races were staged to demonstrate the potential of long-range flight.

Three treks in particular captured the public imagination: the first nonstop crossing of the Atlantic, a race across America and back and the first flight from England to Australia. The Atlantic-crossing, with a prize of £10,000, had been proposed in 1913 by the newspaper magnate Lord Northcliffe, who had also offered the £1,000 prize won by Louis Blériot in 1909 for the first cross-Channel flight. The Atlantic-crossing prize was won in June 1919 by Capt. John Alcock and Lt. Arthur Brown of the newly formed Royal Air Force (RAF), who piloted their modified Vickers Vimy bomber 3,024 km (1,890 miles) from Newfoundland to Ireland (where they landed nosedown in a bog in Galway) in 16 hours, 28 minutes.

The second race, energetically championed by General 'Billy' Mitchell of the US Army Air Service, came to be called the Transcontinental Reliability and Endurance Test. It attracted 63 entrants, 48 of whom attempted the round-trip from New York to San Francisco and back, 15 the journey in the opposite direction. At least for its winner, Lt. Belvin Maynard, who made the journey in less than 10 days in October 1919, the undertaking was a success. But the race also claimed the lives of seven fliers, generating considerable hostile publicity.

A supreme test of endurance

Daring though these enterprises were, they paled in comparison to an England–Australia flight. This was more than a matter of the distance of 17,500 km (11,000-plus miles). It was more even than a question of reliability, though the range of extreme weather conditions,

Bon voyage The Smith brothers (center), their mechanics – Shiers and Bennett – and assembled supporters before the start of their 1919 flight.

coupled with gruellingly long hours in the air, would be an unprecedented test for even the sturdiest machines, to say nothing of their crews, all still in exposed cockpits.

Rather, it was that once away from Europe, the machines would be flying over lands that in many cases were not merely hostile – deserts, jungles, and mountains – but which lacked even the most rudimentary facilities for aviation. There would be almost no airfields – meaning, for example, that arranging for spare parts and fuel would prove a true challenge. Further, though aircraft navigation had greatly improved over the preceding decade, it was still uncertain. Maps were scarce and incomplete; none of the machines had radios.

Nonetheless, the benefits of such a contest were clear to the Australian government. Geographically isolated and still, in aviation terms, in its infancy, Australia needed an airlink with Britain to demonstrate that it, too, was a player in this potentially expanding world. So in 1919 the Australian prime minister, Billy Hughes, announced a £10,000 prize for the first crew to complete the journey. The stipulations were exacting. Only Australians could enter, and only if they flew machines built within the British Empire (which effectively meant Britain). Further, the attempt would have to be completed before the end of December 1920 and take no more than 30 days.

The race – and the prize – were won by two brothers, Capt. Ross Smith and Lt. Keith Smith of the Australian Flying Corps. Leaving London on 12 November, they landed in Darwin 27 days and 20 hours later on 10 December. They were accompanied by two sergeants – their mechanics – Wally Shiers and Jim Bennett. In truth, the Smith brothers were always the most likely winners. Both were experienced pilots, Ross in particular, having served with distinction in the Middle East, where he was briefly Lawrence of Arabia's personal pilot and twice won the Military Cross (MC) and three times the Distinguished Flying Cross (DFC). Further, they not only had a machine of proven reliability, the same model Vickers Vimy that had been used by Alcock and Brown earlier that year, but they also had the full backing of the Vickers Vimy company.

Freezing temperatures and turbulence

Leaving England, they ran into heavy snow. By the time they made their first landing at Lyon, France, the controls of their machine had frozen almost solid and their plane was encased in ice. Two days later, en route to Cairo from Rome, they ran into such severe turbulence over the Appenines that their machine dropped and lurched by up to 150 metres (500 ft).

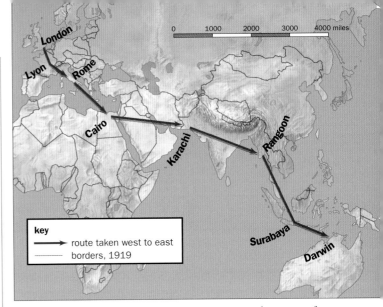

The Smith brothers' epic flight in 1919 was an extraordinary test of endurance – for both man and machine.

Once over the Middle East, the journey proceeded more smoothly. Karachi, 8,000 km (5,000 miles) into the journey, was reached in 13 days. But leaving Rangoon, torrential rain forced them to make an unscheduled stop at Singora on the Malay Peninsula on a treacherously sodden stretch of ground. They were able to take off from a similarly sodden Surabaya in Indonesia only after improvising a runway with bamboo mats.

High price of failure

The Smiths' achievement is made more impressive when compared to the fate of the other entrants in the race. Only one other aircraft made it to Darwin, a de Havilland DH9 piloted by Lts. Ray Parer and John McIntosh. They were the last to leave London on 8 January 1920. It took them 206 days to reach Darwin.

Fifty days after leaving London on 21 October, the Sopwith piloted by Capt. G. C. Matthews had made it only to Vienna. Likewise, it took a Kangaroo commanded by Capt. G. H. Wilkins 19 days to cover the 1,440 km (900 miles) to Rome. Capt. 'Dodger' Douglas, who had boasted he would reach Australia in only 10 days, crashed 9.5 km (6 miles) after taking off from Hounslow aerodrome, his overladen Alliance ploughing into an orchard. Both he and his copilot died.

There was one unofficial entrant, a Frenchman, Etienne Poulet, the only man in the field to be entirely self-financed. Despite leaving Paris (rather than London) almost a full month before the Smith brothers, when he reached Delhi, his lead had been cut to one hour. After three abortive attempts to leave Rangoon, 57 days after leaving Paris, Poulet reluctantly pulled out.

New York to Paris nonstop

CHARLES LINDBERGH | **20–21 May 1927**

When he landed at Le Bourget airport outside Paris at 10:22 P.M. on 21 May 1927, Charles Lindbergh became the first man not just to fly nonstop from New York to Paris but to fly the Atlantic solo. He was instantly transformed into perhaps the most famous person in the world, fêted wherever he went. As a flier – meticulous, visionary, and consistently courageous – he had no equal.

American daring personified Charles Lindbergh and his single-engine lightweight airplane – *Spirit of St. Louis.*

In 1919 Raymond Orteig, a French-born hotelier in New York, put up a $25,000 prize for the first man to fly nonstop between New York and Paris. At the time, it seemed beyond the reach of any flier. Even by the mid-1920s it remained a fearsomely distant goal, despite the rapid advances in aircraft design and performance then taking place. Increasingly, however, the question was not whether it could be won but when and by whom.

Clearly, any such flight would have to be made from west to east to take advantage of the prevailing westerly winds over the North Atlantic. The first flight over the Atlantic by three US Navy Curtis flying boats in May 1919 was not only firmly based on this presumption but also that it could only be achieved in a series of giant hops: from Newfoundland – the nearest point on the North American mainland to Europe – to the Azores and from there to Lisbon. Even so, only one of the three aircraft finished the trip. The total flying time was 26 hours, albeit spread over 15 days.

The following month, when Alcock and Brown made the first nonstop crossing of the Atlantic (*see* p. 22), they, too, were concerned that their route be the shortest possible – the 3,024 km (1,890 miles) from Newfoundland to the west coast of Ireland. They made it, but their flight was considered the limit of what crew and machine could manage.

Both flights, unthinkable even 10 years earlier when a cross-Channel flight of 35 km (22 miles) seemed daunting enough, were impressive. But a nonstop New

Lindbergh's bird's-eye view The *Spirit of St. Louis* en route from California to New York via St. Louis on 10 May 1927, shortly before Lindbergh's epic trans-Atlantic flight.

By 1926 he had decided to attempt the Orteig prize. As he would later write, 'Why shouldn't I fly from New York to Paris?... I have more than four years of aviation behind me, and close to two thousand hours in the air. I've barnstormed over half of the forty-eight states. ...Why am I not qualified for such a flight?'

His preparation for the flight was meticulous. He raised the necessary funds – $15,000 – from the St. Louis Chamber of Commerce, promising that if he were successful, the resulting fame would naturally reflect on the city and help make it a hub of future aviation in America, a prediction that would prove accurate. Believing no suitable aeroplane already existed, he had one built by the Ryan Airline Corporation in San Diego. From the start, and entirely counter to prevailing opinion, Lindbergh insisted that he wanted a single-engine plane – and that he would fly solo.

His logic was that a multi-engine machine would mean less safety, not more. 'Three engines means three times the chance of engine failure,' he asserted. Further, more engines might mean more power, but they also meant greater weight and hence reduced range. For the same reason, he argued against a second pilot. One man was perfectly capable of making the trip in Lindbergh's view; a second would only be dead weight.

York–Paris flight was more challenging still, at 5,744 km (3,590 miles), almost double the distance Alcock and Brown had flown.

It was naturally assumed that if any such flight were possible, it would be attempted by a multi-crewed multiengine plane. The risks of a single-engine plane piloted by a single flier taking on such an immense distance, much of it over water with no serious prospect of rescue in the event of ditching, seemed almost too obvious to be worth spelling out.

> Why shouldn't I fly from New York to Paris? ... I have more than four years of aviation behind me, and close to two thousand hours in the air. I've barnstormed over half of the forty-eight states ... Why am I not qualified for such a flight?
>
> Charles Lindbergh

In pursuit of the Orteig prize

Lindbergh's credentials as an aviator and challenger for the Orteig prize were impeccable. A natural bent for engineering was reinforced by two years at the University of Wisconsin. But he left college early, drawn by a love of flying. In 1924, at the age of 22, he joined the Army Air Service, graduating as the top pilot in his class the following year. For two years he worked as a mail pilot, pioneering the route between St. Louis and Chicago and cultivating a reputation as one of the most reliable and innovative pilots in the service.

Weight-saving

From the start Lindbergh was obsessive in his determination to save weight, ruthlessly rejecting any item he considered unnecessary. He refused to take a radio or parachute or to have navigation lights installed. He designed a new pair of lightweight flying boots; in place of

Crowds flock to catch a glimpse of Lindbergh Having flown from Paris, the American aviator is welcomed by an enthusiastic crowd in Brussels before continuing on to London.

a traditional leather seat, a wicker one was used (though he did allow an inflatable cushion). Even those parts of his maps he wouldn't need were cut off. Every 2.7 kg (6 lb.) saved meant one extra gallon of fuel, and it was fuel that was going to get Lindbergh and his machine to Paris.

By the same kind of compelling logic, Lindbergh had the main fuel tank placed in front of, rather than behind, the pilot. His point was that if there was an accident, he had no desire to be sitting between the engine and a tank of highly flammable fuel. But it meant he had no view forward: In place of the usual cockpit windscreen, there was now only a bank of instruments and the fuel tank. Though a small periscope was installed, Lindbergh could see where he was going only by sticking his head out of the small windows to either side. Flying blind in this way placed a premium on pilot skills.

> *It is the greatest shot of adrenaline to be doing what you have always wanted. You almost feel like you could fly without the plane.*
>
> **Charles Lindbergh**

Tests before takeoff

The aircraft, christened *Spirit of St. Louis*, was ready on 28 April 1927. During the following fortnight, Lindbergh went through a series of graduated tests, which culminated on 10 May with a 14-hour flight to St. Louis. Two days later he made a seven-hour flight to New York, setting a new transcontinental record of 21 hours, 12 minutes.

All that was needed now was a suitable break in the weather. On 19 May the decision was made to go the next morning. Overnight, the youthful Lindbergh was unable to sleep. A damp dawn found him at New York's Roosevelt Field on Long Island, where a crowd 500 strong had gathered. At 7:52 A.M. the *Spirit of St. Louis* took off, lumbering into the air with its huge fuel load. To the onlookers it seemed the machine might not make it. Lindbergh had no such doubts. Though he cleared a telephone line at the end of the field only by about 6 metres (20 ft), he had, he said, '… a fair reserve of flying speed.' He then throttled back to his cruising speed, a little over 145 km/h (90 mph), heading northeast to Boston, Nova Scotia, Newfoundland, and, beyond it, the wastes of the North Atlantic.

Only four hours after takeoff, over the Gulf of Maine, he began what would prove a constant battle with fatigue. To clear his head, he dropped to within 3 metres (10 ft) of the water. Ten hours into the flight, a still drained Lindbergh

The apostle of aviation

It is a truism to say that the 20th century saw the birth of mass media and global celebrity. But the instant fame Lindbergh was subjected to was without precedent. His reception in Paris was astonishing. In America it was overwhelming. When he returned on a US warship on 11 June, he was greeted by President Coolidge. New York gave him a tickertape parade attended by 4 million.

Lindbergh brilliantly exploited this exposure, immediately beginning a six-month aerial tour of America in the *Spirit of St. Louis,* determined to preach that the country must embrace aviation. He made a total of 148 flights, visiting 92 cities in 49 states. He travelled almost 2,080 km (1,300 miles) in parades.

In December he made a 27-hour flight to Mexico City from Washington, touring Central and South America and the Caribbean. (In the photograph above he is meeting General Alvarez in Mexico.) On 4 April 1928, the *Spirit of St. Louis* flew for the last time, from St. Louis to Washington.

The French challenge

Lindberg's Atlantic crossing marked the moment when America regained the lead in aviation over Europe. But it was not for lack of competition from European aviators, French above all. The first challenge came from World War I flying ace René Fonck (right, with Igor Sikorsky) in September 1926. Flying a largely untested and overloaded three-engine Sikorsky S-35, Fonck crashed on takeoff at Roosevelt Field, the machine exploding in a huge fireball. Fonck and his copilot miraculously survived; the other two members of his crew were killed.

Another French attempt was made the following May by Charles Nungesser – like Fonck, a World War I flying ace – and François Coli in an open-cockpit biplane, *L'Oiseau Blanc*. Perversely, they attempted the flight east to west, from Paris to New York, against the prevailing wind. They left Paris on 8 May and were last reported over the west coast of Ireland. They were never seen again.

❛When [flying] alone I perform those little coups of audacity which amuse me. ❜

René Fonck

was skirting the southern coast of Newfoundland. The next land he would see would be Ireland, almost 3,200 km (2,000 miles) away. An hour later, when night fell, he climbed to 2,250 metres (7,500 ft).

Not the least remarkable aspect of Lindbergh's achievement was that, however reliable it was, the *Spirit of St. Louis* was an exceptionally unforgiving aeroplane, demanding constant attention from its pilot. Lindbergh called it 'a living creature … high strung and balanced on a pinpoint. If I relax pressure on stick or rudder for an instant, the nose veers off course.' Yet veering off course was precisely what he could not afford. A successful landfall on the Irish coast was entirely dependent on following his compass course exactly while making what could be no more than an educated guess at his wind drift.

Fighting fatigue

As the night wore on, Lindbergh climbed higher, to 3,000 metres (10,000 ft). Even so, he was unable to avoid a huge cloud bank. Ice began to form on the plane, and bitter cold was now added to the overwhelming tiredness consuming him. Rather than close the windows to keep warm, he left them open in the hope the cold would keep him awake.

Flying east at this latitude and time of year, dawn came early. Yet, if anything, Lindbergh only felt more exhausted. He found himself drifting into sleep, jerking himself awake. Ominously, he realized he had begun to hallucinate. The crisis passed: his near irresistible need to sleep had gradually disappeared. An hour later he saw and circled a group of fishing boats. He shouted to ask the way to Ireland. He received no answer.

Lindbergh in Paris A photomontage of the *Spirit of St. Louis* in the skies above Paris, France – the culmination of Lindbergh's flight from New York.

An hour later, 27 hours into the flight, Lindbergh made his landfall over Ireland. He was less than 4.8 km (3 miles) off course. Within four hours he had crossed the French coast over Cherbourg, 320 km (200 miles) from Paris. A little before 10 P.M. local time, well into his second night, he saw the lights of the French capital. As he arrived over it, he exultantly circled the Eiffel Tower.

When he landed, there were an estimated 100,000 people waiting for him. Car headlights lit the runway. He had flown 5,776 km (3,610 miles) in 33 hours, 30 minutes and 30 seconds at an average speed of 171 km/h (107 mph). He had had no sleep for 55 hours.

The first crossing of the Pacific

CHARLES KINGSFORD-SMITH	31 May–9 June 1928

Of all the pioneer aviators of the 1920s and 1930s – the golden age of long-distance record-setting – the soft-spoken Australian, Charles Kingsford-Smith, was the most prolific, the holder at one time of 11 world records. But his most impressive achievement was the first crossing of the Pacific in 1928. It demanded extraordinary endurance and a new level of navigational accuracy.

The list of Kingsford-Smith's achievements is impressive. He wasn't just the first man to cross the Pacific, he was the first to cross it in both directions, from east to west in 1928 and from west to east in 1934. He flew from Australia to England twice, from England to Australia once, all in record times. He made only the second east–west crossing of the Atlantic, shortly before completing one of the first circumnavigations of the globe, albeit spread over two years. He made the first nonstop flight across Australia and the first flight from Australia to New Zealand and back again.

But no flight caught the public's imagination more than his 1928 Pacific crossing. It appeared doomed, however, even before it could be attempted when the first financing fell through.

There was no doubting his credentials as a flier. With Charles Ulm, who would be his copilot on the Pacific flight in June 1927, he had already flown the entire Australian coastline – 12,000 km (7,500 miles) – in 10 days and 5 hours, making a new record.

The fight to secure funding

Suitably impressed, the government of New South Wales promised to back Kingsford-Smith and Ulm, who then made their way to America, where they hoped to buy a Fokker Tri-motor. Once there, pleading a financial crisis at home, the New South Wales government withdrew its offer. Their prospects seemed grimmer after the widely publicised Dole Race from California to Hawaii in August 1927 resulted in 10 fatalities among the crews of the eight planes that competed.

Kingsford-Smith and Ulm nonetheless convinced a Californian businessman, G. Allan Hancock, that their

Smithy supreme Kingsford-Smith (centre) on arrival in Croydon, near London, after an Australia–England flight.

Final flight There were few aviators of the heroic age more fearless than Kingsford-Smith, a man of almost infinite resource in the air. Here he leaves London on what would prove his tragic last flight in 1935. He disappeared over the Bay of Bengal.

attempted flight was worth backing. With his support they bought a Fokker Tri-motor, which they named the *Southern Cross*, and recruited the two remaining members of the crew, the Americans Harry Lyon, who would navigate, and Jim Warner, who was a radio operator. The credibility of the attempt was underlined when they completed a 50-hour proving flight above San Francisco.

> **❝The only time an aircraft has too much fuel on board is when it is on fire.❞**
> Charles Kingsford-Smith

They left on their epic flight on 31 May. The first two legs, from Oakland to Hawaii and Hawaii to Fiji, proved straightforward, as much a test of fortitude as of piloting, even if on the second leg strong headwinds slowed their progress and there were problems with the starboard engine. Hawaii was reached on 1 June after a 27-hour, 28-minute flight, Fiji on 3 June after 34 hours and 30 minutes in the air. It was as much a triumph for navigator Harry Lyon as for the two pilots, a point the Australians were quick to make.

Ironically, what should have been the least demanding final leg to Brisbane proved to be the toughest. Terrifying rainstorms made accurate position-finding impossible and forced Kingsford-Smith and Ulm to fly blind at wave-top height.

When the coast of Australia was reached, the crew discovered they were more than 160 km (100 miles) off course. Nonetheless, in three legs they had flown 11,822 km (7,389 miles) in 83 hours and 38 minutes at an average speed of 140 km/h (88 mph).

The first female solo crossing of the Atlantic

AMELIA EARHART | **20–21 May 1932**

Along with England's Amy Johnson, the American Amelia Earhart was rocketed to prominence as one of a handful of pioneering female fliers in the early 1930s. If their sex explained much of their glamour-driven fame, both were determined to be taken seriously as aviators first. Earhart's most startling early achievement was her solo Atlantic crossing in 1932.

Touchdown Amelia Earhart waves to the crowd that had gathered in Londonderry, Northern Ireland, on 21 May 1932. Earhart's journey was the first solo flight across the Atlantic and the longest nonstop solo flight by a woman.

Alcock and Brown may have made the first non-stop Atlantic crossing by air in 1919 (*see* p. 22), but even 13 years later there was nothing routine about flying the Atlantic, particularly solo. Engine failure, despite advances in reliability, remained a risk, with little likelihood of surviving a forced landing. The natural hazards of the journey – icing and adverse weather – were matched by the exhaustion of piloting a small plane for many hours in cockpits that were cramped and uncomfortable and filled with a permanent deafening background of engine noise.

Women take to the skies

Amy Johnson made a solo flight from England to Australia in May 1930, an astonishing achievement for a woman whose longest flight had been the 320 km (200 miles) between Hull and London. Johnson had never flown over water. Though she failed to beat the record of 15 and a half days set by the Australian Bert Hinkler in 1928, her time of 19 and a half days was nonetheless remarkable. More importantly, she had shown that for stamina and determination in the air, a woman could be the equal of any man. She was not a natural flier with instinctive piloting skills any more than Amelia Earhart.

Earhart's 1932 solo Atlantic crossing was not her first Atlantic crossing. In 1928, when she had only a handful of modest records to her name, she was invited to fly as a passenger on a west–east Atlantic crossing being made by two American fliers, Wilmer Stultz and Louis E. Gordan, in a Fokker F7 christened *Friendship*.

Earhart's participation was a publicity stunt, and she knew it. It had been largely cooked up by the man she would later marry, New York publisher George Putnam, anxious that a woman should fly the Atlantic for the first time. She would later say that she had been a mere 'sack of potatoes' during the flight – a passenger, nothing more.

Celebrity status

Nonetheless, when *Friendship* touched down in South Wales on 19 June, 20 hours and 40 minutes after leaving Newfoundland, Earhart's fame was immediate. She capitalised on it shrewdly, writing a best-selling book about the flight, becoming a leading figure in aviation journalism in the United States and with a fledgling airline – New York, Washington and Philadelphia Airways – the first female executive in American commercial aviation. In 1929 she also organized the first long-distance air race for women, from Los Angeles to

The heroine returns Amelia Earhart acknowledges the cheers of the crowd in New York City on 20 June 1932. The tickertape parade was arranged to celebrate her historic solo flight across the Atlantic, which was completed a month earlier.

Cleveland – dubbed the Powder-Puff Derby. Earhart finished third. Her championship of female aviation would prove tireless.

But her heart was set on a long-distance record. A solo Atlantic crossing remained her priority. At this stage Lindbergh was still the only pilot to have flown the Atlantic solo. Five years to the day after his epic feat, Earhart set out to match him.

Her starting point, however, was Newfoundland, about 2,400 km (1,500 miles) closer to Europe than his. It was from here, in her scarlet Lockheed Vega, that the 34-year-old Earhart took off early on the morning of 20 May 1932. She never reached Paris. The weather was consistently bad, with strong winds buffeting the plane throughout and freezing temperatures threatening to ice up the fuselage. Not only did her altimeter break, meaning she could only estimate her altitude, but fuel started leaking into the cockpit. At one point flames leaped from the exhaust of her single engine.

'Where am I?'

Uncertain of her position and nearing the limits of her endurance, she realised she would have to put down on the first available land. It turned out to be several hundred miles off her course, a soggy cow pasture near Londonderry, Northern Ireland. As she clambered

Earhart's disappearance

Earhart had long wanted to make a round-the-world flight, the ultimate challenge in long-distance flying. Her celebrity made raising the necessary funding relatively easy: $40,000 was made available for a twin-engine Lockheed Electra, equipped almost as a 'flying laboratory' with state-of-the-art navigation equipment. She received full backing from the US government.

On 1 June 1937, at the second attempt (a previous attempt in March had ended in failure), Earhart, accompanied only by navigator Fred Noonan, set off. She had decided to fly in the opposite direction, from west to east, leaving the Pacific legs till last. By 29 June, having crossed the Atlantic, Africa and much of Asia, they had reached Lae in New Guinea. The Pacific was ahead. Earhart and Noonan left Lae on 2 July, their destination the small island of Howland, 3,563 km (2,227 miles) away.

Both fliers were reaching the end of their tethers. Earhart, who had earlier experienced dysentery, was said to be unusually wan and listless. Noonan, erratic and irascible, was faring little better. On the other hand, a series of US naval ships had been posted under their route to monitor progress and to radio position reports. Despite intermittent radio contact with Earhart and Noonan – deeply poignant in retrospect – they would prove no more than spectators.

Theories of varying degrees of implausibility have been put forward to explain Earhart and Noonan's disappearance. The most obvious explanation is that an exhausted Earhart and Noonan, failing to find their tiny island destination and out of fuel, were forced to land in the sea, where they inevitably perished.

Lady Lindy, the Queen of the Skies Amelia Earhart, pictured in the place she felt most at home – an aeroplane cockpit. Loved by the press and adored by the public, she was the perfect mix of glamour and daredeviltry. No wonder her death seemed so shocking to so many.

wearily from her machine, a man approached her. 'Where am I?' she asked. He replied: 'In Gallegher's pasture. Have you come far?' She had: 3,241 km (2,026 miles) in 15 hours and 18 minutes. It was the longest nonstop solo flight then made by any woman.

It's not easy today to grasp the impact Earhart's flight made both in Europe and America. She became, and would remain until her death in 1937, as famous and as sought after as any Hollywood star. It was a status she enjoyed. Tall and willowy – the press had already dubbed her Lady Lindy after her supposed resemblance to Lucky Lindy Lindbergh – she was trans-formed into a fashion icon as much as a flying one (she designed her own range of clothes 'for the woman who lives actively'). The focus of unrelenting media attention, she was showered with honours and always in demand.

Yet she remained first and foremost a flier. In late August that same year, she set a new transcontinental US record, flying from Los Angeles to New Jersey in

19 hours, 5 minutes. The following year, she improved the record to 17 hours, 7 minutes.

Among her other record flights was one from Hawaii to Oakland, California, made in January 1935 in 17 hours. She was not only the first solo pilot to fly the 3,276 km (2,048-mile) trip, she was the only pilot to have made a significant solo Pacific flight as well as to have flown the Atlantic solo.

Her iconic status, powered by a collective hysteria,

> ❝ Amelia Earhart came perhaps before her time ... the smiling, confident, capable, yet compassionate human being, is one of which we can all be proud. ❞
>
> Walter J. Boyne

helps explain the frenzied reaction when she and naviga-tor Fred Noonan disappeared in the Pacific in July 1937 as they neared the end of their round-the-world flight. The US government spent more than $4 million looking for Earhart and her companion. What really happened continues to be one of aviation's most puzzling myster-ies (*see* box opposite).

The first man to fly solo around the world

WILEY POST | 15–22 July 1933

Wiley Post was a key figure in the transformation of aviation from the barnstorming days of the 1920s to the evermore high-tech business it had become by the late 1930s. His belief that technology was the way forward paid off in two record-breaking round-the-world flights, in 1931 and 1933. On the second, an epic of endurance, he became the first man to fly around the world solo.

Writing of Post's proposed solo round-the-world flight in 1933, the *New York Times* sourly commented that, 'He will ride around the world on radio waves while the robot flies the plane.' It was a comment that did less than justice to Wiley's instinctive understanding that if aviation were to establish itself as a practical means of long-distance passenger travel, it urgently needed a reliable long-distance navigation system.

The original *Winnie Mae* F. C. Hall's daughter on the left, F. C. Hall on the right. Between them are Post (in dark suit) and his navigator, Harold Gatty.

An unlikely record-breaker

Post was an unlikely champion of such a high-tech approach. He was an Oklahoma oil hand with little formal education (and a criminal record), whose first flying experience came when, with no experience whatsoever, he volunteered to be a stunt parachutist for a travelling flying circus (Burell Tobbs and his Texas Topnotch Fliers). Moreover, in 1926 he lost his left eye in a drilling accident. But this did not rule out a career in aviation, in which judgment of distance was an essential requirement for any pilot. Post used other means, such as the heights of buildings, by which to gauge distances.

Paid $1,800 as compensation for the loss of his eye, Post used it to buy an aeroplane with which he gave flying lessons and ferried local oilmen around. By the following year, he had been taken on as the personal pilot of a local millionaire oilman, F. C. Hall, who in 1928 bought a Lockheed Vega, then perhaps the most advanced single-engine, enclosed-cockpit machine available. A downturn in business forced Hall to lay off Post, but in 1930 he took him on again and bought a second Lockheed Vega. Like the first, it was named after Hall's daughter, Winnie Mae.

Hall had bought the new machine not so that he could be flown around faster and more comfortably by Post but because he recognized that Post was a flier of genius. To his lasting credit, Hall had effectively set himself up as the backer of his pilot's attempt to set a new round-the-world record.

A week in the air An exhausted Wiley Post clambers from the cockpit of *Winnie Mae* following his solo round-the-world flight on 22 July 1933. A throng of supporters and newsmen were on the runway at Floyd Bennett Airport, New York, to greet him.

The need for speed

If accurate navigation was key to any such attempt, airspeed was hardly less important. Post had the new *Winnie Mae* modified and a 500-horsepower Wasp engine installed, giving it a top speed of close to 320 km/h (200 mph). It was an emphatic success. In August 1930 Post flew *Winnie Mae* in the National Air Race Derby between Los Angeles and Chicago, covering the distance in 9 hours, 9 minutes and 4 seconds, a time proudly painted on the side of the machine.

Post, flying with Tasmanian-born Harold Gatty, one of the world's most accomplished and innovative air navigators, began his first round-the-world attempt in New York on 23 June 1931. The immediate goal was to beat the existing round-the-world record of 22 days. This was unlikely to prove a formidable hurdle. The time had been set in 1929 by the German airship, the *Graf Zepplin*, which cruised at no more than a stately 112 km/h (70 mph), though admittedly it could maintain this for several days at a time. Post and Gatty smashed the *Graf Zepplin's* time and completed their flight in 8 days, 15 hours and 51 minutes, returning to New York on 1 July to a tumultuous reception.

The flight had been a milestone in more ways than one. Post and Gatty had prepared meticulously. As with any long-distance record attempt at the time, less time on the ground meant more time in the air; similarly, the longer the individual flights were, the faster the overall time of the trip. But long-hop flying of this kind took a huge toll on any crew, rapidly reducing them to exhaustion. Post therefore followed a rigorous fitness regime before the flight and, crucially, accustomed himself to sleeping for short periods only.

> ❝ I cut the emergency switch just in time to keep *Winnie Mae* from making an exhibition of herself by standing on her nose. That would have been fatal to our hopes. ❞ Wiley Post

Under pressure

Wiley Post's fascination with the technical elements of flight led him to the belief that the higher a plane could fly, the faster it would go by virtue of the fact that the thinner air at high altitudes meant less air resistance to slow the plane. At the same time, thinner air made engines, starved of oxygen, less efficient. The answer to this was simple: a super-charger, one of which Post had fitted to the *Winnie Mae* in 1934.

The cabin of *Winnie Mae* was too flimsy to be pressurized, so the answer was a pressure suit for the pilot. The result looked more Jules Verne than space age, not least the canna-balised diver's helmet, but it was the first practical pressure suit (see picture above from test flight, February 1935). On his first flight on 5 September 1934, rigged out in this creation, Post reached 12,000 metres (40,000 ft). On later flights he reached up to 15,000 metres (50,000 ft). These high-altitude flights confirmed the existence of the jet stream, winds blowing at high speeds in the upper atmosphere. Although first observed in the 19th century, these winds were assumed to be no more than localized, possibly freak effects. Post's intuition that higher altitudes meant higher speeds was now understood.

In March 1935 Post rode the jet stream on a flight in the *Winnie Mae* from Burbank, California, to Cleveland, Ohio, at an average speed of 446 km/h (279 mph), covering more than 3,200 km (2,000 miles) in just over 7 hours. At times his speed reached 544 km/h (340 mph), this in an aeroplane with a theoretical maximum speed of less than 320 km/h (200 mph).

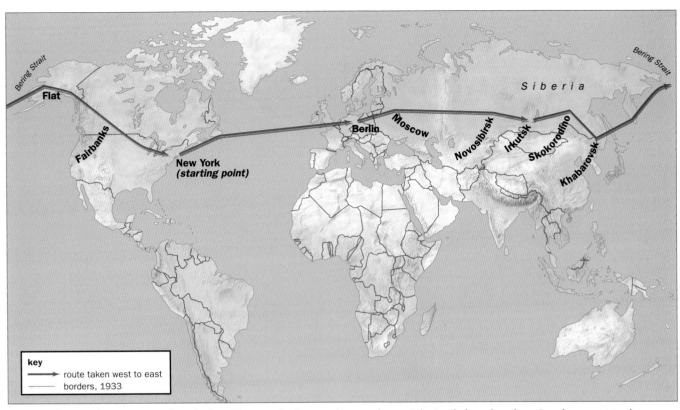

Post chose his route because it was relatively short. However, facilities on the ground across Siberia, Alaska and northern Canada were minimal.

The problems of long-distance flying in this period were often unexpected. In Biagovyeschensk, Siberia, a sodden landing strip prevented takeoff for 14 hours. In Alaska, attempting to take off from a beach, the soft sand effectively tripped the plane up, damaging the propeller (which Post ingeniously beat back into shape with 'a wrench, a broken-handled hammer and a round stone'). A waterlogged runway at Edmonton also caused delays. But the pairing of Post and Gatty nonetheless proved a resounding success.

One-man epic

In planning his solo round-the-world effort in 1933, Post naturally drew on his and Gatty's experiences two years earlier. For one thing, he intended to follow broadly the same route: eastwards from New York to Europe and then across the Soviet Union and Siberia to the Bering Sea and Alaska, from where he would head southeastwards across Canada and the northern United States to New York. Not only was this a relatively short route, about 24,800 km (15,500 miles), it included only one major ocean crossing, the Atlantic, and this at the very start, when Post would be at his freshest. He stopped only 11 times on the entire journey, three times fewer than he and Gatty had.

Two new pieces of technology helped the solo flight: a radio-homing device that significantly eased his navigational worries, and a gyroscope that served as an early form of automatic pilot. This meant that for long periods the *Winnie Mae* could fly itself, allowing Post to rest and, more importantly, to navigate.

Twenty hours' sleep in a week

The flight nevertheless proved gruelling almost beyond endurance. The first leg was a 26-hour marathon to Berlin, the first-ever direct New York–Berlin flight. Heavy fog, coupled with frequent breakdowns of the gyroscope, made much of the vast haul over the Soviet Union a navigational nightmare. By the time he had reached the Bering Sea, Post had been reduced to tying a heavy tool to one finger to stay awake. Every time he nodded off, the tool would fall, jerking him awake. In Flat, Alaska, a heavy landing badly damaged the *Winnie Mae*.

Nonetheless, not only did Post complete his one-man epic, confounding those who claimed it was impossible (and those who asserted it was Gatty who deserved the real plaudits for the 1931 flight), he did it in 7 days, 18 hours and 49 minutes, almost a full day faster than in 1931. He calculated he had had just 20 hours' sleep during the entire flight.

The first man in space

YURI GAGARIN | **12 April 1961**

The successful launch of *Sputnik*, the world's first artificial Earth satellite, by the Soviet Union in October 1957 established Russia's clear supremacy over the United States in spaceflight. The lead was reinforced in April 1961 when the Soviet Union sent the first man ever into space, Yuri Gagarin. Though the flight itself was shrouded in secrecy, the Soviets readily proclaimed their scientific triumph.

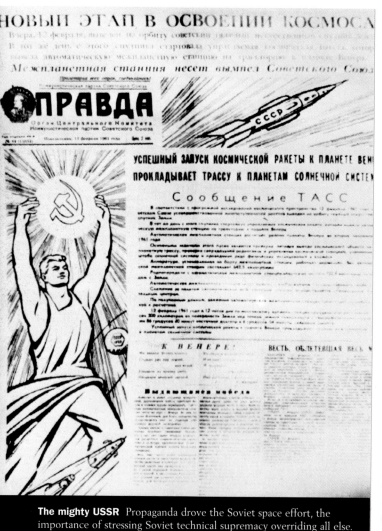

The mighty USSR Propaganda drove the Soviet space effort, the importance of stressing Soviet technical supremacy overriding all else.

The launch of *Sputnik* profoundly shocked the United States. That they should always enjoy a technological lead over the Soviet Union was an article of faith for most Americans, a natural reflection of the superiority of capitalism over communism. To be forced so publicly into second place in the new and unexpected battleground of space was shocking.

America's subsequent efforts to compete with the Soviet Union in space took place in the full glare of publicity – both failures and successes. Soviet failures went unreported. In repeated blazes of precisely orchestrated global publicity, a succession of Soviet achievements in space gave the Russian space effort an aura of invincibility.

Battle for the stars

The Soviets' lead in spaceflight, however, would prove illusory. By the mid-1960s America's space agency, NASA, had all but closed the gap on the Soviet Union. By the end of the decade, as the Apollo moon-landing programme gathered pace, American superiority was unmistakable. In fact, even before the 27-year-old Gagarin's epoch-making flight, the 'space gap' was much smaller than it looked. NASA had actually scheduled its first manned flight for 24 March 1961, 19 days before Gagarin's flight. NASA, however, finally decided on one last unmanned test flight on that date. It went perfectly. Had NASA followed its original plan, the first man in space would have been an American rather than a Russian.

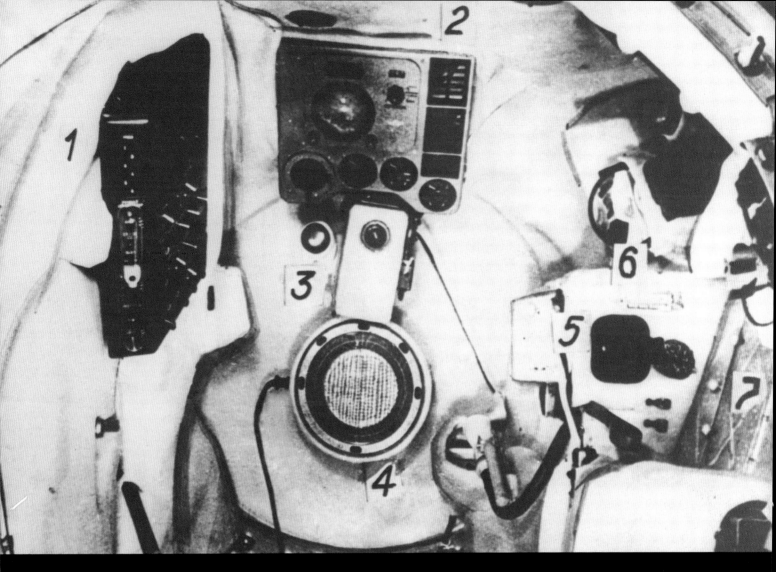

Vostok 1

Whatever their technical sophistication, the planners of the first Soviet flights were exceptionally cautious when it came to the cosmonauts' role. In effect, *Vostok 1* (the capsule's interior is shown above) flew itself, with Gagarin no more than a passenger. Just as in the United States, there were widespread fears among engineers that the strain of spaceflight would prove too much for humans.

The cosmonauts were chosen more for their physical resilience and calmness under pressure than for piloting skills. (As part of his training, Gagarin was subjected to 13Gs on a centrifuge and was locked in a soundless, lightless room for 24 hours.) Gagarin, too, had the advantage of being only 1.5 metres (5 ft 2 inches). This not only saved weight but also space in a cramped spacecraft. In the event of a breakdown in the automatic control system, Gagarin was provided with a key in a sealed envelope, which would allow him to assume direct control of the ship.

❝ Poyekhali! – Let's Go! ❞

Gagarin's cry as *Vostok 1* lifted off

Soviet space factory A Vostok capsule being assembled late in 1965. By this time the Soviet space effort was already being overhauled by America's vastly better-funded and much more technically advanced programme.

But it would have been something of a hollow victory. When, on 5 May, Alan Shepard became the first American in space, it was atop a hastily converted Redstone rocket, originally designed to carry nuclear weapons, which generated no more than 35,000 kg (78,000 lb.) of thrust. This was barely enough to carry Shepard and his Mercury capsule into space at all, much less into orbit around the Earth. His flight was no more than a suborbital hop. Its maximum height was 184 km (115 miles); its maximum speed was 9,760 km/h (5,800 mph). Shepard was weightless for only 5 minutes as his spacecraft looped into near space, curving up and then back towards the Earth. He travelled less than 480 km (300 miles), from Cape Canaveral, Florida, to a landing point near the Bahamas. From launch to splashdown, the flight lasted 15 minutes.

Gagarin's flight

By contrast, Gagarin's flight was a true venture into space. His 4,730-kg (10,430-lb.) spacecraft, *Vostok 1* (meaning East), was propelled by a converted R-7 missile whose 32 engines produced 405,000 kg (900,000 lb.) of thrust. It took off from the Baikonur launch complex in central Russia at precisely 9:07 A.M., rapidly accelerating the Russian cosmonaut to 28,260 km/h (17,660 mph), subjecting him to six times the force of gravity and into Earth orbit. The lowest point of his orbit was 180 km (112 miles), its highest point 326 km (204 miles).

Gagarin made a single orbit of the Earth, which lasted 89 minutes, hurtling through both a spectacular sunset and sunrise. During both the ascent and orbit,

> ❝ The spaceship put in orbit, and the carrier-rocket separated, weightlessness set in. At first the sensation was to some extent unusual, but I soon adapted myself ... I maintained continuous communication with Earth. ❞
>
> Yuri Gagarin

the spacecraft functioned flawlessly. Gagarin, the first man to experience weightlessness, was notably calm, transmitting a continuous commentary to the flight controllers on the ground. Weightlessness, he reported, was 'relaxing.' He added, 'The sky looks very, very dark and the Earth is bluish.' His comments may have lacked profundity. What was remarkable was that they were being made at all.

The only moment when the craft functioned less than perfectly came during reentry, a fact acknowledged only many years later. A strap on the equipment module, which contained life-support systems and the retro rocket to brake the spacecraft for the return to Earth, failed to separate from the crew compartment holding Gagarin. The two craft tumbled wildly until the rogue strap burned up in the heat of reentry. Thereafter, the landing proceeded smoothly, with Gagarin notching another dramatic first as the first man to experience the terrifyingly high temperatures generated by a spacecraft plunging from orbit back to Earth.

Soviet success

From liftoff to landing, his flight took exactly 108 minutes. News of it was instantly beamed around the world by a Soviet Union determined to wring every last drop of propaganda triumph from its technological masterstroke.

Characteristically, the Soviets refused to give out any technical details of Gagarin's flight. Their secrecy hid a telling detail. Soviet spaceflights routinely landed only within the Soviet Union. The greater technical difficulties of bringing a spacecraft down on land rather than in the sea were considered justified by the reduced risk of the craft falling into hostile hands. But in these first flights, as no cosmonaut would be able to survive the violent impact of landing on land, the pilots were ejected from the capsule 7,000 metres (23,000 ft) above the ground, floating down by parachute. As records in manned spaceflight were given international recognition only 'if the pilot remains in his craft from launch to landing,' the Soviets kept this fact quiet for many years.

Gagarin landed near the Volga river, 24 km (15 miles) south of Saratov. An old woman, her granddaughter and a cow saw him first as he floated towards the ground under his billowing parachute in his brilliant orange suit. The woman, startled, asked if he had come from outer space. 'Yes,' replied the cosmonaut. 'Yes, I have.' The cold war race to the stars had begun.

Yuri Gagarin

9 March 1934	Born at Gzhatsk 160 km (100 miles) north of Moscow
1955	Joined Soviet Air Force
1960	Selected as one of the USSR's first 20 cosmonauts
9 April 1961	Informed he had been chosen to make the first manned spaceflight
12 April 1961	Flight of *Vostok 1*; Gagarin promoted from 2nd lieutenant to major during the flight
1961	Awarded Order of Lenin and named Hero of the Soviet Union
1962	Serves as deputy to the Supreme Soviet
1963	Promoted Commander of the Cosmonaut Group
27 March 1968	Killed in routine training flight in MiG-15

The first man on the Moon

NEIL ARMSTRONG – *APOLLO 11* | **20 July 1969**

Only the United States could have landed a man on the Moon in 1969. No other country had the necessary combination of technological and manufacturing might and political determination to make such an audacious effort. As important, only America could afford the prodigious cost. Even so, it stretched the technological means of the world's most powerful nation to their limits.

Mission accomplished Neil Armstrong back in the lunar lander at the end of his historic moonwalk.

Cold war politics inspired the American decision to send a man to the Moon. John F. Kennedy's response in 1961 to the Soviet Union's early lead in spaceflight – that the United States would commit itself to landing a man on the Moon 'before this decade is out' – instantly and dramatically raised the stakes between the only two countries capable of spaceflight.

JFK's mission

Whether intended or not, it was a brilliantly shrewd shift of emphasis: directly challenging the Soviet Union where it was weakest, while moving the ground back to where America was strongest. The goal had been made explicit. It was a challenge neither side could refuse.

Manufacturing capacity was key. Less than 20 years before Kennedy's declaration, American industry had risen to the challenge of World War II, transforming Depression-hit industries to produce weapons, armaments, guns, planes and ships on a gargantuan scale. Almost exactly the same spirit infused the space effort. The numbers were inevitably smaller. In 1942 practically the entire American economy was turned over to weapons production. In 1960 no more than a fraction of America's stupendous economic output was devoted to the space race. But it was impressive enough and vastly more than the Soviet Union could provide. By the mid-1960s more than 500,000 Americans, in factories across the country, were working to put a man on the Moon.

'We have liftoff' Cape Kennedy, Florida, 16 July 1969. *Apollo 11* takes off amidst an explosion of flame, smoke and noise. America is on its way to the Moon. History is being made. Pictured are a small number of the crowds that had flocked to Cocoa Beach to witness the launch.

German intelligence

This immense effort was backed by a scientific expertise the Soviet Union struggled to match. Here again, World War II provided a boost. By the end of the war, pursuing Hitler's dream of the rocket-powered terror weapons he believed would bring the Allies to their knees, Germany had established a clear lead in rocket technology. The key members of the teams responsible for these weapons were rounded up by the Americans in 1945 and taken to the United States.

For most of the 1950s, they were left to toil in obscurity at Huntsville – inevitably known as Hunsville – Alabama. Now, pressed into service on behalf of the American space effort and funded as never before, they, under the leadership of Werner von Braun, came up with the most terrifying flying machine of the 20th

> ❛ We had hundreds of thousands of people all dedicated to doing the perfect job, and I think they did as well as anyone could ever have expected. ❜
>
> Neil Armstrong, on the successful Moon landing

century: the Saturn V rocket. It was a three-stage monster, 109 metres (363 ft) high. Its first stage burned for no more than two and a half minutes yet consumed 2.25 million litres (500,000 gallons) of kerosene and liquid oxygen at a rate of 20 tons a second and produced over 3.3 million kg (7.5 million lb.) of thrust, the equivalent of a small atomic bomb.

The Soviet Union had no effective response. Though its own super rocket, the N-1, was even larger, producing 4.4 million kg (9.9 million lb.) of thrust, it could never be made to work. On each of its four trial launches, it blew up, scattering debris over a 48-km (30-mile) radius.

Three-part programme

The American attempt to land on the Moon was based on three programmes. The first – Mercury – was essentially

Mission control The astronauts who flew to the Moon were no more than the tip of a vast operation back on the Earth. At its heart was Mission Control in Houston, Texas, from where every aspect of the mission was minutely scrutinized.

huddled in their cramped cabin, the crew broadcast indistinct black-and-white television pictures from the Moon to Earth on Christmas Eve 1968 and read from the Book of Genesis as the whole world watched.

NASA may have demonstrated that it could put men into orbit around the Moon, but the technical challenges of actually landing on the Moon remained formidable. In part, they were answered with the flights of *Apollo 9* and *10*, the first tests of the Moon-landing vehicle itself – the LM, or Lunar Module. *Apollo 9*, an Earth-orbit test, flew in March 1969; *Apollo 10*, only the second Apollo mission to go into lunar orbit, flew two months later. Pulses were set racing during *Apollo 10* when the LM, flying only 14.5 km (9 miles) above the lunar surface, suddenly tumbled out of control, prompting an involuntary 'Son of a bitch … What the hell happened?' from copilot Gene Cernan. Within eight seconds it was under control. The rest of the mission was flawless.

Apollo 11 Moon landing

Apollo 11, the first Moon-landing mission, took off on 16 July 1969. In command was Neil Armstrong, one of the few nonmilitary astronauts on NASA's roster. With him were Buzz Aldrin, who would accompany Armstrong to the lunar surface, and Michael Collins,

a rushed response to the Soviet's early lead, intended to show that America could at least send men into space. The second – Gemini – though still an Earth-orbit programme, was much more ambitious, its goal to rehearse the key aspects of manned spaceflight that would be needed to send a man to the Moon. The third was Apollo, the Moon-landing programme itself.

The Apollo programme began slowly. There were technical hitches and delays. In January 1967 it reached its nadir when, in what should have been a routine test of the three-man command module, the vehicle that would take the astronauts to the Moon caught fire and incinerated the three astronauts on board.

Paradoxically, what might have been its death knell, instead reinvigorated the programme. In November of the same year, the first unmanned launch of a Saturn V took place. The following October the first manned Apollo flight triumphantly passed every test. Over Christmas 1968 NASA pulled off its greatest coup yet when *Apollo 8* was launched. It was a hugely ambitious mission – not just the first manned launch of a Saturn V, but the first flight to the Moon itself.

On 24 December the three-man crew of *Apollo 8* were placed into a precise lunar orbit. While they

> ❝ That's one small step for man, one giant leap for mankind. ❞
>
> Neil Armstrong

who would stay in the command module, code-named *Columbia*, in lunar orbit while Armstrong and Aldrin flew the LM, the *Eagle*, to the Moon itself. A small army of flight controllers in Houston, site of the manned spacecraft centre, monitored their progress.

On 20 July, shortly after midnight Houston time,

Man on the Moon

The mission controllers of *Apollo 11* were nothing if not cautious. And they had reason to be. Landing on the Moon was a monumental risk. The consequences of failure were almost too terrifying to contemplate. The prospect of 'losing the crew' always haunted NASA.

As a result, the first moonwalk was conservative. It lasted just two and a half hours. Buzz Aldrin, second onto the lunar surface and first off it, was outside for only 90 minutes. The astronauts were forbidden to go more than 90 metres (300 ft) from the lunar lander.

Nonetheless, in addition to hammering a US flag into the surface (which was famously blown over when the LM's upper stage blasted off from the surface) and conducting a notably stilted conversation with President Nixon, Armstrong and Aldrin still managed to conduct a number of basic experiments. These included collecting a series of rock samples (21 kg [47 lb.] in all), laying out a solar-powered seismometer to monitor 'moonquakes' and taking 'core samples' by means of a metal tube hammered into the ground.

They left the Moon less than 22 hours after landing on it.

The end of Apollo

Five additional Apollo missions landed on the Moon after *Apollo 11*. The last was *Apollo 17*, in December 1972. In all, 12 men made it to the lunar surface. All safely returned to Earth.

When the programme was cancelled in 1972 – it had originally been intended that there would be at least a further three Moon-landing missions – it was over-concern that so ambitious a programme would surely go wrong at some point, as it nearly did on the flight of *Apollo 13* (**see** pp. 224–229). Even within NASA there were calls for the cancellation of the programme after the flight of *Apollo 11*.

More particularly, having achieved its stated aim, there was increasing political reluctance across the country – especially given the cost of the Vietnam War – to fund more Moon landings. This was scarcely a surprise. The Apollo programme was staggeringly expensive. The total cost, still disputed, is conservatively estimated to have been around $24.5 billion.

Armstrong and Aldrin in the *Eagle* had separated from *Columbia* and were beginning their final preparations for the landing itself. The physics of the manoeuvre were straightforward. From an orbit 14.5 km (9 miles) above the Moon and at a point approximately 300 km (190 miles) from their landing point, Armstrong and Aldrin, travelling close to 5,000 km/h (3,000 mph), would fire their descent engine. As it slowed, they would make a controlled fall toward the Moon. At this point all the astronauts had to do was monitor the descent. All the flying would be done by the onboard computer.

At about 105 metres (350 ft) above the lunar surface – it was up to Armstrong to gauge the precise point – Armstrong would take control and fly the LM down to the Moon itself. The LM was possibly the least responsive flying machine ever designed, sluggish and skittish. But Armstrong had no doubts he could execute a successful touchdown.

While still in orbit around the Moon, there were immediate problems when the radio link between the *Eagle* and Houston began to drop out. Not only had the ground controllers lost contact, the data that should have confirmed the status of the LM's systems was only patchy. In this blur of static, the decision to land was made.

The *Eagle* has landed

At 3:06 in the morning Houston time, Armstrong and Aldrin fired their descent engine. In the vacuum of space, there was no sound. But both astronauts felt themselves being gently pushed backward as the engine built up to maximum thrust.

Almost at once, Armstrong radioed that checkpoints on the lunar surface were appearing two seconds ahead of time. Was the *Eagle* following a rogue trajectory of its own? Then three times during the descent the computer signalled alarms. Neither Armstrong nor Aldrin were sure what they meant. There was almost as much doubt in Houston. Yet each time, Houston gave the go-ahead to continue.

Three hundred metres (1000 ft) above the lunar surface, Armstrong realised the computer was taking the *Eagle* directly into a boulder-filled crater. He keyed in new landing coordinates. At 105 metres (350 ft) up, he assumed direct control himself. At 90 metres (300 ft) he

had still not found a place to land. By 60 metres (200 ft) there were approximately only 90 seconds of descent fuel left. But now Armstrong had found his landing site. He manoeuvred cautiously toward it.

In Houston the flight controllers, reduced to little more than spectators, had fallen silent, gripped by the drama taking place almost 400,000 km (250,000 miles) away.

Six metres (20 ft) above the surface, Aldrin called '30 seconds', meaning that there were no more than 30 seconds of fuel left. Aldrin's next call was: 'Contact light'. Seconds later the *Eagle* had landed.

The grainy black-and-white television pictures of Neil Armstrong and Buzz Aldrin on the Moon in July 1969 have many of the same archival qualities of the few surviving movie images of the early pioneers of flight. Hazy and jerky, they belong to another age. Given that they are now almost as close chronologically to 1927,

> ❝ When the *Eagle* landed I was speechless – overwhelmed, like most of the world. I think all I said was "Wow! Jeez" Not exactly immortal. ❞
> Walter Knonkite, CBS news anchor

when Lindbergh first flew the Atlantic, as to our own age of instant, digital communication, this is not surprising.

The technological and political revolutions that have taken place since the last Moon landing in 1972 have allowed the creation of an International Space Station. NASA announced in 2006 that it would create a manned lunar base by 2024.

First man on the Moon Iconic photograph, taken by Buzz Aldrin, of Neil Armstrong's first footprint on the surface of the Moon.

The first nonstop round-the-world flight

DICK RUTAN AND JEANA YEAGER | 14–23 December 1986

In December 1986 Americans Dick Rutan and Jeana Yeager achieved a feat widely assumed to be impossible. Flying a radical aeroplane designed by Rutan's brother, Burt, they not only made the first nonstop round-the-world flight, they did it without refuelling. It gave them the record for the greatest distance ever flown nonstop: 39,978 km (24,986 miles).

Conventional aircraft design had always held that no aeroplane could circle the globe nonstop on a single fuel load. The immense quantity of fuel needed would weigh so much it would require massive engines just to get into the air. But these in turn would require so much more fuel again that still larger engines would be needed. And so on. It seemed an impossible task.

Burt Rutan's typically bold solution, first jotted on the back of a napkin in a restaurant in 1981, claimed that if the machine was aerodynamically efficient and light enough, not only could it be fitted with relatively smaller engines, which would not only weigh less and

Pilots at ease Jeana Yeager and Dick Rutan in front of *Voyager* after a test flight in November 1986.

Final test *Voyager*'s most demanding flight before the round-the-world attempt was a four-and-a-half-day test flight up and down the California coast in July 1986. Accompanied by a chase plane, *Voyager* begins this monumental dry run.

need less fuel, but the weight saved in the construction would then allow more fuel to be carried. It was a vicious circle turned virtuous.

The result, developed over five years, was a masterpiece of aircraft engineering, a slim central fuselage flanked by two outriggers linked by a front, or canard, elevator. Two immense tapering wings swept out to either side. It was built of a composite material of graphite, Kevlar, and fibreglass, immensely strong yet ultra-lightweight. At either end of the main cabin were two engines, both driving propellers – one to pull, the other to push.

It looked like an improbable cross between a high-performance multihull yacht and a pre–World War I box-kite plane. In reality it was a brilliantly conceived and executed flying fuel tank.

The plane itself weighed 423 kg (939 lb.) – the average family car weighs somewhere around 1,350 kg (3,000 lb.) – the two engines about the same again. Yet its 17 interlinked fuel tanks could carry 4,365 kg (9,700 lb.) of fuel. When fully loaded, fuel accounted for 72.3 percent of the machine's total weight.

Voyager's drawbacks

It was not designed for comfort. Though it could carry two people, they were huddled in a tiny cabin cum cockpit 2.25 metres (7 and a half ft) long, 1 metre (3 ft) wide, and 1 metre (3 ft) high. It was in this 'horizontal telephone booth' that Rutan and Yeager would spend the nine days it was estimated the trip would take, alternately flying, navigating and resting (sleeping turned out to be a near impossibility).

It was also not an easy machine to fly. It was exceptionally sluggish when fully loaded, calling for very delicate handling. But even with a light fuel load, it was unresponsive, demanding the pilot's full attention. In addition, it was essential to avoid turbulence, not because of any structural weakness but because buffeting reduced aerodynamic efficiency and therefore used more fuel. Rain, too, cut down *Voyager*'s efficiency, increasing drag and fuel consumption.

Maximum tailwinds, minimum turbulence

Given the extreme limits at which *Voyager* would be operating, its route had to be precisely planned. The goal was to have the maximum number of tailwinds and the minimum amount of turbulence. In effect, this meant exploiting the reliable winds of the trade-wind belt around the equator while flying over water as much as possible to avoid the usual turbulence over landmasses in the tropics.

From the meteorological point of view, the ideal moment for the flight was September, for preference with a full Moon. When an accident to a propeller made

Voyager and beyond

For endurance and fortitude the clear heroes of *Voyager* were its pilots. Dick Rutan had flown 325 combat missions over Vietnam, becoming one of America's most decorated fliers. Jeana Yeager, a compelling standard-bearer of the cause of women's aviation in America, had established her credentials as an aviator long before her association with *Voyager*. Together their achievement in piloting so unforgiving a machine over such a vast distance, surmounting endless technical problems while battling mounting fatigue, is hard to overstate.

Yet the real hero of *Voyager* was its designer, Burt Rutan (above). *Voyager* may have brought him to the attention of the wider public, but his ability to 'think out of the box' had already assured him of cult status in cutting-edge aviation circles. Since *Voyager* he has gone from strength to strength, designing the *Virgin Atlantic Global Flyer*, among other planes, a direct descendant of *Voyager*, in which in March 2005 Steve Fossett made the first nonstop, unrefuelled solo round-the-world flight in a time of 67 hours and 1 minute. In February 2006 Fossett made a second nonstop unrefuelled solo round-the-world flight in the *Virgin Atlantic Global Flyer*, setting a new record of 42,222 km (26,389 miles) of continuous flight.

it impossible to meet this original weather window, the meteorologists urged a postponement to the following summer. The project leaders said no, arguing in favour of the earliest possible departure if only to avoid the financial drain of a lengthy postponement.

On 14 December 1986, at 8:01 A.M., *Voyager* fully fuelled up (a process that took 6 hours) and took off from Edwards Air Force Base in California. Edwards had been chosen because of its reliably windless weather and clear skies as well as its 4,500 metres (15,000 ft) runway, which was one of the longest in the world. And *Voyager* needed an extremely long runway. It rose into the air after a takeoff run lasting 2 minutes, 6 seconds with just 240 metres (800 ft) of runway remaining.

Doomed to failure?

There were fears that the flight was doomed almost as soon as it had begun. Both wing tips, which, when loaded, hung down to the ground when the plane was stationary, had been damaged during takeoff. An inspection from an accompanying plane suggested the damage was trivial. Rutan and Yeager reported that *Voyager* was handling normally. With the all-clear given, *Voyager* headed out over the Pacific.

Flying at its optimum height of 2,400 metres (8,000 ft) (which took 3 hours to reach) and at a sedate 200 km/h (120 mph), *Voyager* passed Hawaii by nightfall. As the fuel load decreased, the front engine was shut down. But ahead, over the Philippines, was a typhoon.

The risks posed by this storm were brilliantly exploited by the ground-based meteorological team and the crew. Altering *Voyager*'s course to the north, they not only avoided the storm but took advantage of the strong easterly winds to its north to slingshot *Voyager* towards the Indian Ocean.

Africa, the only major landmass to be crossed on the journey, was the next hurdle. A series of unpredictable thunderstorms forced the now exhausted Rutan and Yeager to climb close to *Voyager*'s maximum height of 6,000 metres (20,000 ft), using precious fuel in the process. Rutan later likened *Voyager*'s crossing of Africa to, 'Flying through a redwood forest, dodging around and between the massive trunks.' As they emerged over the

Three pioneers Yeager and Rutan flank Brian Allen, the first man to fly the English Channel in a pedal-powered plane.

Atlantic, both pilots were 'crying openly with relief'.

The Atlantic crossing provided some respite. But nearing the coast of northern Brazil, a sudden thunderstorm came close to flipping the machine over. Worse followed. After crossing Mexico, Rutan and Yeager swung out over the Pacific before heading back to Edwards in an attempt to avoid reported headwinds, hoping to skirt and fly under them. As they descended, the fuel in the near-empty tank they were using slopped forward, feeding only air into the rear engine. It stopped.

> *Just like when early airplanes were flying in 1910, we didn't know what the benefits were but we were doing it because it's fun.*
>
> Burt Rutan on *Voyager*

Rutan radioed, 'We've just lost the back engine and I can't start it or the front engine.' In four frantic minutes the *Voyager* dropped more than 900 metres (3,000 ft) before, fuel restored, the rear engine fired again. Headwind or not, the crew gradually brought *Voyager* back to its normal cruising altitude.

The weather gods thereafter relented. At 8:06 A.M. on 23 December, *Voyager* touched down at Edwards under a flawless sky. There was just 48 kg (106 lb.) of fuel left in the tanks.

The first solo nonstop round-the-world balloon flight

Steve Fossett was not the first to fly nonstop around the world in a balloon. That was achieved by an Anglo-Swiss team, Brian Jones and Bertrand Piccard, in March 1999 in their *Breitling Orbiter III*. But to multirecord-breaker Fossett, it was the solo flight around the world that was the real goal. It would take him 10 years and six attempts to achieve it.

The difficulties of flying nonstop around the world in a balloon are legion. It is not just a matter of endurance but of controlling the balloon's direction. Any balloon will go only where the wind takes it. There are just two ways the pilot can exercise even limited control. The first is to choose the most favourable winds, delaying departure accordingly and hoping the wind will continue during the course of the flight. The second, once under way, is to climb or descend in the hope of better conditions. Neither carries any guarantee.

This limits round-the-world flights to two options. In the Northern Hemisphere there is a weather window in December and January with a reasonable expectation of westerly winds around the globe. In the Southern Hemisphere there is a similar window, between June and August, with the same expectation. In both cases it means flying at high altitudes to take advantage of the jet stream. If this means high speeds, it also means temperatures as low as −40°C (−40°F). As well as the risk of icing up, temperatures this low work directly against the basics of balloon flight.

The complexities of balloon flight

The are two types of balloon: hot-air and helium. The former works on the simple principle that warm air rises;

Balloon man Fossett gets set for departure, waving to supporters before securing himself in his capsule.

Final preparations Members of Steve Fossett's support team make final checks and adjustments prior to the launch of *Spirit of Freedom* in June 2002. At 50 metres (180 ft) high the balloon was bigger than those used on his five previous attempts at a solo round-the-world trip.

the latter that helium is lighter than air, though it, too, needs to be warm to generate the most lift. A hot-air balloon could never carry enough fuel for more than a day. A helium balloon has greater range, but as it cools at night, ballast has to be dropped to maintain height. As the gas warms the following day, the balloon then climbs too high. To maintain the correct altitude, helium has to be released, thereby reducing the balloon's lift the following night.

The solution is to use a combined hot-air and helium balloon, with the helium in a self-contained cell above a conventional hot-air cone, both double skinned for insulation and strength. This has the advantage that during the day relatively little fuel is needed to heat the air, while at night, when the air has to be heated, it also

> ❛ This is the oldest form of aviation in the world – ballooning – and yet it [a solo round-the-world flight] hasn't been done yet. ❜
>
> **Steve Fossett**

warms the helium above it, generating further lift.

On Fossett's fourth attempt, in August 1998, he was brought face to face with another reality: balloons are fragile. Nine days and 22,400 km (14,000 miles) into the flight, he ran into a thunderstorm. It ruptured the balloon's skin. The balloon fell 9,000 metres (29,000 ft) into the Coral Sea, where Fossett spent 23 hours on a life raft before being rescued.

Sixth-time lucky

Fossett's sixth attempt (like his fifth) was made from Western Australia. By now he had his biggest-ever balloon, 50 metres (180 ft) high. The helium cell had a capacity of 56,663 cubic metres (200,000 cu ft), the hot-

The record man

Since the early 1990s Steve Fossett, born in Tennessee in 1944, has demonstrated an extraordinary capacity for record-breaking in a variety of endurance sports: aviation, gliding, airships, sailing and ballooning. By late 2006 he had set no less than 116 records, of which 76 still stood.

As well as being the first man to fly nonstop around the world in a balloon, in February–March 2005 he also became the first person to complete a solo nonstop round-the-world flight in a powered aircraft, the *Virgin Atlantic Global Flyer*. The flight, made at an average speed of 550 km/h (340 mph), took him 67 hours. The following February, again flying solo, he broke the absolute nonstop world distance record for any aircraft, flying 41,467 km (25,766 miles) in 76 hours and 43 minutes.

His sailing records are scarcely less remarkable, among the highlights are the then fastest east–west crossing of the Atlantic, 4 days and 17 hours, set in October 2001 on his multihull *Playstation*, and in 2004 a record round-the-world time of 58 days and 9 hours, also on *Playstation*.

Almost as an afterthought, he drove in the Le Mans 24-hour car race and swam the English Channel. In 2007, driving a rocket-powered car, he plans to set a new world land-speed record, his goal 1,280 km/h (800 mph).

Speaking in 2006, he said, 'I plan to be setting and breaking records indefinitely.' You can be sure he means it.

air cone of 2,831 cubic metres (100,000 cu ft). Around the Kevlar-and-carbon capsule were festooned 38 tanks of propane and ethane. The capsule itself, 8 metres (5 ft) square and 2 metres (7 ft) high, was unpressurized, so Fossett would need to wear an oxygen mask for much of the flight. An autopilot maintained altitudes; communications and navigation equipment provided links with mission control in St Louis, allowing weather updates and position finding. Sanitary facilities began and ended with a bucket. Fossett took off at 9:37 A.M. on 19 June 2002.

Riding a 'tenacious jet stream', in the first two days he covered more than 5,600 km (3,500 miles). Two days later, storms blocked his path. To avoid them, he dropped to 120 metres (400 ft), slowing to 32 km/h (20 mph). He avoided the storms, but downdrafts threatened to force the slow-reacting balloon into the sea. He called it 'the most crucial day so far'.

By 27 June he had cleared the Andes, enduring a series of abrupt leaps and dives, the autopilot overcompensating to downdrafts by sending the balloon dangerously high, from where, as it rapidly cooled, it went into high-speed dives. It took 3 hours to regain stability, but he was halfway there.

Drifting south

By 1 July Fossett had cleared South Africa. The wind then began to push him south, worryingly close to Antarctica. If the record was looking more and more certain, so was the prospect that Fossett would miss Australia altogether. He did.

Thirteen days, 8 hours and 33 minutes after takeoff, he crossed the longitude of his starting point. He had circled the globe. But he was still several hundred miles from land. It took him another 35 hours to fight his way north, landing in Queensland after flying 33,195 km (20,626 miles) in 14 days, 19 hours and 51 minutes.

Alone in the skies Steve Fossett's *Spirit of Freedom* pictured shortly after launch from Northam, Western Australia, on 19 June 2002. Almost 15 days later, having covered 33,195 km (20,626 miles), he touched down in Queensland, Australia.

SpaceShipOne: The first private venture into space

BURT RUTAN	June–October 2004

Since the 1960s it was believed that manned spaceflight could only be the preserve of superpower governments. In June and October 2004 *SpaceShipOne*, a private venture, changed this view. In two flights the ship, brainchild of Burt Rutan, reached 102,891 metres (337,569 ft), then 112,041 metres (367,591 ft). These were the margins of space itself.

The impetus behind the flights was the $10 million Ansari X-Prize. Its goal was to provoke new ways of looking at spaceflight, specifically to escape the idea that only governments could afford to send men into space. To win the prize, two flights had to be made within two weeks, each reaching 100 km (62 miles) above the Earth, the internationally recognised boundary of space.

Ansari's initiative provoked a felicitous coming-together of California-based Burt Rutan, whose cutting-edge designs had made him the most forward-looking aircraft designer in the world, and Paul Allen, cofounder of Microsoft, a billionaire with a continuing commitment to technological innovation.

Rutan had begun looking at ways to send a man into

Set to soar *SpaceShipOne*'s first flight, on 21 June 2004. This photograph was taken moments after separating from its launch plane, *WhiteKnightOne*. From there it would blast to the fringes of space.

space as early as 1996. His twin goals were safety and simplicity. If these could be properly mastered, there was no reason why routine low-cost spaceflights should not follow. In part, it was the prospect of space tourism that appealed to Rutan, but even more exciting was the challenge of designing a workable, reusable space vehicle.

Over the following five years, Rutan came up with a solution that was as elegant as it was practical. The task was obvious: to devise a low-cost means of projecting a vehicle into space that could then be flown back to Earth without subjecting it to the stresses of a conventional reentry.

Rutan's goal

The first part of the solution was unashamedly borrowed from the X-15 programme, an American attempt (between 1959 and 1968) at suborbital spaceflight. Similar to the way the X-15 rocket plane was launched in the air from a B-52 bomber, Rutan proposed to bolt his craft to a mother ship – *WhiteKnightOne* – that would carry it to 15,250 metres (50,000 ft). Once released, it would blast upwards under its own rocket power for slightly more than a minute. With the engine shut down, the craft would continue to glide upward for another minute, passing the 100-km (62-mile) barrier before beginning its descent. Weightlessness would last about three and a half minutes.

Rather than plummeting back to Earth in a ball of fire, the rear part of the wing and twin tails would tilt upwards, slowing the ship and stablising it to create a 'shuttlecock' – or, as Rutan liked to call it, 'care-free' – reentry, the ship automatically positioned at the correct angle, in effect flying itself. The wings would then return to their flight position, and the ship would glide back to land. It was a bold idea. And it worked.

70 miles high

SpaceShipOne made a test flight into space on 21 June 2004, reaching a height of 101.1 km (62.82 miles). By September, Rutan was confident that the two flights to win the Ansari X-Prize could be made. The first was on 29 September and reached 102 km (63.38 miles). There was some concern during the ascent, when the craft rolled 29 times, but its climb was otherwise unaffected. As soon as the wings and tail were deployed upwards, the rolling stopped. On 4 October it flew again, reaching 112 km (69.59 miles) and its highest-ever speed, Mach 3.09 (3,518 km/h/2,198 mph), after the longest firing of the rocket yet: 84 seconds. It was a spectacular vindication of Rutan's vision.

SpaceShipTwo

Almost as soon as *SpaceShipOne* had completed its third flight into space, Rutan, backed by British billionaire Sir Richard Branson, announced plans for a second, larger ship – *SpaceShipTwo* – capable of carrying up to nine people into space: two pilots and seven paying passengers.

The first commercial flights are scheduled for 2008. The passengers will be able to move around the ship during weightlessness. The fully pressurised double-skinned cabin also means that it will not be necessary to wear space suits. It will take off and land from the Mojave Airport Civilian Flight Test Center in California.

Infinitely more challenging still are plans for *SpaceShipThree*, an orbital passenger-carrying vehicle. Suborbital spaceflight requires speeds no greater than Mach 3. Orbital flight, by contrast, requires speeds of Mach 25 – 28,000 km/h (17,500 mph), resulting in much greater stresses during reentry.

❝ Our success proves without question that manned spaceflight does not require mammoth government expenditure. It can be done by a small company operating with limited resources and a few dozen dedicated employees. ❞

Burt Rutan

2
Ice & Snow

The Northwest Passage attained

ROALD AMUNDSEN | **26 August 1905**

On 26 August 1905, Roald Amundsen, a Norwegian, became the first man to complete a seaborne crossing of the Northwest Passage. It had taken him almost two years and included some remarkable sled journeys. His success, achieved with a crew of only six, ended almost a century of expeditions to navigate what by then had become one of the most elusive – and alluring – of geographical goals.

As early as the 16th century, the existence of an easily navigable 'northwest' passage to the north of the newly discovered North American continent, linking the Atlantic and Pacific oceans, had lured sailors and merchants seeking a new route between Europe and the presumed riches of the Orient. In a series of epic voyages, the Davis Strait, Baffin Bay and Hudson's Bay were discovered. But by 1616 attempts to force a route through these ice-choked northern seas had been abandoned.

They were resumed at the end of the Napoleonic Wars when the British Royal Navy, overmanned and underemployed after the defeat of Napoleon, began a series of attempts to find a navigable route through the Northwest Passage. Following the ill-fated expedition led by John Franklin in 1845, during which both his ships were crushed by ice and the entire party died, interest in the Northwest Passage languished.

When Northwest Passage interest revived, the focus had shifted from daring human exploration to scientific inquiry. In 1900 the 29-year-old Roald Amundsen used research and careful planning to assemble his own expedition to take on the Northwest Passage.

A new approach

Amundsen epitomised the new approach to Arctic exploration. Where the Royal Navy had trusted in its traditional virtues of large ships and large crews, Amundsen opted for a very small team on an equally small ship. Amundsen's vessel, the *Gjoa*, universally derided as too small for so arduous a voyage, was only 21 metres (70 ft) long. True, short of money, his choice of vessel was limited. But it reinforced his approach to polar exploration: that small, motivated teams of specialists, expertly led and with clear goals, were much more likely to succeed in hostile environments than larger expeditions. In June 1903 Amundsen and his crew left Norway for the Northwest Passage.

The two years Amundsen spent in his quest highlight the qualities that would make him possibly the most

Alaska-bound After completing the Northwest Passage, Amundsen sled 960 km (600 miles) to Eagle City, Alaska, to break the news.

remarkable explorer of the 20th century. Two traits dominated. First, his recognition that in such alien environments no trouble was too great to attend to, particularly nursing and soothing the egos and anxieties of his team. Second, he instinctively understood that survival in such extreme conditions required learning from those native peoples who had lived in such conditions for thousands of years – the Inuits.

Rational and clear-headed, Amundsen recognised the risks of his journey. This meant accepting setbacks with equanimity, but it also meant taking advantage of good fortune. And good fortune was with the *Gjoa* in the early part of the expedition. Having reached the northern entrance of Peel Sound in late August 1903, an area that had consistently been reported as an ice barrier through which no ship could sail, he found it ice free.

By early September, with winter advancing, Amundsen located a near-perfect berth for the *Gjoa* on the eastern coast of King William Island. He named it Gjoafjord. Here, as the ice advanced again, he settled in for what he assumed would be his winter quarters. The Arctic ice, always unpredictable, held Amundsen's ship there for two years.

Locating the Magnetic Pole

With the *Gjoa* gripped by the ice, Amundsen, whatever his worries for the future of his ship, embarked on a series of sled journeys. Most important, he located the Magnetic Pole and found that it had shifted decisively

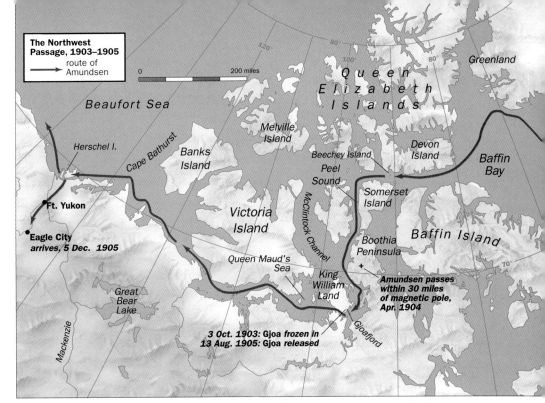

Roald Amundsen's traversing of the Northwest Passage took in excess of two years, much of it spent stricken by ice at Gjoafjord.

Inuit on *Gjoa* It was through the Netsilik Inuit that Amundsen properly began to understand how to survive in the Arctic. They were frequent visitors to the ship and they taught him to sled with dogs.

> **My boyhood dream ... A strange feeling welled up in my throat. I felt tears in my eyes.**
>
> Amundsen, on reaching the end of the Passage

since it was first identified by James Ross in 1831. And, most significantly, his grasp of the imperatives of survival in polar regions was transformed into something close to a life force. 'I could imagine no purer life,' he later wrote. 'It was all I had ever sought.'

On 13 August 1906, the ice in Gjoahaven suddenly retreated. The *Gjoa*, afloat once more, headed west toward the Pacific, picking its way along the treacherous coast of northern Canada. When on 26 August a ship was sighted, it was clear the legendary passage had been achieved.

Farthest south: *Nimrod* expedition to Antarctica

ERNEST SHACKLETON	1907–1909

On 9 January 1909, four men (Ernest Shackleton, Frank Wild, Eric Marshall and Jameson Adams) planted a Union Flag on the bitter, windswept wastes of the South Polar plateau. They were 155 km (97 miles) from the South Pole. They had struggled, on foot, almost 1,120 km (700 miles) to reach this desolate spot.

To return to their base, they now faced the same distance again. Half rations, bitter cold and ebbing strength confronted them. But against all odds, they made it. The leader of this struggling group was an Irishman named Ernest Shackleton. By turns inspirational and infuriating, he was among the most extraordinary figures of the 'heroic age' of polar exploration. By the then standards of British polar exploration, he was a veteran, having been a member of Robert Scott's 1902–1904 Antarctic expedition. It scarcely amounted to serious training. Scott had arrived in the Antarctic with no experience of polar exploration and a belief that no environment, however hostile, could defeat a British naval officer.

Bias against skis, sleds and dogs

Shackleton, a merchant marine officer, may have been less rigid than Scott, but his ignorance of polar exploration was equal to Scott's. And, like his predecessor, he proved to be a slow learner. Both had a bizarre prejudice against skis, clearly the most efficient means of travel on snow and ice. Both were similarly biased against dogs to pull sleds.

For his expedition, Shackleton proposed to import ponies to pull his sleds. It was a decision taken without any evidence to support it and against the repeated advice of the greatest explorer of the age, the Norwegian Fridtjof Nansen.

These technical limitations were abetted by Shackleton's personality. He was a man of restless energy and high ambition. Yet he was inconsistent in his goals, forever drawn to new adventures, rushing impulsively from project to project in pursuit of fame and money.

His Antarctic expedition was hastily arranged in just seven months (horrifying Roald Amundsen, who believed that two years were needed to put together any such venture). The expedition was never properly funded. When Shackleton arrived in Antarctica in January 1908, there was no guarantee that there would be enough money to allow his ship, *Nimrod*, to return the following year to collect the party.

To add to these anxieties, Shackleton was forced to go

Trapped The shattered nature of the Antarctic pack ice is highlighted by this image of *Nimrod* beset in the ice.

Farthest south (left to right) Adams, Wild and Shackleton; Marshall took the picture. There is some doubt Shackleton really did get to within 155 km (97 miles) of the Pole. The position was worked out by dead reckoning from the last known position, 96 km (60 miles) to the north.

Faced with the prospect of either an ignominiously early return or drastically reducing rations, Shackleton chose the latter. The food was now to be eked out to last 110 days. The average daily distance goal dropped to 20 km (12 ½ miles). On 9 November that was exactly the distance made. By 25 November Shackleton had passed Scott's farthest point south, set in 1902. To reach it, Scott had averaged 5 km (3 miles) a day; Shackleton was now averaging 21 km (13 miles) a day. Spirits rose accordingly. The following day, however, Frank Wild noted in his diary: 'I am beginning to think we shall get to the Pole alright, but am doubtful about getting back again.'

By 1 December, still trekking southwards, only one of the four ponies was still alive (the others were shot after they were no longer able to work). This provided fresh meat for the party but increased the loads to be pulled. Already, Shackleton was reporting that '…we are very hungry.'

back on a promise to Scott that the expedition would stay away from Scott's old base in McMurdo Sound. Shackleton's mood – and prospects – were dampened further en route to Antarctica by a running feud with *Nimrod*'s captain, Rupert England, who was suffering a nervous collapse. The party that eventually landed at McMurdo Sound on 29 January 1908, was thoroughly demoralized.

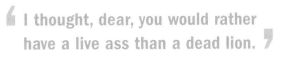

> ❝ I thought, dear, you would rather have a live ass than a dead lion. ❞
>
> Ernest Shackleton to his wife, Emily, after turning back 97 miles short of the Pole.

Early setbacks

On 29 October 1908, having endured a more or less trouble-free winter, Shackleton left for the Pole. The distance, to be covered entirely on foot, was 1,195 km (747 miles) each way. He had food for a party of four for 91 days, calculated on an expected progress of 26 km (16 ½ miles) a day. After nine days of struggling over crevasses with the ponies repeatedly sinking into the snow up to their stomachs and having to be rescued, the party had made 86 km (54 miles), an average of 9.5 km (6 miles) a day.

Until this point, Shackleton's party had been travelling on the Ross Ice Shelf, a vast sheet of sea ice, hundreds of metres thick. By Antarctic standards it was easy to cover. But ahead loomed a mountain range that would have to be climbed to reach the Pole.

Here Shackleton showed the remarkable side of his character. The greater the challenge, the more heroically he rose to it. Over the next month, he led, cajoled, encouraged and bullied his men up a 3,300-metre (11,000-ft) climb of the vast Beardmore Glacier,

The return to McMurdo Sound

On 20 January 1909, making their way down the Beardmore Glacier, Shackleton and his party were 21 km (13 miles) from their next food depot. They had supplies for one day. If they made the depot, they would then pick up a further five days' food, which was intended to take them to the next depot, 160 km (100 miles) off. This was a distance it had taken 14 days to cover on their way up the glacier. Now they had to do it in five. That evening Shackleton collapsed.

By 26 January they were still 32 km (20 miles) short of the second food depot. When they finished breakfast that morning, there was no food left. Late in the afternoon Eric Marshall, the expedition doctor, handed around 'Forced March' pills – cocaine tablets. It was their final throw.

By midnight the depot was in sight, perhaps 3 or 4 km away. At this point Frank Wild collapsed. 'Repeated kicking' failed to wake him. Marshall set off on his own, returning within an hour with what food he could carry. By now, the party had not eaten for 40 hours. It was, wrote Shackleton, 'The hardest and most trying day we have ever spent ... and which will ever stand in our memories.' Such were the tiny margins by which he and his party survived.

The picture above shows (left to right) Wild, Shackleton, Marshall and Adams aboard *Nimrod* after their harrowing return journey.

pathfinding every step of the way. On 7 December the last pony died when it plunged into a crevasse, depriving the men of a further source of food.

A matter of survival

On Christmas Day they were 400 km (250 miles) from the Pole. There was one month's food left. The ration was reduced again. The body temperatures of all four men were now 2 degrees below normal. By 3 January, with 288 km (180 miles) still to go, it was clear the Pole was unattainable. But if it couldn't be reached, Shackleton was determined to get within 160 km (100 miles) of it. All nonessential items were now dumped, and rations were reduced again in pursuit of a 'final dash'. On 9 January

Two sides to Shackleton In civilian life Shackleton was a clear misfit. Away from civilisation he was revered by his men, clear thinking and tough.

1909, four shivering figures planted their flag 155 km (97 miles) from the South Pole. They now faced the drudgery of retracing their steps . If they failed to reach any of their inadequately marked depots before their limited food ran out, they would die. They all knew it.

Shackleton and his three men returned to McMurdo Sound on the very day the *Nimrod*, their relief ship, was due to leave. 'I cannot describe adequately the mental and physical strain,' he later wrote. It is hard to know whether Shackleton was grotesquely reckless, allowing his pursuit of fame to warp his judgement about unacceptably high risks, or whether he was touched by a kind of genius for survival in the most hostile environments. Either way, his attempt to reach the South Pole in 1908–1909 remains among the most inspiring – and terrifying – of all journeys.

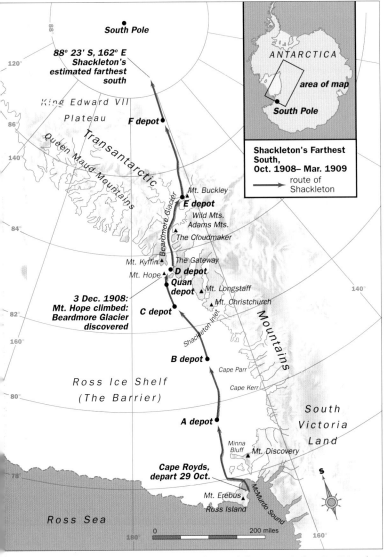

Shackleton's party made a round-trip of almost 2,240 km (1,400 miles) in Antarctica in 1908–1909. They failed to make the Pole, but all of the men survived.

> **No person who has not spent a period of his life in those stark and sullen solitudes that sentinel the Pole will understand fully what trees and flowers...and running streams mean to the soul of a man.**
>
> Ernest Shackleton

Dual claims to have reached the North Pole

DR. FREDERICK COOK AND ROBERT PEARY | 1908–1909

On 1 September 1909, the American explorer, Dr. Frederick Cook, emerged from the Arctic wastes to announce that on 21 April the previous year he had reached the North Pole. Five days later a second American, Robert Peary, claimed that he, too, had reached the Pole, on 6 April 1909. Each denounced the other as a fraud. Who could claim priority? More to the point, could either?

Cook', in the words of the Danish explorer Peter Freuchen, 'is a liar and a gentleman. Peary is neither.' It seemed – and seems – an accurate summing up of the dispute between the two, and the claims made by them and their supporters. The supporters were principally newspapers, the *New York Herald* backing Cook and the *New York Times* Peary. The papers had staked large sums on their men as part of a circulation battle, and the finger-pointing was very public.

Both men should have had credible claims to have reached the Pole. Peary's expedition was the eighth he had made to the Arctic. On his previous expedition, in 1906, he had come within 278 km (174 miles) of the Pole. Cook's first Arctic journey, in 1891, had been made with Peary, and he accompanied Peary on a later attempt to reach the Pole in 1902. He was also a member, with Roald Amundsen, of the *Belgica* expedition of 1897–1899, the first to spend the winter in Antarctica.

Different methods

Their attempts on the Pole in 1908 and 1909 were radically different. Cook travelled light, with two Inuits, two sleds and 26 dogs. Peary, by contrast, planned a military-style operation, intending to 'force' his way to the Pole. He took 24 men, 19 sleds and 133 dogs. The men were to blaze a path for Peary as well as to prepare the return route, each one turning for home at predetermined intervals. The last party left Peary, poised for his 'final dash', 213 km (133 miles) from the Pole.

Peary on the march His teams were precisely organised and highly professional, their depots at exactly spaced intervals. His party had 24 men, 19 sleds and 133 dogs. He was the first to recognise that winter was the best moment to travel if the Pole was to be reached.

> **The Pole at last!!! The prize of three centuries, my dream and ambition for 23 years. Mine at last.**
>
> *Peary at the North Pole*

The case against Cook was that the proof he supplied to back his claim was flimsy. He produced no astronomical observations, which he would have had to made to fix his position. Furthermore, based on his own figures, the food he took with him could scarcely have lasted 42 days, let alone the 84 he claimed to have spent in covering the 1,760 km (1,100 miles) to and from the Pole.

Knud Rasmussen, a Danish explorer, described Cook's proof of the Pole as ' … impudent … the most childish sort of attempt at cheating.' Roald Amundsen added a sad postscript: '… I was forced to come to the conclusion that my old comrade was lying.'

Did either explorer make the Pole?

The case against Peary is less clear cut and largely rests on the improbably high daily distances he made on his return. His distance to the Pole – 661 km (413 miles) – had taken 27 outward marches at an average of 24.5 km (15 ¼ miles) each. On his return, however, Peary claimed to have covered the same distance in 16 marches, an average of 41 km (25 ½ miles) each. This is not an impossible figure, but it is an unlikely one. In his defence, Peary claimed that the rationale behind his return journey was that he would be travelling light on a premarked route.

If the case against Cook has always looked watertight, that against Peary will almost certainly never be proved. The most probable conclusion is that neither man actually reached the Pole – but that Peary was at least close to it.

Faker The mystery of Frederick Cook is why such a successful explorer should have so transparently faked his claims to have reached the Pole.

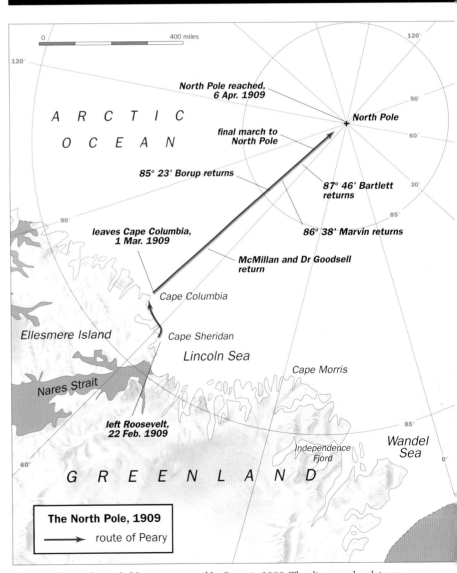

The map shows the probable route covered by Peary in 1909. The distances he claims to have made on the return leg seem unlikely although not impossible.

The winter trek to Cape Crozier

EDWARD WILSON, HENRY BOWERS AND APSLEY CHERRY-GARRARD

June–August 1911

On Robert Falcon Scott's Antarctic expedition of 1901–1904, a colony of Emperor penguins was discovered. The expedition's scientific leader, Edward Wilson, believed they were a key point in the evolution of birds and reptiles. To prove it would mean examining their eggs, which hatched in midwinter. On Scott's second expedition (1910–1913) Wilson organised a three-man party to collect them.

It is hard to imagine the horrors of winter travel in the Antarctic. Winter is a time of permanent darkness and extreme cold that numbs the senses. In such terrifying conditions survival is not dependent on character and determination but on preparation and technology.

Wilson's party – himself, Henry 'Birdie' Bowers and Apsley Cherry-Garrard – were poorly equipped. All they could offer was a combination of *esprit de corps* and a belief that the scientific imperatives of what they were setting out to achieve justified the agonies of their journey.

Horrors await Left to right: 'Birdie' Bowers, Edward Wilson, Apsley Cherry-Garrard just before leaving for Cape Crozier.

The distance to be covered was not great, about 107 km (67 miles) each way, most of it over what, in the summer, was the relatively easy travelling of the Ross Ice Shelf. They had two sleds with a total of six weeks' provisions. They had no skis and they were man-hauling, each pulling about 112 kg (250 lb.).

Freezing conditions

The three men left on 27 June. By the following day, as they left the comparative warmth of the sea-ice, temperatures plummeted. On the night of June 29, it was –54°C (–65°F), the following night –60°C (–76°F). On 6 July, it was –60.5°C (–77°F) at noon. In such low temperatures sled runners can no longer melt the snow over which they pass. As a result, not only were the men sinking deep into the snow with each step, the effort of pulling the sleds became intolerable. By 30 June they were forced to relay: to take one sled, leave it and come back for the second. To travel 1 mile, they had to walk 3.

They made 5.25 km (3 ¼ miles) that day. The following day it took them eight hours to travel 4 km (2 ½ miles). Over the next seven days they travelled 19 km (12 miles), twice managing less then 3.25 km (2 miles) a day. It took 19 days to make Cape Crozier, an average of 5.5 km (3 ½ miles) a day.

Camp work was a nightmare. What might normally

'Good God! Here is the Crozier party!' These were the words that greeted Wilson (left), Bowers (centre) and Cherry-Garrard (right) on their return to Cape Evans on 1 August. Considering what they had endured, they survived remarkably unscathed.

take two hours, loading and unloading sleds, putting up and taking down the tent, was now taking nine hours. The string around the mouth of the tent was frozen into a wirelike consistency. Even the food bags were proving almost impossible to open. To touch any piece of metal was to guarantee frostbite. Matches proved incredibly hard to light. Writing was a near impossibility: as the men's breath instantly froze, so any piece of paper would be covered by a film of ice. Their feet were permanently numbed with cold, the skin splitting, and all three had huge fluid-filled blisters on their fingers. Inevitably, the fluid froze with agonizing results. 'Sometimes,' wrote Cherry-Garrard, 'it was difficult not to howl.'

Their woollen balaclavas were effectively soldered to their heads with ice, their clothes frozen equally rigid.

> If we had been dressed in lead we should have been able to move our arms and necks and heads more easily than we could now. If the same amount of icing had extended to our legs I believe we should still be there, unable to move.
>
> Cherry-Garrard on the hazards of their frozen clothing

Emerging from the tent one morning, Cherry-Garrard glanced upwards. His clothes had frozen solid, forcing him to spend the whole morning with his head locked skyward.

Yet their worst moments were always in their reindeer sleeping bags. It frequently took an hour to force their way into them, hammering and battering at the rigid, unyielding fur. The bags then slowly thawed, leaving the men in ice water. Less than a week into the journey, Cherry-Garrard was writing of '… a very bad night: a succession of shivering fits which I was quite unable to stop, and which took possession of my body … until I thought my back would break.' All suffered the agonies of cramping.

Their desperately slow progress and the extreme cold also meant they were using their fuel at an alarmingly high rate. They had started with six 4.5-L (1-gallon) tins. By 13

The Igloo

The decision to build an igloo once the three men arrived at the nesting grounds was sensible on paper: It would be larger and warmer than the tent; further, they could heat it with their blubber stove knowing that the 'oily black filth' it produced would not matter in a temporary structure. In practice it turned out to be a near catastrophe.

The structure was simple. The walls were built of rocks banked with snow. One of the sleds was used as a ridge pole, over which a sheet of thick canvas was stretched, its edges tied to rocks and weighed down with snow blocks. Further snow blocks were placed over the roof to anchor it yet more firmly. An immediate drawback was that however much snow was piled in and around the rock walls, it was impossible to prevent fine particles of drift and grit finding their way into the hut. Socks, gloves, jerseys, and other items of clothing,

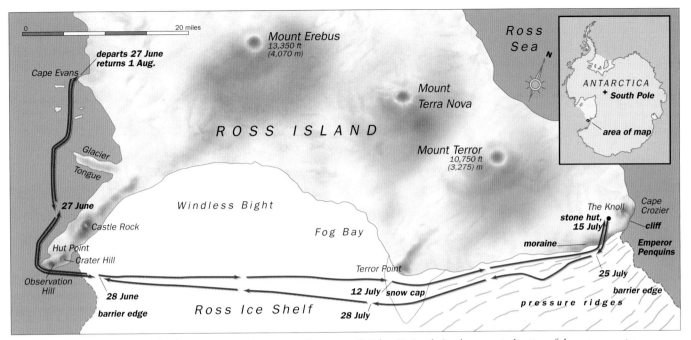

The Cape Crozier party's painfully slow progress on their outward journey – 3–5 km (2–3 miles) a day – was indicative of the extreme winter conditions in the Antarctic.

July, before they had even reached Cape Crozier, only two were left. Compounding their anguish, they then became lost in vast, confusing waves of pressure ice. Unable to navigate in the dark or to see crevasses, they could only plod doggedly onwards, trusting to luck and to Providence.

Reaching the eggs

Finally at Cape Crozier, they built a canvas-roofed igloo, more spacious than their tent, before picking their way through pressure ice and clambering over ice cliffs to where the birds nested 6.5 km (4 miles) away. It took two visits before they could reach the birds. They collected five eggs, two of which Cherry-Garrard broke almost immediately. But they had what they had come for. On the return trek, they became lost. 'As we groped our way back that night,' wrote Cherry-Garrard, 'sleepless, icy and dog-tired in the dark and the wind and the drift, a crevasse seemed almost a friendly gift.'

It was now that their travails began in earnest. First, oil from their blubber stove, which they were using to save their small reserve of fuel, was spat into Wilson's eye. He lay groaning all night, convinced his eye was lost. Then a blizzard swept away their tent, pitched outside the igloo.

> **As we groped our way back that night, sleepless, icy and dog-tired in the dark and the wind and the drift, a crevasse seemed almost a friendly gift.**
>
> Cherry-Garrard on the his way down off the ice cliffs

The next day it blew the roof off the igloo. For 48 hours they lay in their bags, without food, contemplating certain death. As the storm died, Bowers embarked on a search for the tent. He found it, scarcely damaged, half a mile away. 'We were so thankful we said nothing', wrote Cherry-Garrard.

Their return passed in a blur of exhaustion, the men sleeping as they walked. Bowers fell into a crevasse to the limit of his harness. Their clothes were rapidly being reduced to rags. The cold remained relentless. Yet it is an extraordinary testament to underlying loyalty the men felt to one another that, in the face of so futile an epic of suffering, they remained unendingly cheerful. 'I never heard an angry word', wrote Cherry-Garrard.

Missing link

Less than a year later Wilson and Bowers died on Robert Falcon Scott's doomed South Pole expedition (*see* p. 74). The three eggs were delivered by Cherry-Garrard to London's Natural History Museum in 1913, where they were subsequently examined and shown, as Wilson had suspected, to provide a key link in the evolution of birds and reptiles. Cherry-Garrard was forever haunted by the death of Scott. He died in 1955.

The South Pole attained

ROALD AMUNDSEN
AND ROBERT FALCON SCOTT

1909–1911 and 1910–1912

On 14 December 1911, the Norwegian Roald Amundsen, leading a team of four, became the first man to reach the South Pole. It took him 55 days to cover the 1,128 km (705 miles) to the Pole from his base at the Bay of Whales. With abundant supplies in hand, it then took him only 42 days to make the return journey. It was perhaps the most precisely planned and executed polar journey ever made.

Amundsen's success can be painfully contrasted with the simultaneous attempt made on the South Pole by Captain Robert Scott of the Royal Navy. Amundsen had a single goal in mind: the Pole. Scott led an expedition with largely scientific goals. The Pole was the most obvious of these goals, but it was not the only one.

A chance meeting The two expeditions on 4 February 1911. Scott's *Terra Nova* is in the distance, Amundsen's *Fram* in the foreground.

Radically different philosophies

Scott believed that any successful attempt on the South Pole demanded the largest possible numbers. His party totalled 34. Officers and scientists (in effect, honorary officers) lived separately from the 'shore-party men', with the expedition's hut divided in two by a wall built from packing cases. In contrast, Amundsen's nine-man party was entirely civilian and all shared the same conditions, living and working together. Amundsen was the party's leader. In all other respects, nothing differentiated him from the other members.

The two expeditions had radically different approaches to polar travel. Scott, despite his experiences of the Antarctic on a previous expedition in 1901–1904, persisted in his dependence on man-hauling the sleds of supplies, a method of travel the Norwegians regarded with undisguised contempt.

Scott refused to accept the value of dogs to pull sleds. He had taken dogs with him in 1901–1904 and would do so again reluctantly in 1910, but not knowing how to use them properly, he had never benefited from their skills. Worse, because Shackleton had taken ponies with him on his 1907–1909 Antarctic expedition, when he had got to within 155 km (97 miles) of the Pole, Scott decided that he, too, would take ponies.

Both parties planned to make for the Pole from the Ross Sea, travelling over the Ross Ice Shelf – the Barrier – before climbing the Transantarctic Mountains to the

Amundsen versus Scott – rivalry or pragmatism?

Amundsen was not just a consummate professional, he had an absolute goal in mind: the North Pole. It was one fixed almost from the start of his career as an explorer. Amundsen went south for an equally straightforward reason: that the North Pole had apparently already been reached by an American, Robert Peary, in 1909. By this point Amundsen's own plans for an attempt on the North Pole were already well advanced. He had his ship, *Fram*; he had his men; and he had (most of) the necessary financing.

When he left Norway in the summer of 1911, it was ostensibly for Alaska and a planned North Polar drift and attempt at the North Pole. In reality, he had already decided to make an attempt on the South Pole. He had told almost no one. In Madeira, apparently en route for Cape Horn and from there to the Berring Strait, he informed his stunned crew that their goal was the South Pole. Their next landfall was Antarctica. With Amundsen now beyond reach, his brother and business manager, Leon, broke the news. The telegram he sent to Scott, by then in Australia, was a masterpiece of understatement: 'Beg leave to inform you Fram proceeding Antarctica.'

Emotions were heated. Many Norwegians were embarrassed by their countryman's apparently underhanded tactics; most Englishmen were outraged. Sir Clements Markham, president of the Royal Geographical Society and Scott's particular champion, wrote indignantly that '… he [Amundsen] has been deliberately forming a plan to steal a

South Pole attained Amundsen proving himself at the South Pole by use of sextant and artificial horizon. The four navigators in the party each signed the others' navigation books as proof the Pole was reached. Amundsen's final position was later shown to have been accurate to within 180 metres (200 yards).

3,300-metre (11,000-ft) Polar Plateau. As on his earlier expedition, Scott was based on Ross Island in McMurdo Sound at the western end of the Ice Shelf. Amundsen, daringly, made his base on the eastern end of the Ice Shelf.

For Scott the advantages seemed clear. Not only was McMurdo Sound known to him, but Shackleton three years before had pioneered the route from the same base up the Beardmore Glacier to the Polar Plateau. All Scott had to do was follow in Shackleton's footsteps. In reality, McMurdo had significant drawbacks. It was 96 km (60 miles) farther from the Pole than Amundsen's base; in addition, reaching the Barrier meant a 24-km (15-mile) journey on sea ice followed by an exceptionally difficult trek past pressure ice (ice that is pushed by winds and tides and, when rammed against other ice floes, splits and fissures under the pressure of millions of tons) and crevasses.

Amundsen, on the other hand, merely had to step out of his winter quarters to see the Barrier, flat and inviting, stretching in front of him.

Moving supplies

Before the Antarctic winter set in, both parties needed to move supplies onto the Barrier, where they would be left to support the polar attempts the following spring. Their relative performances in these depot-laying journeys give a chilling indication of the parties' respective strengths and weaknesses.

Scott intended to take 1 ton of supplies to 80° south, about 272 km (170 miles) from his base. It took him and 12 men 24 days of weary struggle, during which two of their eight ponies died, to reach a point 48 km (30 miles) short of 80°. On his return, four more ponies died. Amundsen made two depot journeys. On the first, he reached 80° south and returned to his base in five days. On the second, late in the season, he set down two further depots, at 81° and 82° south. In effect, Amundsen had moved his departure point 240 km (150 miles) closer to the Pole than Scott. His farthest depot, at 82° south, was marked by 60 flags; Scott's solitary depot was marked by one.

When Amundsen and Scott began their polar

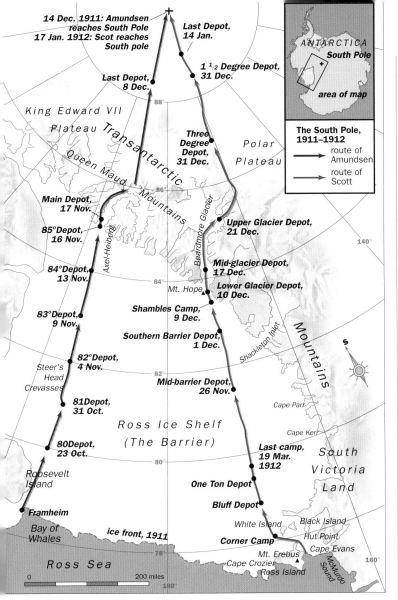

The routes of Amundsen and Scott in 1911 and 1912. For Amundsen there was glory, for Scott tragedy.

Map labels:
14 Dec. 1911: Amundsen reaches South Pole
17 Jan. 1912: Scot reaches South pole
Last Depot, 14 Jan.
1 ½ Degree Depot, 31 Dec.
Last Depot, 8 Dec.
King Edward VII Plateau
Three Degree Depot, 31 Dec.
Polar Plateau
Transantarctic
Queen Maud Mountains
Main Depot, 17 Nov.
85° Depot, 16 Nov.
Axel-Heiberg
Beardmore Glacier
Upper Glacier Depot, 21 Dec.
84° Depot, 13 Nov.
Mt. Hope
Mid-glacier Depot, 17 Dec.
Lower Glacier Depot, 10 Dec.
83° Depot, 9 Nov.
Shambles Camp, 9 Dec.
Southern Barrier Depot, 1 Dec.
Shackleton Inlet
82° Depot, 4 Nov.
Steer's Head Crevasses
Mid-barrier Depot, 26 Nov.
Mountains
81 Depot, 31 Oct.
Cape Part
Cape Kerr
Ross Ice Shelf (The Barrier)
80 Depot, 23 Oct.
Roosevelt Island
Last camp, 19 Mar. 1912
South Victoria Land
One Ton Depot
Bluff Depot
Framheim
Bay of Whales
ice front, 1911
White Island
Black Island
Corner Camp
Hut Point
Cape Evans
Ross Sea
Mt. Erebus
Cape Crozier
Ross Island
McMurdo Sound
0   200 miles

Inset map:
ANTARCTICA
South Pole
area of map
The South Pole, 1911–1912
→ route of Amundsen
→ route of Scott

to travel 24 km (15 miles) a day. It took Amundsen five hours to make this distance, with halts every hour to mark the route and rest the dogs. It took Scott more than 10 hours to cover the same distance with a single halt for lunch. Scott was additionally disadvantaged, at least until the foot of the Beardmore, by using three different methods of travel: tractors (the drivers were reduced to man-hauling after the machines failed), ponies and dogs. As all travelled at different speeds, staggered starts were consistently required. If nothing else, it was a logistical nightmare.

Once at the Beardmore, however, with the last of the ponies shot and depoted to feed the return parties, and the dogs sent back to McMurdo, the real horror of Scott's journey began: man-hauling. Henry Bowers, perhaps the most indefatigable of Scott's men, eternally cheerful, immensely hardworking, wrote of the ascent of the Beardmore that it was '… the most back-breaking work I have ever come up against … The starting was worse than the pulling as it required from ten to fifteen desperate jerks on the harness to move the sled at all.' Ultimately, the effort would prove too great.

> It was a sheer marvel … that the dogs accomplished today. 17 miles [27 km] with 5,000 ft. [1,500 m] climb. Come and say that dogs cannot be used here.
>
> Roald Amundsen

journeys the following spring, their differences were thrown into even starker relief. Amundsen had 1,128 km (705 miles) to travel, pathfinding all the way from 82° south, knowing he had to find a way up and across the Transantarctic Mountains. He left on 20 October and reached the Pole 55 days later, averaging 20 km (12 ¾ miles) per day. Scott had 1,224 km (765 miles) to travel to the Pole, 1,069 (668) already pioneered by Shackleton. Because his ponies were vulnerable to the cold, he was forced to leave later, on 1 November. He reached the Pole on 17 January. It had taken him 78 days at an average of 15.5 km (9 ¾ miles) per day.

Amundsen's superiority

These discrepancies in performance hid a more brutal reality. Assuming good weather, both parties expected

Scott at Cape Evans Suspicious and distant, Scott was the only man in his party to have his own cabin.

Beasts of burden

As Scott's party made their uncertain way across the Barrier towards the Beardmore Glacier, Lawrence 'Titus' Oates wrote in his diary, 'Scott realises now what awful cripples our ponies are and carries a face like a tired seaboot in consequence.'

There is a striking comparison with the attitude of Amundsen and his team to their dogs. Amundsen (his dog camp pictured above) depended on his dogs for his and his team's lives. He also recognised that the life of a dog counted for less than that of a man. Hence the decision to kill most of them for food once they had reached the Polar Plateau. Of the 18 that remained, the relationship between men and animals was perhaps stronger than ever. One of Amundsen's team, Oscar Wisting, took his lead dog, Colonel, back with him to Norway. Colonel died many years later. Of him, Wisting wrote, 'It was as if I had lost one of my own, so much did I miss him.'

Man-hauling takes a toll Man-hauling not only meant much longer on the march to do the necessary daily mileage, the men gradually starved. Their full 'summit' ration was 4,500 calories a day, at least 1,000 less than required. It also greatly increased the risks of dehydration.

It took Scott almost two weeks to climb the Beardmore. It took Amundsen four days to climb to the same height up what he named the Axel Heiberg glacier. On 21 November, as he reached its summit, Amundsen wrote, 'It was a sheer marvel … that the dogs accomplished today. 27 km [17 miles] with 1,500 metre [5,000 ft.] climb. Come and say that dogs cannot be used here.'

Amundsen had started with 52 dogs. The same evening, whatever his debt to them, he had all but 18 shot. He needed the meat to feed the men and remaining dogs, which he now divided into two teams. He had 438 km (274 miles) to go.

The return journey

When Amundsen left the South Pole on 18 December, having spent four days taking precise astronomical sights to fix his position, Scott was scarcely halfway up the Beardmore Glacier. By the time Scott arrived at the Pole,

> **❝ … that Englishmen can still die with a bold spirit, fighting it out to the end. ❞** Robert Falcon Scott

the Norwegians were racing back across the Barrier, making 30 and 50 km a day and scattering unwanted food and clothing behind them. When Amundsen reached his base at the Bay of Whales on 26 January, Scott's party, already weakening, was still on the Polar Plateau, 1,032 km (645 miles) from its base.

Their subsequent deaths would show, as Scott wrote, shivering and starving in his tent on the Barrier, '… that Englishmen can still die with a bold spirit, fighting it out to the end.' Scott's attempt to reach the South Pole was heroic in every sense. But his death and those of his companions were the result of his profoundly wrong-headed belief that man-hauling could compete with sleds pulled by dogs. Man-hauling killed Scott as surely as Amundsen's success was ensured by his dogs. The irony was that Scott's epic suffering, recorded in his diary, made Amundsen's achievement look almost prosaic. It was not, but his careful planning and use of cold-adapted sled dogs made it seem so.

The first ascent of Everest

SIR EDMUND HILLARY AND TENZING NORGAY | 29 May 1953

From the 1920s, British mountaineers led the way in the attempted conquest of Mount Everest. Despite the daunting challenges they faced, successive expeditions inched their way closer to the summit. In 1953 a ninth expedition was launched. On 29 May two of its members, New Zealand-born Sir Edmund Hillary and Nepal-born Tenzing Norgay, stood on top of the world.

Top of the world Tenzing Norgay on the summit of Everest – 11.30 A.M., 29 May 1953 – photographed by Hillary.

The original impetus for the British determination to conquer Everest came from Francis Younghusband, president of the Royal Geographical Society (RGS), from 1919 to 1923.

In tandem with the Alpine Club, the RGS sponsored expeditions in 1921, 1922 and 1924. Speculation remains rife that on this last expedition, George Mallory and Andrew Irvine, whose last camp was less then 600 metres (2,000 ft) from the summit, may have reached the top. When last seen, they were reported to have been 'going strong'. Neither made it down. Interest lapsed until 1931, when the RGS again took the lead. Four expeditions followed, in 1933, 1935, 1936 and 1938. World War II then ended further attempts on the mountain.

The Nepalese route

All these expeditions had tackled Everest from Tibet to its north. The Chinese invasion of Tibet in 1950 sealed the country's borders and brought an abrupt end to that route. British interest in climbing Everest again had started as early as 1947, with the RGS and the Alpine Club once more taking the lead. But it was clear that any future attempts on Everest could only be made from Nepal to the south.

In 1951 the RGS sponsored an expedition to reconnoiter a southern route. It was led by Eric Shipton, who had been on all four of the Everest expeditions in the 1930s and who was acknowledged as the world's leading Everest expert.

Height of Mount Everest

When, in 1852, the British surveyors of India espied through their telescopes and sextants a huge mountain to the north 240 km (150 miles) away, they called it Peak XV. They measured it at exactly 8,839 metres (29,000 ft). For fear that such an exact number would be thought no more than an estimate, two feet were arbitrarily added to the height.

Bizarrely, there has since been no universal agreement as to the precise height of Everest (southwest face pictured above). In 1955 an Indian survey team measured Everest at 8,848 metres (29,028 ft). But in May 1999 an American expedition, using a GPS device, recorded that the summit was 8,850 metres (29,035 ft). In October 2005 a Chinese expedition then claimed, after what they asserted had been the most accurate measurement of the height of Everest, that it was 8,844 metres (29,017 ft) high.

In part these differences reflect the difficulty of precise measurements at such high altitudes. In part they are the result of a curious difference of opinion. The Chinese measurement in 2005 was based on the rock at the summit of Everest; the American measurement in 1999 on the snow at its summit, necessarily several variable feet higher.

Final push Hillary (left) and Tenzing on the Southeast Ridge on 28 May, about to leave for Camp IX. This was their final camp just below the South Summit at 8,370 metres (27,900 ft) and the final effort for the summit itself the following day.

Its results were promising, suggesting a viable route if only a way could be found across the chaotic Khumbu Icefall, a shattered mass of ice and crevasses between 5,250 and 5,850 metres (17,500 and 19,500 ft).

The Swiss find a way to the south

As it turned out, there was a route, and it was discovered the following year by a Swiss expedition, which then pushed on to pioneer a way across the next obstacles, the snow fields of the Western Cwm (a cwm is a shallow snow valley) and, beyond these, the Lhotse Face, another treacherously iced ascent 7,350 metres (24,500 ft) high. The Swiss then went farther still, pushing on to the South Col, 7,800 metres (26,000 ft) high. From here the way to the summit seemed clear.

They came tantalizingly close to success. A final effort was made by two climbers, Raymond Lambert and the man who would partner Hillary in 1953, Tenzing Norgay, a Sherpa climber. They were less than 300 metres (1,000 ft) from the summit when cold and exhaustion forced them back. To the British it was a rude shock. Not only had a new route been pioneered, but Lambert and Tenzing had set a new highest record. British primacy on Everest was looking shaky.

But the British held a crucial card. Access to Everest was tightly controlled by the Nepalese government. In 1952 only the Swiss expedition had been allowed onto the mountain. In 1953 only the British were given access. If they now had the field to themselves, however, it was clear others were snapping at their heels. There was a sense that the 1953 expedition represented a last chance for final success.

Hunt blazes the trail

It was in this heated atmosphere that the decision was made to replace Eric Shipton as leader of the expedition with John Hunt. Hunt's credentials as a climber, in fact, never approached Shipton's. As an organiser, however, he was unsurpassed. And organisation, as Hunt and the RGS had clearly seen, was – as it remains – the key to Everest.

Compared to many of the world's classic climbs, Everest presents no insuperable difficulties. Technically it is relatively undemanding. But its dangers are real: altitude and weather. The latter is violently unpredictable: stable conditions can be transformed into vicious white-outs and bitter winds in a matter of hours. Above 7,800 metres (26,000 ft), thin air and intense cold take a relentless hold, making the most modest physical effort nearly intolerable. Judgments can become warped. In Himalayan terms this is the Death Zone. Three days is the most anyone can expect to survive at such heights.

Hunt planned his expedition meticulously. For the first stage, a 272-km (170-mile) trek from Kathmandu to the foot of the mountain, he used 350 porters to carry the expedition's supplies. When the ascent proper began, he whittled his team down to 23 Sherpas (native porters), under the leadership of Tenzing, and 14 climbers.

The climb

By 21 May the South Col had been reached. Six days later, the final camp had been established. It was 8,370 metres (27,900 ft) high. On 29 May, at 6:30 A.M., after a sleepless night shivering in their tent, Hillary and Tenzing made their bid.

'I was absolutely certain that Tenzing and I could do this', Hillary later said. By 9 A.M., they had reached the South Summit, a precipitous snow ridge from which sheer drops fell away to either side. Inching their way along, they came up against what is now known as the Hillary Step, a steep spur of rock and ice 16.5 metres (55 ft) high. It was painstakingly climbed. Once over it, Hillary, in his own words '... continued hacking steps along the ridge.'

Vertical limit Hillary gingerly picking his way along an aluminum ladder over a snow crevasse above Camp III in the Western Cwm.

> I wouldn't say that the final push was fun ... But, you know, this was Everest, so we felt we had to push it a bit harder than we would ordinarily.
>
> Sir Edmund Hillary

What followed seemed almost anticlimactic. Almost without realising it, they were on the summit, 'a symmetrical, beautiful snow cone,' as Hillary called it. The two men shook hands. Hillary then removed his oxygen mask and, '... took photographs down all the leading ridges just to make sure I had plenty of evidence we had made it to the top.' Tenzing, a Buddhist, left sweets and biscuits on the summit; Hillary, a crucifix he had been given by Hunt. Fifteen minutes later they began their descent.

The first man they met as they descended was George Lowe, earnestly waiting for news. 'How did it go?' he asked. Hillary replied, 'Well, George, we knocked the bastard off.'

Hillary was knighted by Queen Elizabeth II for his feat, for Tenzing there was simply fame.

The crossing of Antarctica

VIVIAN FUCHS AND SIR EDMUND HILLARY	**November 1955–19 January 1958**

Science was the prime impetus behind the Commonwealth Trans-Antarctic Expedition of 1955–1958, not least the desire to contribute to the International Geophysical Year. But it was the intended crossing of Antarctica itself that captured imaginations. Despite lavish funding and the widespread use of modern technology, it proved a vastly more arduous enterprise than many expected.

Iron will Vivian Fuchs brought a potent combination of planning, experience and determination to the expedition, bulldozing all obstacles aside.

The expedition, conceived and led by Vivian Fuchs, consisted of three principal thrusts. The first, which left London in November 1955 and arrived in the Antarctic late the same year, was the landing of a small party at Vahsel Bay on the Weddell Sea, where it would spend the winter of 1956. The second was a larger party, led by Fuchs, which in January 1957 would join the party already at Vahsel Bay and winter over in Antarctica before beginning the crossing of the continent in November. The third, led by the co-conqueror of Everest, the New Zealander Sir Edmund Hillary, was to land on the opposite side of Antarctica, at McMurdo Sound on the Ross Sea, early in 1957. It, too, would winter over before beginning a depot-laying journey towards the South Pole. It would carry supplies for Fuchs's party to pick up as they made their way to McMurdo after they had reached the Pole. Hillary's team was not intended to go on to the Pole but to return to base once the depots had been laid.

Technologically well equipped

If it was an ambitious programme, it was at least well supplied. Fuchs, who had already spent two years in Antarctica, was fully aware of the continent's relentless hostility. Technology, in his view, was the key to overcoming it. The Weddell Sea party accordingly had 11 land vehicles: four Sno-Cats; four cargo-carriers called

Welcoming party 19 January 1958, 3.2 km (2 miles) from the South Pole, Fuchs's convoy approaches the US base at the Pole. In the foreground, stars and stripes flying, is an American convoy coming out to meet them carrying Hillary and base commander, Admiral Dufek.

Weasels; and three tractors – one, a Muskeg specifically built for snow travel, the other two modified versions of Ferguson farm tractors. The Ross Sea party had a single Weasel and five Fergusons. Though both parties also took dogs, these were a backup means of transport, clearly valuable but intended principally to be used in the event of major mechanical failures.

The expedition also had four aircraft: an Otter, capable of carrying over 1,575 kg (3,500 lb.) of cargo; a Beaver, which could carry over 900 kg (2,000 lb.); and two smaller planes, known as Austers. These aircraft were central to Fuchs's plans. They were to be used not just for reconnaissance and route-finding but for depot laying and the construction of a forward base, South Ice, 440 km

> **Some of the monstrous caverns we have discovered beneath the innocent surface ... would have accepted a double-decker bus ... As the vehicles rumble over the booming caverns below, it is with a sense of some considerable relief that each driver reaches the far side.** Vivian Fuchs on the journey to South Ice

(275 miles) south of the main base, known as Shackleton, at Vahsel Bay. Three men were to spend the winter in this lonely outpost, making meteorological and other observations.

The landing of the first party at Vahsel Bay turned out to be exceptionally testing. The expedition's ship, *Theron*, was beset in the Weddell Sea for almost a month and extracted with major difficulty. With the season now so late, when *Theron* reached Vahsel Bay, the unloading of the expedition's 300 tons of stores took priority, and there was no time to construct the team's hut before winter set in. The eight men left behind were forced to spend the winter in one of the 6-m (21-ft) -long plywood crates used to transport the Sno-Cats.

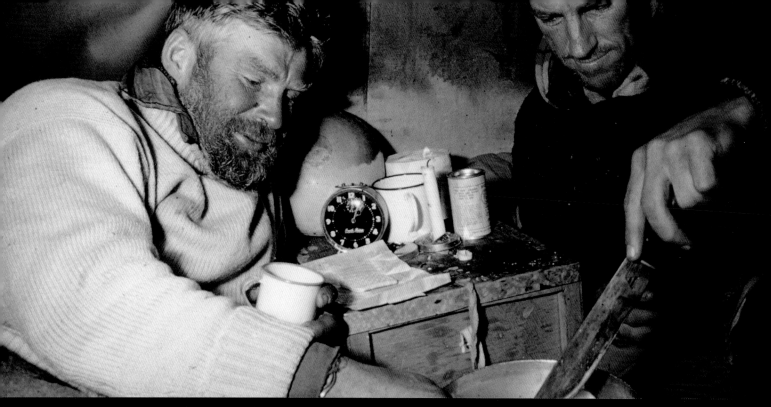

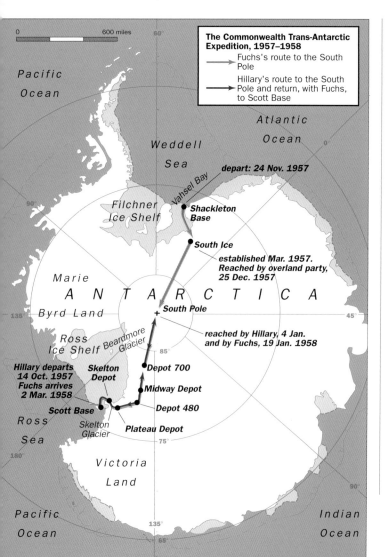

The Commonwealth Trans-Antarctic Expedition, 1957–1958

→ Fuchs's route to the South Pole

→ Hillary's route to the South Pole and return, with Fuchs, to Scott Base

Pacific Ocean

Atlantic Ocean

Weddell Sea

depart: 24 Nov. 1957

Filchner Ice Shelf

Shackleton Base

South Ice

established Mar. 1957. Reached by overland party, 25 Dec. 1957

Marie

A N T A R C T I C A

Byrd Land

South Pole

reached by Hillary, 4 Jan. and by Fuchs, 19 Jan. 1958

Ross Ice Shelf

Beardmore Glacier

Depot 700

Hillary departs 14 Oct. 1957 Fuchs arrives 2 Mar. 1958

Skelton Depot

Midway Depot

Scott Base

Depot 480

Ross Sea

Skelton Glacier

Plateau Depot

Victoria Land

Pacific Ocean

Indian Ocean

Arrival in Antarctica

The expedition's fortunes subsequently improved. By January 1957 both main parties had arrived in Antarctica, Fuchs at Shackleton Base, Hillary at Scott Base in McMurdo Sound. Work was immediately begun on depot laying and, at Vahsel Bay, on establishing South Ice, a base that was to be supplied by air. South Ice was completed and manned by a three-man party in late March.

When the main journeys began the following spring, Hillary's party had the easier task: a circuitous but, in Antarctic terms, less-than-demanding climb up the Skelton Glacier to the Polar Plateau and, from there, a relatively straightforward 800-km (500-mile) trek to the last depot, 800 km from the Pole. Fuchs, by contrast, was immediately faced with almost 480 km (300 miles) of treacherous crevasse-strewn territory that he had to cross twice, first on a preliminary journey to South Ice to mark the route and then, having flown back to Shackleton Base, with the main 12-man party.

Fuchs left on the preliminary journey on 8 October. By 28 October, the date he had hoped to arrive at South Ice,

While Hillary's trek to the Pole was the longer route, Fuchs's path was strewn with crevasses and much more demanding.

Tecnological assault The aggressive use of technology on the largest possible scale was the key to the successful crossing of Antarctica. In the face of the most hostile environment on Earth, the expedition forced its way across the continent.

he was still 240 km (150 miles) short. He arrived on 13 November after 37 days of painfully slow and consistently hazardous progress. It did not bode well.

His route to South Ice now marked, on 24 November, 10 days later than planned, Fuchs set off again, leading the main 12-man party towards the South Pole via South Ice. This time the journey to South Ice took only 29 days but was still a difficult trek with many emergencies that Fuchs laconically later called 'severe crevasse trouble with three major recoveries of Sno-Cats [from crevasses].' When they reached South Ice, however, the worst was over. On Christmas Day 1957, with 25.5 tons of stores, the party left for the Pole itself, 888 km (555 miles) away.

> ❝ Another 30 miles today, but what alabour! The strain ... is rodigious. ❞
>
> Vivian Fuchs, 2 January 1958

The push for the Pole

While Fuchs was battling to reach South Ice, Hillary had already arrived at his final depot, 800 km (500 miles) from the Pole. Here on his own initiative, he decided to carry on to the Pole itself. His reasoning in part was that he could then mark the whole of the return route to McMurdo Sound. But it's also clear that there was an element of competition between him and Fuchs. Once at the Pole, which he reached on 4 January (having led only the third party to reach the South Pole by land), Hillary sent a message to Fuchs advising him to call off the second part of his crossing until the following year and to fly back to McMurdo from the newly established American base at the Pole. It was advice Fuchs did not take to kindly, though press claims of a 'thunderous row' between the two were exaggerated.

Once at the Pole, which he reached on 19 January, Fuchs still had more than half his journey to complete. The journey was not without its difficulties; one member of the party, Geoffrey Pratt, was found unconscious in the cabin of his Sno-Cat, a victim of faulty ventilation. Nonetheless, a slow but steady increase in the party's daily mileages told their story. When they reached Scott Base on 2 March 1958, Fuchs had taken 99 days to travel 3,473 km (2,158 miles) at a daily average of 35 km (22 miles). Considering the frustrations of the first part of the crossing to South Ice, it was a phenomenal performance, and it beat Fuchs's original estimate for the journey by one day.

The crossing of the Arctic

WALLY HERBERT | **21 February 1968–22 June 1969**

In the mid-1960s Wally Herbert, a British explorer, aged 34, planned to walk across the Arctic Ocean from Alaska to Spitsbergen, Norway, via the North Pole. It called for four men to spend 16 months on the unstable ice of the Arctic Ocean travelling on foot close to 6,400 km (4,000 miles), almost half of the time in pitch darkness and appallingly low temperatures, to pursue a largely quixotic goal.

Herbert's premise was simple: that a small party, setting out from Point Barrow on the north coast of Alaska and making for Norway's Spitsbergen Island on the opposite side of the polar basin, could exploit the drift of the pack ice in the Arctic Ocean to reduce its total travel time. Admirable in theory, perhaps, the real trek immediately ran up against insuperable obstacles.

Not the least obstacle was the distance, close to 6,080 km (3,800 miles). The Arctic has limited travelling seasons. Permanent darkness and extreme cold rule out

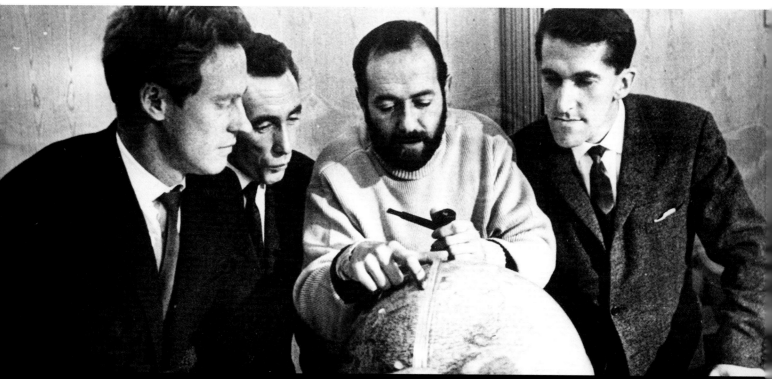

Plotting success The expedition members pose for the press before leaving for Alaska and their 16-month ordeal across the Arctic. From left to right, Roy Koerner, Alan Gill, expedition leader Wally Herbert and Ken Hodges.

winter travel. Rising temperatures and melting ice hamper summer travel. There is a brief window in September and a rather longer one in the spring, when the ice is firm and daylight is returning. But given that any average daily distance was unlikely to exceed 24 km (15 miles), these windows are not long enough to complete the journey.

Wintering over

It became clear to Herbert that the only way the trip could be made was by spending the winter on the ice. Given the unpredictable nature of the Arctic ice pack, wintering over was extremely dangerous.

It also posed logistical problems. Four men with, as Herbert proposed, 40 dogs would require vastly greater supplies than they could carry. The only answer was to airlift supplies to them at prearranged intervals. The Arctic Research Laboratory and the Royal Canadian Air Force agreed to make the supply drops. The planning of this formidable operation was hard enough. Raising the necessary financial support was even harder.

The expedition left Point Barrow, where the men and their 40 dogs had spent the winter, on 21 February 1968. They immediately found themselves in a maze of pressure ice (ice that is pushed by winds and tides and, when rammed against other ice floes, splits and fissures under the pressure of millions of tons). Eight days later the floe they had camped on split without warning. The following day, a ridge of ice, 'with blocks weighing several tons tumbling from its summit', bore down on their camp, forcing a six-hour struggle through the night to escape it.

Mission accomplished 22 June 1969. Bearded but otherwise remarkably fit after their 476 days on the ice, Hedges (left) and Herbert (centre) talk to Peter Buchanan, captain of HMS *Endurance*, the ship that picked them up.

> ❝ The mush ice was in constant movement. Several times I was about to set foot on the crossing when it would suddenly boil up: green blocks the size of bungalows would rise out of the stew of ice debris and collapse with a dull thud back into the mush. ❞
>
> Wally Herbert, 26 April 1968

Falling behind schedule

By early March the expedition, falling dangerously behind schedule, reached firmer ice. The drift that should have been taking them towards the Pole, however, was now taking them away from it. By 11 April, when they were 400 km (250 miles) from Point Barrow, they discovered they were only 1 mile farther north than they had been three days before. Herbert realised that if they were unable to establish their summer camp far enough north, their drift would take them farther still from the Pole. He began to worry that they might end up as much as a year behind their schedule, potentially drifting helplessly past Greenland to certain death in the North Atlantic. At times they were only able to travel 2.4 km (2 miles) a day, 'fighting for every mile'.

The last week before they reached their summer

The winter hut

Once parachuted in on 25 September 1968, the expedition's hut was rapidly assembled. However bleak its setting, the hut, small though it was, proved remarkably workable. In the centre was a stove: typically, if the temperature at the roof of the hut approached 32°C (90°F), at head height the temperature was generally around 15°C (60°F) and at ground level 0°C (32°F). Each corner was allocated to one man, whose territory it became.

Despite having to dismantle, move and re-assemble the hut after the original floe it stood on broke up in October, the winter passed painlessly, chores shared, the dogs tethered outside, surrounded by drifted-over supplies.

For Herbert the only bad moment came when the hut was left as the floe broke up towards the end of February 1968. It would clearly either be crushed or sink. 'Abandoning that hut', he wrote, 'was for me deeply moving.'

Herbert was at the mercy of the frozen seas during the Arctic crossing. Drifting ice initially put him 560 km (350 miles) behind schedule. Further, life-threatening problems arose when the floes began to melt.

camp on 4 July was 'physically the hardest of the whole journey … a losing struggle with the drift – a hopeless effort to travel north-west.' The men were exhausted, four dogs had been lost and some equipment was failing.

The summer camp, Meltville, was aptly named. It was a curious semi-soggy mass of 'jostling and fracturing ice'. Here, in two pyramid tents and a 'marquee' made of parachutes, the party waited until September and the final push north to its winter quarters. During the two months, Herbert wrote a 12,000-word article for an American magazine. To transmit it, he had to crank a hand generator for 57 hours to provide sufficient power for the radio.

They were on the move again on 4 September. They settled down for the winter on 25 September and the next day received their largest drop yet, 28 tons of supplies, among them the 4.5 x 4.5 metres (15-ft by 15-ft) prefabricated hut, in which they would spend the next five months. A month later their floe split. It took 10 days to sled the expedition's supplies and hut to a new site.

Homeward bound Despite worsening ice conditions with the approach of summer, progress once the Pole had been reached was swift, a stark contrast to the travails of the early days of the expedition.

The final push

By spring their position was bleak. The drift, favourable until November, had since carried them 192 km (120 miles) farther from the Pole, putting them 560 km (350 miles) behind schedule. To reach the Pole and then, crucially, to make Spitsbergen before the ice broke up in June, meant a trip of almost 2,400 km (1,500 miles) in 100 days, approximately the same distance it had already taken almost a year to cover.

Their final departure, on 24 February, was not propitious. Their floe began to disintegrate. Men and dogs alike were forced to leap gyrating ice in search of better surfaces. The first three weeks were dismal. The fatigue, wrote Herbert, was 'crippling', food was short and temperatures were consistently below –45°C (–50°F). But they were now making sustained progress. From travelling 'like old men', Herbert now reported the going as 'exhilarating'.

On 5 April they reached the North Pole. But there were still more than 960 km (600 miles) to Spitsbergen

> ❝ I would be most grateful if you would inform Her Majesty The Queen that the first surface crossing of the Arctic Ocean has been acccomplished. ❞
>
> Wally Herbert's note to Sir Miles Clifford, 29 May 1969

and only 60 days to cover them. All nonessential gear was dumped, rations for men and dogs increased and travel time stepped up to 10, sometimes 12 hours a day. Warmer weather brought an end to the numbing temperatures but also foretold the breakup of the ice.

On 26 April while they were travelling on apparently benign ice, a floe suddenly tilted upwards, tossing men and dogs into the frozen sea. It was the closest the expedition came to losing a sled and a dog team. As May began, fog further hampered progress. Though land was sighted on 23 May, polar bears now became a serious menace, packs of them stalking the party.

By late May, the ice had become so unstable that it was clear Spitsbergen itself could not be reached. But other land could. On 29 May two of the party scrambled ashore on the desolate granite wastes of Vesle Tavleoya or Little Blackboard Island off the coast of Spitsbergen. The first crossing on foot of the Arctic Ocean had been made.

Everest without oxygen

REINHOLD MESSNER AND PETER HABELER | 1978

That Everest could not be climbed without supplemental oxygen had long been assumed. At such immense heights it was as much as any human could do to survive at all, let alone to contend with the physical efforts of climbing the world's highest mountain. In 1978 two men – an Italian, Reinhold Messner, and an Austrian, Peter Habeler – turned this accepted wisdom on its head.

Extreme exposure Messner shows reporters his frostbitten thumb, incurred during prepartions for his climb with Habeler.

Messner and Habeler were prime exponents of the Alpine style of climbing. When Everest was first climbed in 1953 (*see* p. 80), it was as a result of an almost military-style siege of the mountain, in which large parties laid depots and established camps at ever higher points up the mountain, paving the way for a final push to the summit by a single pair of climbers, who were naturally climbing with oxygen.

Aggressive climbing technique

What Messner and Habeler proposed was radically different. In the Alps they had already established a reputation for aggressive climbing, in the process setting record times for ascents of the Matterhorn and the Eiger and demonstrating a relish for demanding precision

> Everest – by fair means – that is the human dimension, and that is what interests me. In reaching for the oxygen cylinder, a climber degrades Everest. A climber who doesn't rely upon his own skills, but on apparatus and drugs, deceives himself.
>
> Reinhold Messner, 1978

climbs in which technique was all. In 1970, with his brother Günter, Messner climbed the world's fourth-highest mountain, Nanga Parbat, 8,125 metres (26,658 ft) high. Their descent showed that mountain climbing is an inherently high-risk business. Günter Messner was killed in an avalanche, and Reinhold Messner, severely frostbitten, lost seven toes.

At this stage not even Messner was convinced such vast mountains could be tackled without oxygen. There had long been a belief, however, that the purer the climber's approach – the fewer aids he took – the more fulfilling and worthwhile the success. This wasn't just a matter of climbing ethics; there were practical benefits, too. Even in the 1920s George Mallory, who remains the most famous casualty of Everest, reported that, 'The climber does best to rely on his natural abilities, which warn him whether he is overstepping the bounds of his strength. With artificial aids, he exposes himself to the possibility of sudden collapse if the apparatus fails.'

In 1960 and 1961 Sir Edmund Hillary had conducted a series of experiments on Everest that apparently demonstrated that oxygen levels at the summit, less than a third of those at sea level, were barely enough to sustain life at all. Sustained exposure to oxygen levels this low were thought not merely to temporarily incapacitate but to risk long-term brain damage.

Nonetheless, 'lunatics' or not, Messner and Habeler in 1975 made an attempt without oxygen on Gasherbrum 1 in the Himalayas, at 8,068 metres (26,470 ft) the 11th-highest mountain in the world. It proved gruelling in the extreme. But they made it. The obvious question remained: could Everest be climbed in the same way?

Morning climb Messner embarks on a climb from Camp II, situated at the foot of the southwest face of Everest. The daily grind, according to Messner, was one of 'ploughing through knee-deep snow, the tired stiff movements on leaving camp and the scorching heat just before midday.'

> I am nothing more than a single narrow gasping lung, floating over the mists and summits.
>
> Reinhold Messner

In 1978 Messner and Habeler made their attempt.

Though determined to bring their Alpine technique to bear on Everest, climbing alone and with a minimum of equipment, not even Messner and Habeler could take on the mountain entirely unsupported. In March 1978 they joined an Austrian expedition, with whom they began a methodical ascent to the higher reaches of the south face of Everest, establishing camps en route in the way that had now become orthodox. They planned to make their assault from Camp 3 – 7,467 metres (24,500 ft) high – at the base of the Lhotse Face, which they reached on 23 April.

The final climb began badly. The night before, Habeler came down with food poisoning. The following morning, with two Sherpas, Messner pushed on without him. At 26,000 feet (7,925 metres on the South Col, a storm trapped the three men. After two days, with food running out and their tent badly damaged, Messner and the Sherpas were forced back. The attempt, Messner said, appeared 'impossible and senseless'. Nearing exhaustion,

Everest alone

In 1980 Messner made a solo ascent of Everest without oxygen. Arguably, it was the single most remarkable climb ever made, a feat of endurance and determination without parallel. More astonishing still, Messner made it from the north of the mountain, pioneering a route never before climbed.

On the summit he remained typically clear-thinking, recognising that he had been reduced to the limits of his physical capacity. Yet the state of absolute, almost inhuman exhaustion in which he found himself had simultaneously induced a condition approaching what he called 'spiritual abstraction'. 'I no longer belong to myself', he later wrote.

That Messner was driven is clear. It has been suggested he suffered a permanent sense of guilt after his brother, Günter, was killed on Nanga Parbat in 1970. Such speculation will always remain just that. In 1986, Reinhold Messner became the first man to climb all 14 of the world's highest mountains. He remains the greatest climber of the 20th century, the man who redefined the art of the possible.

Messner and Habeler retreated to the expedition's base camp at 5,395 metres (17,700 ft).

Had the mountain defeated them? Could they try again? Habeler was willing – but only if this time they took oxygen. Messner absolutely refused, asserting not only that he would not climb with Habeler, or indeed with anyone, who had oxygen, but that, if necessary, he would make a solo attempt. Habeler relented, though he managed to get Messner to agree that they should take a token two cylinders of oxygen to be used if either man fell seriously ill – and that in such a dire event both would descend together.

A second attempt

On 6 May they began their second attempt. That evening, they were again at Camp 3, and by the following afternoon at Camp 4 on the South Col at 7,925 metres (26,000 ft) up. Habeler in particular found the height draining. But both were having difficulty breathing, and Habeler suffered from a severe headache and double vision.

They began the final push at 3 A.M. By now even the most ordinary effort was appallingly difficult. To save energy, they agreed not to talk, using hand signals instead. Just getting dressed took two hours.

It took four hours to reach the last camp, Camp 5, at almost 8,535 metres (28,000 ft). From here they made their summit attempt. At this point Messner felt as if he might 'burst apart'. Both were repeatedly falling to their knees, desperate for breath.

Their progress up the Hillary Step, the summit now less than 90 metres (300 ft) away, was agonising, an inch-by-inch upward shuffling. Once above the Hillary Step, they were unable to move more than 3 metres (10 ft) without collapsing, prostrate, onto the snow. Messner later said he thought his mind was now 'dead'.

Messner on the summit after the first solo ascent of the mountain, 20 August 1980. The tripod was left by a Chinese survey team in 1975.

Summit attained

The summit was reached in a daze of exhausted suffering neither could entirely explain. Habeler, certain he had now suffered irreparable brain damage, immediately began his descent. Messner remained, taking photographs and whispering into a tape recorder. Then he, too, began to make his way back down the mountain. He was already paying an alarming price. To take his photographs, he had removed his goggles. The result, predictably, was severe snow-blindness. He was virtually blind by the time he had reached safer altitudes.

Two days later, still dazed and exhausted, Messner and Habeler, contrary to medical science and all practical common sense, reached Base Camp.

The first journey to both Poles

ROBERT SWAN | **1984–1986 and 1989**

On 11 January 1986, Robert Swan, leading a three-man party, arrived at the South Pole having walked exactly 1,400 km (873 miles) in 70 days to reach it. On 15 May, 1989, leading an eight-man party, he arrived at the North Pole, this time having walked approximately 996 km (623 miles) in 55 days. This stalwart Englishman became the first man to have journeyed to both Poles of the Earth on foot.

Arriving at the US Amundsen–Scott base The three-man party – Swan (left), Wood (right) – had arrived from the other direction. But, facing into the Sun, they couldn't photograph it. They were forced to walk around the base and approach it from the other side to capture the moment on film.

Gateway to the Pole Robert Swan (left) and Canadian Gareth Wood (right) refuelling with warm drinks. The Gateway, the entrance to the Beardmore Glacier, discovered by Ernest Shackleton in 1907, the key to the Polar Plateau and the South Pole, can be seen behind and directly between them.

L ord Shackleton, son of the polar explorer and initially resolutely opposed to Swan's attempt on the South Pole, called Swan 'the most persistent young man I have ever met'. He may have understated the case. At university Swan had developed a fascination with Scott's doomed attempt on the South Pole in 1911–1912 (*see* p. 74), seeing it both as immensely gallant and, whatever its failures, oddly inspiring. It became an all-consuming obsession. Swan decided he had to replicate it.

Though Swan's plans for his expedition would change substantially with what at first had been conceived as a tiny venture evolving into a much larger – and significantly more expensive – operation, the goal remained the same: an unsupported walk to the Pole. Unlike Scott, Swan and his team would not then have to make the return on foot: once at the Pole, they would be flown back to their base at McMurdo Sound. But what was planned was nonetheless daring.

Entirely unsupported

Swan and two others (Roger Mear and Gareth Wood) would leave from McMurdo Sound (as had Scott) dragging all their supplies – clothes, tent, sleeping bags and food – on sleds for almost 1,440 km (900 miles). At

> *After a further mile and a half the Amundsen-Scott base became discernible as a faint grey shadow on the horizon.*
>
> **Roger Mear, 11 January 1986**

no point would they be resupplied. They would have no means of making contact with the outside world. If they were to survive, it would be through their own efforts. If their food ran out or their equipment failed, they would simply die.

Fittingly, given Swan's determination to emulate Scott, he and four others over-wintered in Antarctica in 1985 in a hut built just a few hundred yards from that in which Scott had spent the winter of 1911. In late June, the height of the Antarctic winter, three members of the party journeyed to Cape Crozier in a direct duplication of 'The Worst Journey in the World' (*see* p. 70), the epic of pointless suffering undertaken by three of Scott's men in 1911. They made it easily.

On 3 November 1985, 74 years to the day after Scott had begun his attempt on the Pole, the polar journey began. The technical challenge facing them was clear. To

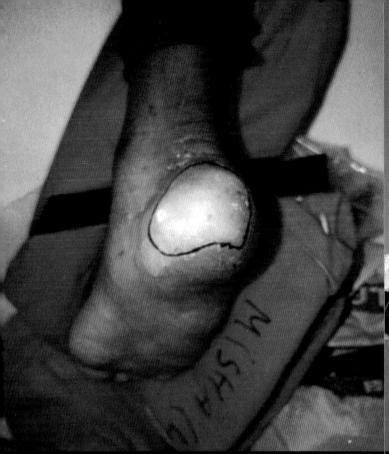

Darryl's heel

Among the team that left Ellsemere Island on 20 March for the North Pole was Darryl Roberts, a 23-year-old African American. His motivation was never in doubt. On the other hand, his inexperience was also obvious. Almost from the start, Roberts developed a persistent blister on his right heel. However carefully treated, it became progressively more serious. Well before the Pole was reached, the expedition doctor, Misha Malakhov, a Russian and easily the most experienced Arctic traveller among the party, was treating Roberts's heel twice daily, before and after every march. Malakov refused to allow Roberts to see his heel for fear that the sight of the vast area of raw skin, rubbed through to the bone, would discourage the young American from continuing.

make the Pole, they would have to travel more than 19 km (12 miles) a day for at least 70 days. It meant around nine hours on the march day in, day out. Anything less and their food would run out.

Battling the elements – and each other

The psychological challenge was more intangible but no less real. In part, this was as a result of the relentless pace needed to make their daily mileages. It also stemmed from the increasingly uncomfortable relations between the three, inevitably highlighted by the inescapable realities of their vulnerability. Swan and Mear, themselves frequently at loggerheads, found Wood's punctilious reticence almost unbearably irritating. For his part, the long-suffering Wood, meticulous and precise, found Swan and Mear intolerably bumptious and overbearing. Relations were frequently strained.

The expedition's professionalism got the party to the Pole five days ahead of schedule.

The South Pole walk raised Swan's profile. He took full advantage. He made the North Pole his next goal.

The North Pole reached It was a moment of supreme vindication for Robert Swan. Few had believed his disparate party could make it. All had approached levels of exhaustion they could scarcely conceive. The elation was overwhelming.

But his motivation was different. The South Pole had been a personal challenge – part homage to Scott, part a desire to prove his own worth. In approaching the North Pole, Swan was attempting something more ambitious and more public. He wanted to reach the North Pole in a blaze of media attention so that he could highlight how man-made climate change was threatening these pristine spaces.

This time he recruited an international team – two Brits, a Canadian, a German, an Australian, an American, a Russian and a Japanese. They would leave from Ellsemere Island in Canada, the nearest land to the Pole, and travel the 960 km (600 miles) to the Pole. They would be resupplied en route by air drops, and they would be air-lifted back after conducting a live television broadcast at the Pole.

Dogged persistence

The early days of the expedition saw team members struggling across a shattered mass of pressure ice. Mileages were low, morale worse. The more experienced members of the team turned on the tyros. All the while, the daily average that had to be made if the Pole was to be reached on time climbed relentlessly. Camping at night, with stoves hissing, sodden clothing strung from the roof of the tent in an attempt to dry it, a tense, often sullen silence reigned. The realities of survival in extreme conditions were clear to everyone.

But they pushed on. As the Pole came closer, the team's efforts increased. As Swan reported, 'We seemed to haul around the clock, pushing beyond the bounds of exhaustion to some strange state where thoughts were scattered all over the place.' And they all made it.

> ❛I was at the North Pole. I could hardly remember how I had got there, the journey was so blurred in my mind.❜
>
> Robert Swan

Rescue at the South Pole

SEAN LOUTITT, MARK CAREY AND NORMAN WONG | April 2001

In April 2001 the Canadian crew of a de Havilland Twin Otter flew to the South Pole to rescue an American doctor, dangerously ill with pancreatitis, at the US Amundsen-Scott base. It was a remarkable piece of aviation. Even in summer conditions there is nothing routine about flying in Antarctica. In the permanent darkness and bitter cold of the Antarctica winter, it was assumed to be impossible.

On 16 February 2001, as the summer's last giant American LC-130 Hercules lumbered off the ice at the Amundsen-Scott base, 59-year-old Dr. Ron Shemenski, physician to the 49 scientists and researchers who would be wintering over at the US base that year, said to a colleague, 'We're going to have a nice quiet time.' With the polar winter setting in, there would be no further flights to the Pole until late October at the earliest. They were on their own.

The first plane to land at the South Pole did so in 1956, a preliminary to the establishment of the US base there. Then and ever since, the base has been resupplied by air. In summer there are up to six flights a day, ferrying personnel and bringing in supplies. Common sense suggested that these flights could not be made in the winter.

The problem is neither the darkness nor the storms, which can be as severe in the summer as in the winter. It is the cold. The average winter temperature at the South Pole is about –60°C (–76°F). In such extreme cold, most aircraft cannot function. Even the fuel freezes.

Medical emergency

In early April Dr. Shemenski passed a gallstone. A series of radio and Internet consultations with colleagues in America confirmed his diagnosis of pancreatitis. Shemenski, aware of the risks of airlifting him out, was reluctant to leave. He was overruled.

The initial plan was to fly in a US Hercules. It was swiftly dropped. Instead, a Canadian company, Kenn

Safe and sound Ron Shemenski in Punta Arenas, Argentina, 26 April 2001 after his rescue from the South Pole. He owed his life to Sean Louttit.

Borek Air (motto: Anytime, Anywhere … Worldwide) was asked if it could help. The answer was yes. On 18 April two eight-seater de Havilland DHC-6 Twin Otter turbo-prop planes, workhorses in the best sense, immensely rugged and dependable, set off from Calgary for the South Pole. By 21 April they had reached the British Antarctic base at Rothera, 2,080 km (1,300 miles) from the Pole. One plane would then fly to the Pole. Bad

Extreme aviation No photograph can do justice to the extreme cold of winter at the South Pole. The weather may have been calm but the temperature when Louttit and his crew landed was almost four times below that of a domestic deep freeze.

weather delayed departure until 24 April, when, at 2:30 A.M., the plane took off. On board were Sean Loutitt, the captain; copilot Mark Carey; flight engineer Norman Wong; and Dr. Betty Carlisle, who would replace Shemenski.

Preparations had been made at the Pole to welcome the plane. The runway was flattened and barrels of burning debris – 'smudge pots' – set out to mark it. Search-and-rescue teams were activated. At 12:04 P.M. the plane successfully touched down. The temperature was –69°C (–92°F). Heaters were immediately placed around the plane and the engines swathed in protective covers.

Deteriorating weather and the extreme difficulty of freeing the plane's skis, which had become rigidly frozen into the snow despite the heaters, meant that the

planned 10-hour stopover at the Pole turned into a 17-hour wait (Loutitt, matter of factly, used the extra time to buy a commemorative T-shirt). But at 4:45 A.M. on 25 April, after the extensive use of heaters and shovels, the return journey began. Ten hours later the plane had reached Rothera. Shemenski was immediately airlifted back to America.

Repeating the impossible

Sean Loutitt, a down-to-earth man, has always shrugged off comments that he and his crew performed a feat out of the ordinary. In September 2003 he repeated the flight from Rothera to the US base at the South Pole to airlift out a researcher, Barry McCue, also suffering from a gall bladder problem. It had been diagnosed at the Pole by the station's doctor, Ron Shemenski.

3
Wind&Water

The last grain race

ERIC NEWBY | **18 October 1938–10 June 1939**

In October 1938 18-year-old Eric Newby started as an apprentice on the Finnish-owned *Moshulu*, a four-masted barque that was among the largest sailing ships then afloat. He had scarcely been to sea before he boarded *Moshulu* in Belfast, bound for Australia. Although no one knew it at the time, he was also about to take part in the last grain race.

By the late 1930s a handful of sailing ships remained in service on the grain route to and from Australia, travelling out in ballast, returning with grain. The grain race was an unofficial annual sailing contest between the vessels headed for Australia, for which there were no prizes. Magnificent or not, these ships had become anachronistic, and their economic survival was precarious. Thirteen ships took part in the 1938–1939 grain race, *Moshulu* among them. There would be no more grain races. World War II, which started on 3 September 1939, killed the trade.

Newby joined *Moshulu* in October 1938 in Belfast. He was immediately ordered to the top of the main mast, 60 metres (198 ft) high. His next job was to clean the lavatories. The following day, woken at 5:30 A.M., he was sent over the side to chip rust off the steel hull. Almost at once, he dropped a hammer into the water. His spirits sank.

Newby had joined *Moshulu* in part because he had wanted to experience the Southern Ocean at its most extreme on a great sailing ship. His ambition was fully met.

Two weeks later, ballasted with 1,500 tons of sand, paving stones, and granite blocks, *Moshulu* headed into the Irish Sea. There were 29 men on board – the captain, three mates, a sailmaker, a carpenter, a steward, a steward's mate, a cook, two men to look after the mechanical winches and 18 foremast hands – divided into two watches, port and starboard. As an apprentice foremast hand, Newby was one of the four most junior men on board. He was the only Englishman, and he earned 10 shillings a month.

Gale in the Southern Ocean, March 1939 Newby's photographs show the battering that *Moshulu* received at certain points of the voyage.

Moshulu was 97 metres (320 ft) long and had 31 sails. The rigging consisted of several miles of rope and wire. Newby had to learn the name of every sail and every line in Swedish, the working language of the ship. Things did not start well. When he was ordered aloft for the first time at sea, it was pitch dark and a crewmate threw up on him.

After almost a week of trying to beat south out of the Irish Sea, the ship headed north around Ireland and into bad weather in the Atlantic. We were, Newby wrote in *The Last Grain Race*, ' … no longer in the 20th century at all.'

As the weather warmed, the men were plagued by hordes of bedbugs. They killed thousands but could never eradicate them. The insects returned to torment the crew on the voyage home.

Speeding to Port Lincoln

On 21 November the ship crossed the equator; on the 29th – storm canvas bent on in preparation for the Southern Ocean – the crew saw their first albatross. By mid-December *Moshulu* was deep in the Southern Ocean, tearing along in a rising wind across vast seas at 13 and 14 knots. 'It was as if the ship had wings,' noted Newby in his book.

In early January, 560 km (350 miles) from their destination – Port Lincoln in South Australia – Newby got into a fight. Finding his cigarette tin defiled, he poured a bowl of custard over the man he thought had done it. The ensuing brawl was brief and violent. Newby established himself in the eyes of the crew as a 'proper strongbody' – someone who wouldn't stand for any nonsense.

The ship reached Port Lincoln on 7 January. It was desolate, windswept and hot – temperatures approached 50°C (122°F). Not only was the crew forced to remain on board, sweltering and listless, but the captain found that grain prices had plummeted. The ship might have to wait a year for a cargo. Then, unloading the ballast, the crew was assaulted for days by a foul stench. Eventually, the remains of two dogs were found under the ballast and had to be removed. When a cargo was at last secured, it took almost seven weeks to load.

Nonetheless, *Moshulu* left Australia on 11 March 1939, carrying 4,875 tons of grain in 59,000 sacks. The last grain race had begun.

By 20 March the temperatures had dropped so much that the captain was issuing rum to the crew at the end of every watch. It was a drink, according to Newby, that 'had the same effect as a blow from a heavy stick'. The barometer was falling steadily.

Life before the mast

Newby had been cheered days after he joined *Moshulu* in Belfast when two other apprentices came on board. One was a Dutchman named Jack Kroner, who spoke fluent English and alternately tormented and delighted Newby. The other was a young American, George White, lured like Newby by the desire to make a great sea voyage under sail. Within days of their arrival, White, sweeping one of the decks, stepped backward into the hold below. He fell 6 metres (20 ft) and broke his leg.

At sea, hazards such as this were commonplace. In the Southern Ocean, Newby, steering with a much more experienced man, found the ship rounding up into the wind, masts and sails shuddering, risking the ship's sudden foundering. Throwing their combined weight against the wheel, Newby and his companion were unable to move it. The captain, first mate, and third mate then threw themselves onto the ship's afterwheel. Very slowly the ship came off the wind and resumed its course. 'The danger was past, but … as the captain turned away, pale and trembling, I heard him sob: "O Christ",' wrote Newby.

Moshulu and the grain race

Though destinations and sailing dates varied, the grain race, never official but always keenly contested, amounted to 24,000 km (15,000 miles) of arduous sailing by a series of heavily laden ships. The record was 87 days, set in 1936 by *Passat*.

Ship	Sailed	Arrived	Days
Moshulu	11 March	10 June	91
Padua	3 April	5 July	93
Pamir	8 March	12 June	96
Passat	9 March	15 June	98
Pommern	20 March	15 July	115
Kommodore Johnsen	26 March	11 July	107
Abraham Rydberg	11 February	11 July	107
Olivebank	20 March	17 July	119
Viking	16 February	15 June	119
Archibald Russell	3 April	2 August	121
Winterhude	22 March	3 August	134
Killoran	13 July	29 November	139
Lawhill	15 March	2 August	140

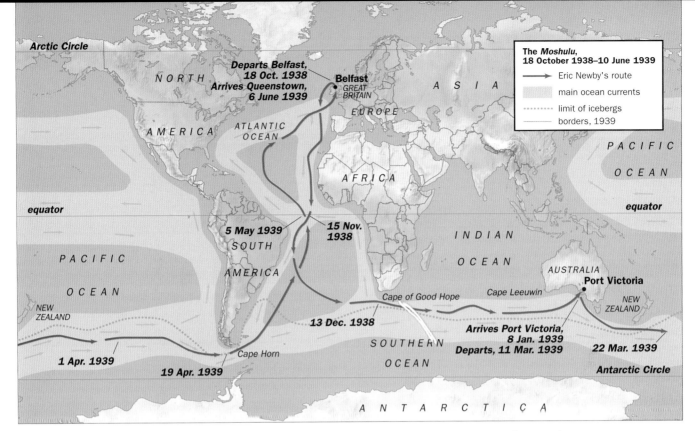

Moshulu followed the classic sailing-ship route from Europe to Australia and back. She completed the return leg in 91 days.

At the mercy of a storm

On 26 March, with the crew struggling to reduce sail, a huge wave broke over the ship, sweeping Newby 15 metres (50 ft) across the deck. He was left, facedown, with his head jammed through a scupper (a drainage hole). As the storm increased, eventually reaching Force 11, the 'wind seemed to be tearing apart the substance of the atmosphere.' Giant waves continued to sweep over *Moshulu*. Everyone – and everything – on board was drenched. Six inches of water rushed across the floor of the forecastle where the crew now struggled to survive. 'We were all of us awed', wrote Newby. The ship was sailing at its limits.

At the height of the storm, Newby was knocked off the upper rigging at night. He fell just 1.5 metres (5 ft) before becoming entangled in the rigging. He at once climbed back up to join his crewmates. 'I felt no fear until much later on', he wrote.

Hubris followed. Encased in layers of clothing against the cold, Newby was ordered to trim the wick of one of the navigation lights that was housed in a domelike glass structure.

Having forced in his head and shoulders, he became stuck. He began, slowly, to asphyxiate. Initially, when the third mate tried to pull him out, he succeeded only in pulling off Newby's boots. But after more attempts the third mate finally was able to free the sailor.

Windless days, steamy heat

Moshulu passed Cape Horn on 9 April. The ship was now rushing north, but it proved illusionary. Approaching the equator, windless days and steamy heat left the crew debilitated. North of the equator more windless days left *Moshulu*, sails slaking, agonisingly short of her destination – Queenstown in the south of Ireland. On 10 June *Moshulu's* anchor finally put down off Queenstown. She had taken 91 days to sail the 24,000 km (15,000 miles) from South Australia. She may not have set an all-time record, but she had won the last grain race.

> ❝The power and noise of this wind was now vast and all-comprehending, in its way as big as the sky, bigger than the sea itself, making something that the mind balked at, so that it took refuge in blankness. ❞

Eric Newby, on the storm in the Southern Ocean, 25 March 1939

The first passage under the North Pole

| USS *NAUTILUS* | 1–5 August 1958 |

The USS *Nautilus*, launched in January 1954, was the world's first nuclear-powered submarine. At a stroke she rendered her rivals obsolete. *Nautilus* was faster, could dive deeper and had a greater range than any conventional air-breathing diesel-powered boat. Her superiority was demonstrated in August 1958 when she made a so-called impossible journey – the first underwater crossing of the Arctic Ocean.

In May 1955, five months after her maiden voyage, *Nautilus* sailed from her home port of New London, Connecticut, to Puerto Rico. She covered the 2,209 km (1,381 miles) in exactly 89 hours, 54 minutes at an average speed of 15.36 knots. The entire journey was made submerged. It was ten times farther than any submarine had traveled continuously underwater.

In February 1957, when the boat underwent its first overhaul – its pressurised water reactor was refuelled – *Nautilus* had already sailed 100,000 km (62,500 miles), half of them submerged, on a single load of fuel. A diesel-powered boat would have required more than 9.1 million litres (2 million gallons) of fuel for the same distance.

A new breed of submarine

Conventional submarines were little more than submersibles – surface vessels able to spend limited periods under water. *Nautilus* was the world's first true submarine: a vessel properly in its element only under water. It could operate safely at 215 metres (700 ft) below the surface. Its maximum submerged speed – 25 knots – was greater than its speed on the surface. Its fuel was almost inexhaustible; the only limit to the time it could spend submerged was the amount of food it could carry for its crew, under the command of Captain William R. Anderson.

Submarine warfare is clandestine. But the *Nautilus* was a technological ace that the United States was determined to play on the global scene – following the launch of *Sputnik* into Earth orbit by the Soviet Union in October 1957 (*see* p. 40). Faced with this Russian success, a headline-grabbing voyage by the world's first nuclear-powered submarine was a convincing demonstration of American technological virility. The attempted voyage – 2,000 miles (3,200 km) under the polar ice cap via the North Pole –

Preparing to dive The crew of *Nautilus* execute a diving manoeuvre during testing in May 1956.

was actively encouraged by President Eisenhower. It was agreed, however, that the voyage would not be announced in advance; it would be publicised only after the fact. The technical details of the mission were planned by scientists from the Naval Electronics Laboratory, including Dr. Waldo Lyon, who accompanied *Nautilus* as chief scientist.

Inches from disaster

In December 1957 *Nautilus* had already made a preliminary voyage to the Arctic, covering 2,212 km (1,383 miles) under the ice and coming within 288 km (180 miles) of the Pole. In June 1958 the first systematic attempt was made. Entering the Arctic Ocean from the Pacific – via the Bering Strait and the Chukchi Sea – *Nautilus* suffered a failure of its gyrocompass and was unable to find a way through the shallow waters of the Chukchi Sea.

> **For the world, our country, and the Navy – the North Pole.**
>
> Capt. William R. Anderson, announcement
> to the crew, 11:15 P.M., 3 August 1958

A second attempt was made late in July. Again, the Chukchi Sea nearly defeated the *Nautilus*. With the ice 18 metres (60 ft) thick in places and the seabed rapidly getting shallower, it took two days to thread *Nautilus* through an imperfectly charted underwater labyrinth. For the 115 men on board under Capt. Anderson, it was a period of high drama. At one moment the lines on the sonar recorder showing the distance to the ice above and the seabed below converged. At a critical moment the ship was simultaneously scraping the seabed below and the ice above. This raised the prospect that the submarine's delicate radio antennas and periscopes might be damaged, leaving the ship to sail blind, and there seemed a real possibility the *Nautilus* would become jammed. It was the largest crisis of the voyage. As engineer Bill NcNally recorded, 'It was the moment of truth. And didn't we just know it!'

America triumphant

Thereafter, in water more than 3.2 km (2 miles) deep, progress was almost anticlimactic. The Pole was passed at 11.15 P.M. local time on 3 August. By 5 August the ship had reached the Atlantic off Greenland having covered 2,945 km (1,830 miles) in 96 hours. America had her triumph.

USS *Nautilus* (SSN-571)

Length: 98.5 metres (323 ft)

Beam: 8.2 metres (27 ft)

Draft: 6.7 metres (22 ft)

Displacement (surfaced): 3,533 tons

Displacement (submerged): 4,092 tons

Maximum speed (surfaced): 22 knots

Maximum speed (submerged): 25 knots

Built: Electric Boat Shipyard, Groton, Connecticut

Launched: 21 January 1954

Maiden voyage: 17 January 1955

Accepted by US Navy, trials complete: May 1956

Decommissioned: March 1980

Total distance sailed: 822,000 km (513,550 miles)

Total dives made: 2,507

Complement: 105 (13 officers, 92 enlisted men)

To the bottom of the seas

TRIESTE	23 January 1960

The Mariana Trench in the Pacific Ocean is the deepest place on the planet, 11 km (7 miles) below the surface of the sea. It is a world of impenetrable darkness where temperatures are scarcely above freezing and where the weight of the water presses down at 8 tons per square inch. *Trieste* reached this profoundly alien environment in January 1960.

The Swiss designer of *Trieste* was Auguste Piccard, a wild-haired visionary – reputedly the model for *Tintin's* Professor Calculus. In the early 1930s he designed a series of high-altitude balloons whose pressurized cabins enabled him to set a number of altitude records, culminating in 1935 at 23,000 metres (72,177 ft). By 1937 he had realised that the same technology could be used to do exactly the opposite – to explore the world's deepest sea beds.

By 1948 he had produced his first deepwater submersible, the *FNRS-2*. That same year in the Mediterranean he established a new depth record of 4,176 metres (13,700 ft). By the summer of 1953, his new submersible, *Trieste*, built in Naples, Italy, was ready.

He called it a *bathyscape*, from the Greek 'bathos', meaning deep, and 'scaphos', ship. The need for structural integrity was absolute; the principles on which it worked were elementary.

An extraordinary vessel

The main body of the submersible was 18 metres (59 ft) long and contained three chambers. The largest, in the center, held 10,205 kg (22,500 lb.) of aviation fuel, which, less dense than water, was naturally buoyant. It was flanked by two flotation tanks containing compressed air. Suspended between them were 9,145 kg (9 tons) of pig iron and, directly below the central tank, a metal sphere, 1.82 metres (6 ft) high and 1.52 metres (5 ft) wide, for the two-man crew. In the words of crew member Lt. Don Walsh, it was 'about the size and temperature of the average household refrigerator.'

To dive, air was released from the end tanks, allowing the weight of the pig iron to sink the ship. To rise to the surface, 2 of the 9 tons of iron were released. Two 2-horsepower electric motors drove the vessel.

Piccard successfully carried out a number of dives in the Mediterranean, reaching a depth of 3,700 metres (12,100 ft). In 1958 he sold *Trieste* to the US Navy, then actively pursuing deep-sea exploration. After extensive modifications, the vessel was shipped the following year to the

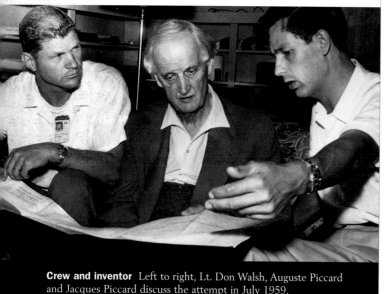

Crew and inventor Left to right, Lt. Don Walsh, Auguste Piccard and Jacques Piccard discuss the attempt in July 1959.

> Indifferent to the nearly 200,000 tons of pressure clamped on her metal sphere, the *Trieste* balanced herself delicately ... on the bottom, making token claim in the name of science and humanity, to the ultimate depths in all our ocean – the Challenger Deep. **Jacques Piccard**

Northern Marianas islands in the western Pacific, site of the Challenger Deep, the deepest spot of the Mariana Trench.

Attempt on Challenger Deep

Six preliminary dives at increasing depths were carried out before, on 23 January 1960, the attempt was made on the Challenger Deep. On board were Jacques Piccard, son of the designer, and Don Walsh of the US Navy. *Trieste* descended at 91 cm (3 ft) per second until 8,230 metres (27,000 ft) was reached. The descent was then slowed to 45 cm (1 ½ ft) per second. Voice contact was maintained with the surface via a sonar communications system that provided a 'faint but clear' signal that took 7 seconds in each direction. The only alarming moment – 'a pretty hairy experience', as Walsh put it – came when the single porthole, made of 15-cm (6-inch) -thick Plexiglass, cracked.

At exactly 1:06 P.M. local time, after a descent of 4 hours, 48 minutes, *Trieste* settled on the bottom, raising 'clouds of fine white silt'. The sea temperature was 3°C (37.4°F), the depth 10,911 metres (35,798 ft).

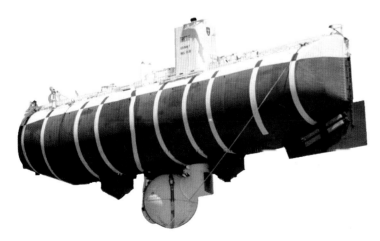

Journey to the deep The real challenge for Piccard was to build a vessel capable of resisting the enormous pressures of the deep seas.

From Nekton to *Thresher*

The initial impetus for the US Navy to buy *Trieste* from Piccard was mainly scientific, but the submersible's military applications were also a consideration. *Trieste* played a central role in the Navy's deep-sea research project, code-named Nekton. During the 20 minutes the vessel spent at the bottom of the Challenger Deep, Walsh reported seeing a white flatfish about 30.5 cm (1 ft) long, a shrimp and a form of jellyfish, making it clear that even the oxygen-deprived waters of the world's deepest seas – the hadalpelagic zone – were capable of supporting complex life forms.

The Navy put *Trieste* to a very different use when USS *Thresher* – first of a new class of nuclear-powered submarines – sank 560 km (350 miles) off the coast of Massachusetts with the loss of all hands during trials in April 1963. It was *Trieste*'s crew that found and identified the remains of *Thresher* 2,560 metres (8,400 ft) under the sea (pictured above).

The first man to sail solo nonstop around the world

ROBIN KNOX-JOHNSTON | 14 June 1968–22 April 1969

Robin Knox-Johnston's epic sailing voyage in the late 1960s disproved one of the apparent certainties of the emerging creed of single-handed sailing: that a solo nonstop circumnavigation was beyond anyone's reach. Knox-Johnston may have seemed an unlikely pathfinder; he struggled for money, and his boat *Suhaili* was more carthorse than thoroughbred. But he redefined the art of the possible.

Knox-Johnston was an ideal candidate to sail around the world. At 29, he was not just young enough to withstand the rigours of the voyage, he had served 12 years in the British Merchant Navy – seven as an officer – at a time when seamanship of the old school was still at a premium. He was also an experienced small-boat sailor. In 1963, while stationed in Bombay with two colleagues, he had a yacht built, named *Suhaili*. She may not have been fast, but at 9.75 metres (32 ft) she was an excellent oceangoing boat – strong and seaworthy. In 1965 they sailed her back to Britain, completing the 11,200 km (7,000 miles) from Cape Town in one leg.

Early planning

By 1967 the idea of a single-handed round-the-world trip had begun to take shape in Knox-Johnston's mind. His motive was partly adventure, but more specifically that someone was bound to make the attempt sooner or later. The most likely candidate seemed to be a Frenchman, Eric Tabarly. Knox-Johnston put it simply, 'By rights a Briton should do it first and in the circumstances he had better get moving.'

Knox-Johnston on the foredeck Under-canvassed, overweight and plodding, *Suhaili* was nonetheless a supreme sea boat – for anyone not in a hurry.

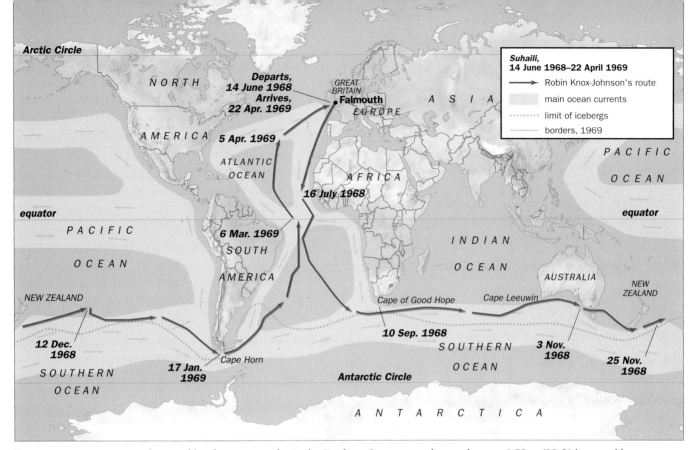

Suhaili,
14 June 1968–22 April 1969

→ Robin Knox-Johnson's route
main ocean currents
limit of icebergs
borders, 1969

NORTH

AMERICA

Departs,
14 June 1968
Arrives,
22 Apr. 1969

GREAT
BRITAIN
•Falmouth
EUROPE

A S I A

PACIFIC

OCEAN

5 Apr. 1969

ATLANTIC
OCEAN

AFRICA

16 July 1968

equator

PACIFIC

OCEAN

6 Mar. 1969

SOUTH

AMERICA

INDIAN

OCEAN

AUSTRALIA

equator

NEW
ZEALAND

NEW ZEALAND

Cape of Good Hope   Cape Leeuwin

12 Dec.
1968

Cape Horn

10 Sep. 1968

SOUTHERN

3 Nov.
1968

25 Nov.
1968

SOUTHERN

17 Jan.
1969

OCEAN

Antarctic Circle

OCEAN

A N T A R C T I C A

Traversing mountainous seas, bitter cold and persistent gales in the Southern Ocean seemed more than any 9.75-m (32-ft) boat could conquer.

Obtaining leave was the least of his worries. Lack of money initially made it seem the voyage would never get beyond the pipe-dream stage. The ideal boat, specially built for the trip, was beyond his means, and potential sponsors were just not interested. By late 1967, all other options exhausted, Knox-Johnston made up his mind: he would make the attempt, underfunded or not, in *Suhaili*.

Knox-Johnston left Falmouth, in the south of England, on 14 June 1968. *Suhaili*, crammed with stores for a year and 'notably sluggish', floated several inches below her designed waterline. Preparations had been so rushed it was only at sea that Knox-Johnston could properly lay out his courses. As important, he was now in a race. At the end of February, the *Sunday Times* in London had launched what it called the Golden Globe Race for the first man to sail non-stop alone around the world. There was no starting date. No one even knew how many would take part. But however staggered and uncoordinated the start, the gun had been fired.

Truly alone – a different age of sailing

Today round-the-world races are full-on sprints with fleets of highly tuned boats, decked out in gaudy sponsors' logos, speeding their way around the globe. Satellite navigation and Internet connections are standard, distances in excess of 560 km (350 miles) a day commonplace.

Ultimate challenge Unflappable and fearless, Knox-Johnston never had any doubt what he was taking on. He also knew expert seamanship was what would see him through.

Slocum's legacy

The immediate inspiration behind Knox-Johnston's solo circumnavigation came from two other English sailors – Francis Chichester and Alec Rose. In 1966–1967 Chichester sailed single-handed around the world on his yacht *Gypsy Moth IV*, stopping only once, in Australia. In 1967–1968 Rose repeated Chichester's voyage on his yacht *Lively Lady*. These were impressive feats.

But the original solo circumnavigator was a Canadian, Joshua Slocum (pictured above). Between April 1895, when he sailed from Boston, and June 1898, when he arrived in Newport, Rhode Island, Slocum undertook an ambitious and arduous single-handed journey around the world aboard a converted 11-m (36-ft) fishing sloop that he named *Spray*.

It was not a nonstop voyage, which explains its three-year duration. But it was the first time an individual had attempted what, at the time, was assumed to be impossible.

The contrast with Knox-Johnston and *Suhaili* is telling. Even sailing at her best, *Suhaili* was hard-pressed to make more than 6 knots. A day's run of 240 km (150 miles) was an achievement. Navigation was a matter of dead reckoning interspersed with sextant sights (weather permitting); communication was dependent on whether the radio would work at all – just making contact with a relay station on shore could take 8 hours.

Taking on water

None of this dismayed Knox-Johnston. These were the realities of small-boat ocean sailing at the time. It was expected that sails would split and have to be hand sewn – not that this did much to ease Knox-Johnston's mood when, deep in the Southern Ocean, endlessly stitching yet again, he sewed the spinnaker to his mustache. It was also a certainty that *Suhaili*, however strong her teak hull, would leak. Even before he had reached the equator, the boat was leaking alarmingly. The solution was for Knox-Johnston to dive overboard, holding his breath, to tack a mixture of hemp and sailcloth into the hull – the whole held in place by a copper strip.

Knox-Johnston's progress across the Southern Ocean was a permanent struggle against cold, fatigue and endless seas. On 6 September the boat was knocked flat. On 13 October, approaching Australia in 'by far the worst weather' he had met so far, he was 'convinced … that the boat would not last long.' By 3 November his self-steering, frequently on the point of failure, finally gave out. He was less than halfway around.

Run aground

Attempting a rendezvous on the south island of New Zealand to drop off mail, he endured almost his worst night yet. Increasingly exhausted, he attempted to find his way through a narrow and largely unlit channel in a rising gale. Ironically, his destination safely made, he then went aground.

> ❝ We are now becalmed. Come on God, give me a bloody break. It's been nothing but calms or gales for weeks. How about some steady winds for a change. ❞
>
> Robin Knox-Johnston, *A World of My Own*, 2 November 1968

Almost home On his last leg to Falmouth on 23 April 1969, Knox-Johnston and *Suhaili* are cheered on by the crew of a British warship. A bath, clean sheets, a cigar and a pint of beer loomed.

He not only faced the prospect of the brutal run to Cape Horn, still several thousand miles to the east, but news that a Frenchman – Bernard Moitessier – sailing a larger and faster boat, was hot on his heels. Rounding Cape Horn on 17 January, his 218th day at sea, Knox-Johnston still had 14,500 km (9,000 miles) to sail.

Suhaili was never built to take on such consistently harsh conditions over so long a period. Yet, with crucial repairs improvised by Knox-Johnston, she plugged onwards resolutely. The same can be said of Knox-Johnston. 'The other part of the team,' he wrote, 'was in good physical shape apart from the inevitable cuts, bruises and blisters.' Endurance was key.

'Completely licked'

Once north of the equator again, 266 days into the voyage, Knox-Johnston smoked his last cigarette. As ever, the sea then had the last laugh. By 11 April, 1,600 km (1,000 miles) from home, *Suhaili* was becalmed off the Azores. 'I feel completely licked,' he wrote. 'I don't think I have felt so low the whole voyage.'

Eleven days later, on 22 April 1969, he crossed the line at Falmouth, 313 days and almost 48,000 km (30,000 miles) after he had set out. He had averaged just over 160 km (100 miles) a day. First on board were the Customs and Excise officers, asking the time-honoured question: 'Where from?' 'Falmouth,' answered Knox-Johnston.

The first solo Atlantic row

John Fairfax was determined to become the first man to row the Atlantic single-handed. As a child, he had been obsessed with the story of George Harbo and Frank Samuelsen, the Norwegian fishermen who in 1896 had reputedly rowed from New York to England. The success of John Ridgeway and Chay Blyth – who in 1966 rowed from Cape Cod to Ireland – provided the final spur.

In the summer of 1966, John Fairfax was determined to turn his dream of a solo Atlantic crossing into reality. It proved depressingly hard. Despite the success of Blyth and Ridgeway, no one seemed interested in supporting him.

An advertisement in the personal columns of *The Times* produced six answers. Three were from 'cranks'; the fourth contained a check for £1; the fifth, an offer to help build a boat; and the sixth was from Sylvia Cook – the woman who in the early 1970s would row the Pacific with him (*see* box).

Britannia and 'a bright light'

Fairfax later said that, so far as 1967 was concerned, Sylvia 'was the only bright light in my life'. It seemed an omen. The following year, Martin Cowling (a business-man) agreed to sponsor Fairfax. The money wasn't gener-ous, but it was enough. *Britannia* was commissioned from the celebrated British dinghy-designer, Uffa Fox.

At 7.5 metres (25 ft) long and weighing 390 kg (860 lb.), *Britannia* was not going to be an easy boat to row, especially when fully loaded. But she was a magnificent sea boat, able to right herself in two seconds if capsized and with a self-draining system that could empty her almost as fast. Given the quantities of water that persistently slopped over her low freeboard, this was a key asset.

It was one Fairfax would need. In 1966 Blyth and Ridgeway had chosen the shortest route across the Atlantic – winds and currents clearly in their favour. Fairfax proposed to row almost double the distance, from

the Canary Islands to Florida – the longest practical dis-tance, given wind and current, he thought he could man-age. The most direct course was around 5,760 km (3,600 miles). Allowing for the vagaries of the wind, Fairfax's likely real distance would be closer to 8,000 km (5,000 miles). Further, rather than merely aiming to make his landfall wherever an erratic course took him, he announced a precise destination – Miami.

Fairfax left Gran Canaria on 20 January 1969. His last night on land had been bad. The prospect of what he was attempting seemed crushing. The farewells with his moth-er and Sylvia Cook the next morning were anguished.

Calm before the storm Fairfax poses nonchalantly while *Britannia* is prepared for shipping to the Canary Islands, the voyage's starting point.

Redoubtable endurance

Fairfax rowed throughout the first night. As dawn broke, he was dismayed to see the bulk of Gran Canaria looming hardly 24 km (15 miles) away. Adding to his woes, the otherwise reliable Northeasterly Trade Winds had given way to strong westerlies. They blew for the next three weeks. Even the most modest progress to the west meant hours of continuous, backbreaking labour.

On February 8 he sighted a ship, *Skauborg*, a Norwegian cargo vessel. Its crew confirmed what his own sights had already told him – that in 19 days he had made just 132 km (83 miles). The captain offered to take him on board. Fairfax refused. As *Skauborg* disappeared over the horizon, Fairfax 'cried without shame'.

The reality of what Fairfax was attempting weighed heavily. He was now rowing for upward of 10 hours a day, approaching absolute exhaustion. The weather was draining, temperatures in excess of 32°C (90°F) alternating with violent downpours and squalls. Progress was limited.

Birthday blues

21 May was his thirty-second birthday. It was a dispiriting day. A fragment of tobacco, hoarded for the occasion, proved too wet to light, and his last tin of raspberries was contaminated. Then, defiantly swigging from a bottle of brandy, Fairfax was washed overboard by a rogue wave, the bottle lost in the depths. But by the next day he was still rowing, determined to keep up his daily stint.

Fairfax had long since developed a curious relationship with *Britannia*, cajoling, abusing and praising the boat by turns. There was no more eager moment for him and his long-suffering little ship when, on 23 June, his 154th day at sea, he spotted Cay Verde, an outlier of the Bahamas, his first land since Gran Canaria. He spent a luxurious day alone on its white sands. By nightfall he was rowing again.

It would take a further 16 days before Fairfax reached Miami, his landfall exactly as predicted. He had rowed 8,547 km (5,342 miles) in 180 days.

The Pacific conquered

'I was definitely not her type, nor she mine.' This was the reaction of Fairfax to meeting Sylvia Cook in 1967. On the other hand, she was, he added, 'a keen rower.' In April 1971 Fairfax and Cook (pictured) began an improbable task – to row across the Pacific.

They left San Francisco on 26 April 1971, their destination Australia. They arrived at Hayman Island, off the Great Barrier Reef, on 21 April 1972, having covered 12,865 km (8,041 miles) in 361 days. They had stopped three times – at Washington Island, Fanning Island, and at the Onotoa Gilbert Islands. In the process any normal conclusion of what a two-man crew – wholly dependent on their own muscle power and resolve – might achieve had been shattered.

Fairfax became the first man to row the Atlantic and the Pacific oceans, Sylvia Cook the first woman to row any ocean.

The impossible voyage

CHAY BLYTH | 19 October 1970–6 August 1971

Robin Knox-Johnston showed it was possible to sail around the world single-handed without stopping (*see* p. 112). The 29-year-old Scotsman Chay Blyth wanted to go one better. Not just to complete a nonstop solo circumnavigation of the globe, but to do it against the prevailing winds and tides of the Southern Ocean. It amounted to a head-on assault on the world's roughest seas.

At the age of 21, Chay Blyth had become the youngest sergeant in the Parachute Regiment, one of the elite units of the British army. It was an outfit that placed a premium on toughness. At 26, having hardly been to sea in his life, he volunteered to row the Atlantic with a fellow member of the regiment, Capt. John Ridgeway. It took them 92 days. Blyth admitted it was 'bloody hard'.

Plotting a course Blyth sailed with instruments then thought state of the art. Today they would seem primitive. But they were enough.

In 1968, having left the army, he attempted to sail around the world on his own. He didn't make it. His boat, *Dytiscus*, little more than a family cruiser, was unequal to the demands of the Southern Ocean. Battered by storms off South Africa, he was forced to pull out. For Blyth the sense of failure was all-consuming. This wasn't how it was meant to be. Challenges were there to be overcome – preferably by precise planning; if necessary, by brute force.

He immediately set about finding a new challenge. It wasn't hard. Robin Knox-Johnston had already sailed nonstop around the world from west to east. If that was a first Blyth could now never claim, there was another still within reach – nonstop around the world from east to west, against the prevailing winds of the Southern Ocean.

The classic sailing route around the world took advantage of the fact that the winds in the Southern Hemisphere are predominantly from the west. If you started and finished in Europe, it made little difference to the first and last legs of a circumnavigation which way you planned to sail. The first leg could only be south across the Atlantic, the last leg north across the Atlantic. It was the middle part of the voyage – the 24,000 km (15,000 miles) or so of Southern Ocean – that counted.

The hazardous Southern Ocean

The Southern Ocean is the most dangerous body of water in the world, a wind-wracked emptiness of gales and ferocious seas. Year round it is swept by depressions

Self-steering The self-steering on *British Steel* proved a persistent headache, simultaneously too complicated and never sturdy enough to be relied upon. It required endless maintenance. In the end, Blyth decided he was better off without it.

that produce waves, traveling at up to 65 km/h (40 mph), their crests up to 182 metres (200 yards) apart. The waves circle the globe relentlessly, uninterrupted by any land. There is nothing regular or predictable about these watery depths. As weather systems pass overhead, wind directions change rapidly and violently. Sea conditions generate giant, unstable peaks of water that can pummel and, on occasion, sink even the largest ships.

Added to this is the bitter cold produced by the Antarctic continent to the south, frequent fogs (despite the gales) and the hazards of icebergs. The farther south you sail, the greater the risks but the shorter the distance; the farther north, the fewer the risks but the greater the distance. In either case the prospect of rescue if you capsize or lose your mast is effectively zero. Midway between Cape Horn and New Zealand, you are farther from land than at any other point on the surface of the globe.

It was across this huge, unforgiving sea that Blyth now proposed to sail in the wrong direction. Even at his best estimate, it would take a minimum of 10 months, during which he would be entirely reliant on his own efforts.

A boat of steel

He needed an exceptional boat, and he got one. In December 1969 the British Steel Corporation agreed to sponsor him. It meant not just generous funding, but as important, a boat built of steel, which Blyth judged essential if it were to withstand the battering it would encounter in the Southern Ocean.

Finding a builder proved much harder. It wasn't until late March 1970 that a contract for the boat could be placed. It was a race against time. Blyth had to leave in October to avoid the Southern Ocean winter. That meant the boat had to be launched by mid-August to allow time for trials. It was a highly stressed Blyth that saw his vessel – 18 metres (59 ft) overall and now christened

Deck design One of the radical design features of *British Steel* was her near flush deck. It was partly designed to allow ease of movement around the boat, more particularly to allow seawater, which frequently crashed overboard, to run off it with the minimum of obstruction.

British Steel – slide down the slipway on 19 August 1970.

On 19 October he crossed the start line. By nightfall, beating down the English Channel, he 'felt more like a zombie than a human being.' But once he had adjusted to the rhythms of life on board, the opening weeks of the voyage presented no particular problems other than the successive breaking of both his running booms (metal spars used to spread out the head-sails when running down-wind). This would slow him on the two Atlantic legs. It also raised doubts about the mast. On the other hand, it was unlikely to make much difference in the Southern Ocean.

The equator was crossed on 14 November, the

> If I ever dream, I'll dream of this storm. The hurricanes in the Atlantic never haunted me, but this one could. I just close my eyes and see those white-blue legions rising and falling, but always advancing.
>
> Chay Blyth, *The Impossible Voyage*, on the Southern Ocean, 29 April 1971

twenty-eighth day of the voyage. By mid-December, Blyth was closing in on the coast of South America, en route to Cape Horn. He was forced to contend with a series of vicious squalls – *pamperos* – that struck with little warning, the wind suddenly screaming at 50-plus knots, on one occasion at 60 and knocking *British Steel* on her beam ends before righting herself.

Rounding Cape Horn

Cape Horn was the first of Blyth's major landfalls, the moment he would face the Southern Ocean proper. At least in theory, it also marked the most southerly point of the voyage (in reality, having rounded Cape Horn, he was forced farther south still by headwinds). The weather, by

Big business?

Chay Blyth's voyage marked a key moment in the transformation of long-distance ocean sailing. What had once been thought the exclusive preserve of enthusiastic amateurs had proved to be a legitimate field for corporate sponsorship. As big business warmed to the possibilities, suddenly a series of ocean races – fully crewed and single-handed – were launched. The first was the Whitbread Round-the-World Race, first held in 1973–1974 [and in 2001 rechristened the Volvo Ocean Race (pictured)]. But perhaps the most lasting legacy of this new realisation was the Vendée Globe, first sailed in 1989–1990.

Times may have tumbled as technology advanced but the risks remain. Two competitors have lost their lives in the Vendée Globe. Three sailors died in the first Whitbread, one in the 1989–1990 Whitbread, one in the 2005–2006 Volvo.

Chay Blyth showed the oceans could be tackled. But they will never be mastered.

Adventure incorporated

For Blyth personally, his round-the-world voyage proved to be a prelude to more than a decade of further endurance sailing events. In 1973–1974 he skippered *Great Britain II* in the first Whitbread Round-the-World Race. In 1974 he skippered *Great Britain IV* to a record time in the Round Britain Race. He was skipper of *Brittany Ferries* in the 1981 two-handed trans-Atlantic race. In 1984, sailing with Eric Blunn on a trimaran, *Beefeater II*, in the New York–San Francisco race, the boat capsized off Cape Horn; Blyth and Blunn spent more than a day on their upturned boat before being rescued.

But his most enduring legacy was the British Steel Challenge (since 1996 the BT Global Challenge), launched in 1989. (Blyth, in hat, is pictured above celebrating with the winners of the 1997 race.) The aim, brilliantly realised, was to allow ordinary people the opportunity to race around the world on professionally skippered yachts. It immediately established itself as the life-changing event Blyth had always hoped for – a rare opportunity for people from a wide variety of backgrounds to test themselves in ways most never experience.

now, was 'bitterly cold'. Already, he wrote, his 'eyes were sore with going to windward; spray was constantly hitting them, and they were red with repeated rubbing.'

A valuable boost to morale was provided 140 km (87 miles) from the Horn by a meeting with HMS *Endurance*. Blyth put on a clean shirt; the captain of *Endurance* sent over two bottles of whisky. And then he was on his own again. The next day, 24 December, Blyth rounded the Horn.

Exhuasting battle

The wind immediately went foul, rising to a full gale. *British Steel* was hit by a 'huge sea', and Blyth was 'hurled across the cockpit', his forehead badly cut. The self-steering was 'smashed beyond repair'. Blythe was forced to steer by hand in freezing temperatures.

A continuing, exhausting battle followed. By 2 January the wind was blowing Force 11 (102–115 km/h) On 7 January Blyth encountered the first of four days of thick fog. It was followed by windless days. The cabin was now permanently sodden, clothes and bedding impossible to dry. As the month wore on, the wind continued to torment Blyth. 'It was either calm or blowing like hell from the wrong direction', he wrote. 'The Southern Ocean seemed to go on for ever.'

February began – and continued – with gales. Nonetheless, by the 14th, now less than 800 km (500 miles) from New Zealand, Blyth had crossed the 180th meridian. He was halfway.

Longing for home

With New Zealand safely rounded at the end of February, Blyth made for Tasmania and a rendezvous to drop off and pick up mail. His mood became curiously unsettled. For once, he was oddly timid, almost nervous. Nonetheless, the mail drop at Tasmania successfully completed, by 12 March he was on his way again. And now he was homebound. He later wrote: 'I could not know but by far the worst stage of the voyage was ahead of me.'

For the first time loneliness set in, his thoughts constantly turning to home. Progress remained reasonable, however. With Cape Leeuwin, the southwest tip of Australia, cleared by the end of March, his next goal was the Cape of Good Hope – and the end of the Southern Ocean.

On 8 April, forced on deck at night due to very high winds and not wearing his safety harness, a wave nearly rolled him overboard. It was the closest call yet. He was

Bailing out Seawater gushes into the cabin. Sodden electronics and sodden living conditions are a fact of life when sailing the Southern Ocean.

becoming very tired, close to punch-drunk. It was now he encountered the worst storm of the journey, at its peak a Force 12 (117–133 km/h) monster that left Blyth dazed and profoundly exhausted. Blyth wrote on 29 April, 'For the first time in my life I've been genuinely frightened. … I'll say, without any embarrassment, I am frightened.' It was the key crisis of the voyage.

The Southern Ocean still hadn't given up. On 13 May the Cape of Good Hope all but reached, a wave broke over the boat and left Blyth 'holding the tiller and steering *under* water.' The water poured off the boat. Seven days later he was back in the Atlantic.

On 6 August 1971, Blyth crossed the finish line at the end of his personal odyssey. He had been at sea for 292 days and had covered 50,000 km (31,000 miles). For sheer bloody-minded endurance, his achievement remains without peer.

The first woman to sail solo around the world

NAOMI JAMES | 9 September 1977–8 June 1978

Hardly two years before she set out to sail nonstop single-handed around the world, Naomi James had never been on a boat. Even a month before she hoped to leave, she had no boat and no sponsor. Yet not only was she on the starting line, she made it back. It wasn't nonstop, but she was the first woman to sail solo around the world.

Naomi James, born and brought up in New Zealand, went to sea by chance. Travelling through Europe by bicycle and trying to learn German, she met Rob James, one of Britain's leading ocean-racing yachtsmen and then skipper of Chay Blyth's *British Steel* (*see* p. 118). He invited her on board. The first time they sailed together, she 'didn't know the front end of a boat from the back,' and she was violently and persistently sick. They married the following year.

Almost at once, Naomi decided she was going to sail around the world. It was an astonishing ambition for so obviously inexperienced a sailor, yet she was very determined. She not only secured the support of her husband, Rob, among the most experienced and successful long-distance sailors in the world, but of Chay Blyth, then – as a result of his 1970–1971 east-to-west solo circumnavigation – perhaps the best-known endurance sailor of all.

Rob James had already taught her the rudiments of boat handling and navigation. Blyth then gave her a 16-metre (53-ft) boat called *Spirit of Cutty Sark*. It was immensely strong and seaworthy. It was also designed to be sailed by a crew of 10.

Courage and inexperience

On 9 September 1977, after only a month of rushed and exhausting preparations, James left. It was the first time she had sailed single-handed.

By now sponsorship of a sort had been secured from the *Daily Express* in London, and the boat was accordingly

Triumph of the farm girl James had unexpected reserves of grit. What she achieved seemed inexplicable in the hard-bitten world of ocean sailing.

re-named *Express Crusader*. The extra money – and profile – made little difference to James's ability to sail. It took her fully three days, never sure of her position, just to clear the mouth of the English Channel. Once into the Bay of Biscay, the wind at last fair, it took her a debilitating hour and a half to manoeuvre the headsails to get the boat sailing downwind.

As she headed south, her mood picked up. Whatever her technical limitations, it was clear that this was a world that suited her. Her ability to sail the boat was clearly improving; her readiness to take on the daily business of renewing and repairing failing gear was also growing. Occasional worries aside, her confidence in her navigation was gradually rising, too.

Failed communication

On 7 October, approaching the equator, her radio failed. It was a potentially devastating blow. The link it had provided with the outside world was a huge boost to morale. On 28 October, 3,2000 km (2,000 miles) from Cape Town, she suffered a further setback. She had on board a kitten, Boris. During a routine sail change, Boris was swept overboard and not recovered.

By 18 November, as she approached the gales and huge seas of the Southern Ocean, her self-steering had disintegrated. It was clear she would have to stop to have it repaired. When, on 19 November, she arrived in Cape Town, her hopes of a nonstop circumnavigation were gone.

It may have been a blessing in disguise. The essential repairs were completed in record time, and James – between bubble baths and nights in clean sheets – found herself hugely refreshed. Her radio had also been fixed. It is doubtful if she could have continued otherwise.

The Naomi James who set off from Cape Town to cross the Southern Ocean on 22 November 1977, was a more accomplished sailor than the timid figure who had begun the voyage in England two months earlier.

An arduous test

It was as well. The Southern Ocean awaited. It was wet, cold, tiring and more often than not, terrifying – but it was clear that not just the boat but James herself could cope. Endless sail adjustments, the risk of icebergs, rapidly changing weather – with gales and calms alternating – and, inevitably, wear and tear on the boat enhanced rather than reduced her ability to keep the boat sailing safely.

On 26 February, still 3,200 km (2,000 miles) from Cape Horn, she capsized. It was 5:00 A.M. The wind was Force 10

Naomi the navigator

A precise measure of Naomi James's inexperience afloat was provided by the navigational errors she made on the first leg of the trip to Cape Town. She had always been conscious of her shortcomings as a navigator, not least worried what Rob, her husband, would make of them.

As she approached the Southern Ocean, she wrote, 'I discovered I'd been making a monumental blunder ... adding the magnetic variation to the compass error!' The net result was to put her 59 degrees off course.

This was a beginner's mistake. James herself wrote that if she had followed her own courses, she would have, 'continued across the ocean in a series of zigzags, probably ending up in Alaska.'

Joke or not, it hardly boded well for someone attempting to find her way across the loneliest oceans in the world. Nevertheless, she never made the same mistake again.

Naomi and Rob: The perfect couple

Briefly, after her circumnavigation of the world in 1978, Rob and Naomi James were the media darlings of the sailing world. She for having sailed around the world, he – already a veteran of two round-the-world races – as not just for being among the most experienced sailors in the world but among the most personable. It was a marriage made in heaven.

In December 1982, routinely skippering a boat back up the English Channel, Rob James fell overboard and drowned. This wasn't just a tragic end for a man who had already established himself as one of the most successful yacht racers of the period, it was devastating for Naomi. She was nine months pregnant when Rob died. Their daughter was born 10 days after his death.

Planning her round-the-world attempt, Naomi had long worried – nearly obsessed – about falling overboard. She rarely imagined the same might happen in the relatively kind waters of the English Channel – nor that its consequences would be so tragically close to home.

(88–101 km/h), the seas mountainous. James, in the cabin, was thrown from her bunk. The boat staggered upright, tons of water pouring from its decks. To James's delight the mast was still intact. With *Express Crusader* then laboriously made safe – pumped out, sails and rigging checked, the worst of the chaos down below put right – James, 'devoid of thought and incapable of feeling', took the helm herself. The key crisis of the journey had been survived.

Emergency repairs

But it was already obvious she would have to stop again. On 24 February, two days before her capsize, a 'clatter on deck' at 6:00 A.M. had James scurrying from the cabin. Part of the rigging holding the mast had collapsed. Three times she climbed the mast to make what, at best, could only be a temporary repair. On 14 March, by now swooping south into the ice-filled waters around Cape Horn, her best efforts at these repairs gave out, the rigging thudding once more onto the deck. Again she was forced up the mast. It was, she reported, 'bitterly cold'. Much more to the point was how long these temporary repairs would last. On 19 March she rounded Cape Horn.

The Falkland Islands, reached on 24 March, provided a vital respite for James. Her rigging was righted, her spirits crucially lifted. Four days later she was off again.

Her homeward trip was a predictable mixture of exhilaration and frustration. The weather eased. It was clear that, barring a serious accident, she would make it home in one piece. Approaching England, a series of windless days – the boat rolling wildly, sails thrashing uselessly – provided a final test of James's endurance, the finish line tantalizingly close but frustratingly hard to reach.

Her joy as she crossed the finish line was all the more remarkable for a woman who, only two years before, had spent her summer shearing sheep in New Zealand.

Head for heights Even in harbour, climbing the mast can be daunting. At sea it can seem an impossibility. Naomi never lacked guts.

The first woman to sail solo nonstop around the world

KAY COTTEE | 29 November 1987–5 June 1988

Australian Kay Cottee was brought up in and around boats. More boat bum than circumnavigator, she seemed an unlikely candidate to make sailing history. But on 5 June 1988, when she brought her 11-metre (37-ft) sloop, *Blackmores First Lady*, into Sydney harbour to a tumultuous reception, she did precisely that. She had become the first woman to sail nonstop single-handed around the world.

There were many tears on Cottee's departure from Sydney on 29 November 1987, for her round-the-world trip. There were even more tears when she came home, and there had been plenty during her voyage. 'Cried myself to sleep … very homesick and crying … cried again … cried my eyes out … set me off crying again …' said her log entries.

Appearances were deceptive. Cottee's apparent vulnerability provided a necessary emotional outlet for a tough-minded woman, who had the advantage of technological improvements for her trip.

First-class support network

There was little that was special about Cottee's boat: sturdy but otherwise a standard production model. But its electronics were remarkable – a telex machine, three radios, two satellite navigation systems, radar, a satellite tracking system, a weather fax machine and three electronic self-steering mechanisms (as well as two wind-operated systems). Given this high-tech equipment, she could routinely maintain contact with home.

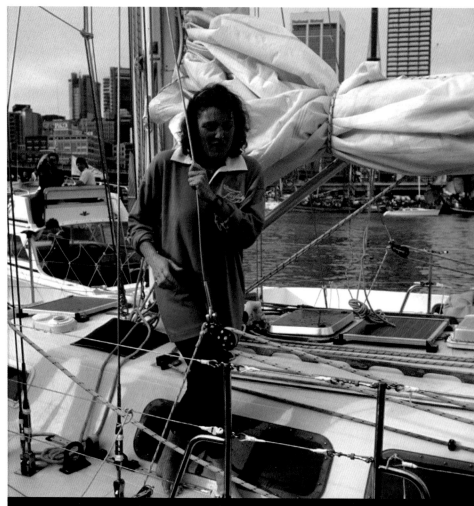

Final checks Cottee prepares to leave Sydney harbour in November 1987. The sophisticated electronics that equipped Cottee's boat were a major boon to her attempt.

Cottee had acquired this state-of-the-art equipment because she had a rare talent for promoting herself. Hence the willingness of Blackmores – one of Australia's leading healthcare companies – to sponsor her. Hence, too, the substantial shoreside team who worked to get *Blackmores First Lady* to the starting line in Sydney on 29 November.

But once aboard *Blackmores First Lady*, she was on her own. Her first days at sea were predictably tough. The adjustment from the frenetic pace of preparation to the reality of being at sea alone with 32,000 km (20,000 miles) and the whole of the Southern Ocean to cross proved daunting.

She soon began to confront the realities of the Southern Ocean and rapidly came to terms with her solitary life. The monster seas and gales she encountered as she proceeded to Cape Horn lifted rather than oppressed her spirits.

A run of ill fortune

Nearing Cape Horn, she was thrown across the cabin, landing on her knee. Swollen and bruised, it would plague her until the end of the voyage. She also cracked the boat's boom. This was a potentially voyage-ending problem. Over the following three months, she worked to fix it. The mend was never ideal. But it held.

Cape Horn rounded, Cottee headed north to the equator. For her voyage to be officially recognised as a round-the-world trip, she had to sail to the Northern Hemisphere. Thunderstorms and calm seas plagued her way north; dolphins and spectacular sunsets left her inspired.

The equator reached, she headed south again for the Cape of Good Hope and home. Off South Africa, the wind gusting to Force 11 (102–115 km/h), she suffered

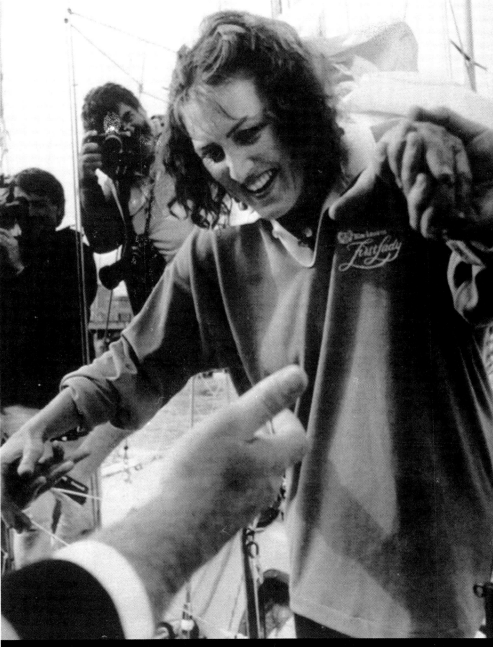

A nation celebrates Kay Cottee was all but unknown in Australia when she set off around the world. She returned on 5 June 1988, to find herself a national heroine, feted on every side.

her most serious challenge. 'Sobbing and shuddering,' she realised she was on a direct collision course with a freighter. Fortunately, the ship changed course at the last minute. She was then immediately washed overboard to the limit of her harness. After climbing back aboard, the crisis averted, she drank 'a very large gin'.

When Kay Cottee crossed the finish line in Sydney, she 'stood alone on the foredeck crying'. The next thing she knew, she was being introduced to Hazel Hawk, the Prime Minister's wife.

Bold man of the sea

JIM SHEKHDAR | **29 June 2000–30 March 2001**

On 30 March 2001, Jim Shekhdar stepped onto the beach on Stradbroke Island, Queensland, Australia. Nine months earlier the 54-year-old Briton had left Ilo, Peru – 12,800 km (8,000 miles) to the east – to row single-handed across the Pacific. His wasn't the first solo crossing of the Pacific by a rower. But it was certainly the most dramatic.

Of all extreme sports, none is more gruelling – mentally as much as physically – than ocean rowing. And no form of ocean rowing is tougher than solo. The odds are stacked against you from the start. Even with winds and currents in your favour, progress is pitifully slow. Assuming reasonable weather, even the strongest rower can manage no more than 10 hours at the oars in a day. On an exceptional day, that might mean 80 km (50 miles). On a trip as long as Shekhdar's, an average of 56 km (35 miles) a day is about the best one can hope to achieve. Over the course of 24 hours, that's about 2.4 km/h (1½ mph).

In bad weather it is often impossible to row at all. This is more than a question of simply waiting out storms (while hoping you haven't been blown too far off course). It raises the prospect of capsizing.

All ocean going rowing boats are self-righting in theory. But as Peter Bird, who spent a total of 938 days rowing across the world's oceans, graphically said, 'The thing about capsizing is that after the first one, it doesn't get any better. The 26th is just as bad.' A French rower, Gerard d'Aboville, capsized 39 times crossing the northern Pacific in 1991.

The realities of long-distance rowing

Shelter is rudimentary at best – it is a tiny cabin, little more than 2 metres (6 ft) long, most of it crammed with navigational and survival gear. Inside, unable even to sit up, you alternately shiver or swelter. A second cabin, at the other end

Confidence of foolhardiness? Shekdahr in St. Katherine's dock, London. He was never in doubt he could row the Pacific. By the end, even his supreme brand of self-belief had been shaken.

A bigger splash Shekhdar was hurled from *Le Shark* when he finally reached Australia, only yards from shore. His boat slammed over in the surf. It was a dramatic and ironic end to the row – Shekhdar having kept the vessel afloat, until that point, for 274 days.

of the boat, provides no shelter because it is filled with food – the solo ocean rower requires a prodigious amount of nourishment, up to 6,000 calories (25,000 kilojoules) a day. Yet he or she is still guaranteed to lose weight – 'every ounce of spare flesh', as Bird put it. Shekhdar lost more than 36 kg (80 lb.) in the Pacific. A fully loaded boat slows progress, ensuring that the hull will soon be encrusted with barnacles, which in turn makes progress slower still.

There are other dangers as well. Threats from sharks and whales – both are capable of sinking a frail boat – are as real as the hazards posed by large ships, whose radar frequently cannot pick out such small craft as rowing boats. In shipping lanes the prospect of being run down is ever present. Even in daylight you may not be seen.

If Jim Shekhdar was in any way alarmed by the prospect of what he was taking on, he didn't show it. In an interview just before his marathon row, he dismissed the dangers. 'I believe I can cope with any situation,' he said. He added, 'I describe myself as arrogant and that's true … I treat life as a game. Calculated risks are part of it.'

> ❝ I looked out of the hatch about three o'clock in the morning having been woken by a large noise and I saw a hundred feet of steel heading straight for me. That was scary, that's the only time in my life I've been affected like that. I was quite wobbly for a week after that. ❞
>
> Jim Shekhdar, on his near miss with a tanker

Stubborn determination

He was very tough. He had already rowed the Atlantic in 1997 from the Canaries to Barbados, though admittedly this was a two-man effort; his partner was an Englishman, David Jackson. Shekhdar's Pacific row took place under the duress of persistent pain from an arthritic hip, which he was due to have replaced shortly before he set off. With typical insouciance he cancelled the long-planned operation.

His persistence – stubbornness to most people – was obvious in his planning for the trip. It took him two years, during which he was repeatedly rebuffed by possible sponsors. Six months before he left, he announced that he had given up any hope of corporate backing.

Mission impossible

'They don't call it the Pacific for nothing. Way down south it gets rough, but in [the] north it tends to be calm. I may be going the wrong route – it may not be exciting enough.' This was Shekhdar speaking before his Pacific ordeal in 2000. In 2003 he decided to see just how rough it could be 'way down south.' He planned to row from New Zealand across the Southern Ocean past Cape Horn to the Cape of Good Hope in South Africa – 18,000 km (11,000 miles) across the roughest seas in the world. His first attempt, on 16 October, in a new, specially built boat, *Hornette* (pictured), lasted hardly 24 hours. A malfunctioning GPS and a broken wind generator forced him back to his starting point, the port of Bluff on New Zealand's South Island.

On 5 November he tried again. Twelve days and 1,180 km (730 miles) into his trip, a violent storm smashed parts of *Hornette*'s superstructure and Shekhdar's spare oars and washed the other pair overboard. Shekhdar, hurled across the boat, cut his head badly. He sent out a distress call and drifted for 30 hours before he was picked up by a government-owned research vessel.

He did not try again.

Struggling from the surf With his daughters on either side, the massed ranks of the media awaiting him, Shekhdar wades ashore after his epic Pacific crossing. He admitted he was looking forward to a beer.

Paradoxically, sponsorship of a kind then began to dribble in. It was never lavish – Shekhdar was forced to bear most of the cost himself – but it was just enough. Shekhdar claimed that the row would be significantly easier than raising the money.

His original plan was to leave from Chile. The Chilean authorities – alarmed at the prospect of his probable failure and the likelihood of his body and shattered boat being washed back onto land – peremptorily turned him down. The Peruvians proved more accommodating (though customs officials there still attempted to charge him for importing his boat, provoking a series of arguments).

The voyage begins

Thus it was from the small port of Ilo in southern Peru that Shekhdar left in his boat, *Le Shark*, on 29 June 2000. Ahead of him was the largest ocean in the world. 'I reckon the first 200 miles [320 km] will be the hardest,' he said before he left. He was wrong.

It was all hard. The distance he was attempting, an empty waste of sea that went on and on, was daunting. He advanced scarcely measurable distances, not just day after day, but month after month.

The crises were also predictable. The most serious was when a tanker came within yards of running him down. It was easily the worst moment of the trip. Over the next week, Shekhdar scarcely slept at all.

At much the same time, his electronics began to fail, his water ran short and his food decreased alarmingly. A shark began to follow him. Then a school of tuna joined the parade. Shekhdar found himself alternately talking and singing to them. He later claimed to have been able to recognise most of the fish.

He kept his course, however. Australia finally loomed before him. His arrival provided an unexpected moment of drama. With family and press gathered on the beach to watch his triumphant final few strokes, his boat was flipped over in a swell 182 metres (200 yards) from the shore, and Shekhdar was unceremoniously dumped into the water. He emerged, struggling out of the surf, a long white beard prominent. The journey had taken him 274 days.

Race against time

Britain's Ellen MacArthur is one of the outstanding sportswomen of all time. On 7 February 2005, she sailed a 23-metre (75-ft) trimaran, *Castorama B&Q*, to a new single-handed round-the-world record of 71 days, 14 hours, and 18 minutes. MacArthur, just 1.5 metres (5 ft 2 inches) and then 28 years old, was competing in a world dominated by men. She took them on and comprehensively defeated them.

When she was 18, MacArthur contracted glandular fever. Enforced idleness provided a natural opportunity for reflection. By the time she recovered, MacArthur had made her up her mind: she would become a professional sailor. She meant it.

Kingfisher MacArthur sails *Kingfisher* into Southampton on 15 February 2001. She came in second in the Vendée Globe race, beating a stellar cast of male single-handed sailors.

Decisions taken by MacArthur have an appealing simplicity. They are absolute.

She wrote 2,500 letters to potential sponsors. She received two replies, both turning her down. Undeterred and recognising that sailing was much more widely supported in France than in England, she decamped to Brittany, spending three impoverished years in a French dockyard, living in a portable plastic shed that contained hardly more than a mattress and a kettle.

From the dockyard to success

Persistence proved its own reward. At 22 she had mustered enough support to enter her first trans-Atlantic race, from Quebec, Canada, to St. Malo, Brittany, sailing a 6.4-metre (21-ft) boat, *Le Poisson*. She finished third. The following year, in the same boat, she entered the French Mini-Trans-Atlantic race. She came in only seventeenth. But the sailing world was beginning to take notice. The French retail giant, Kingfisher, agreed to sponsor her in the 1998 single-handed Route du Rhum race from St. Malo to Guadeloupe in the Caribbean. It was the first time she had taken on the big league. It was also the first time she had had a competitive boat. She finished first in her class.

The big breakthrough came in 2001. By now Kingfisher had become serious about MacArthur, agreeing to provide her with a state-of-the-art 18-metre (60-ft) vessel for the Vendée Globe, the world's premier single-handed round-the-world race. MacArthur finished second, a mere day behind one of the leading lights of the ocean-racing world – Frenchman Michel Desjoyeaux. But behind her was a stellar cast of some of the world's leading single-handers. All but one were men. Her time around the world of 94 days and 4 hours was the second fastest ever. She also became the youngest person, male or female, to complete a nonstop circumnavigation. The following year, sailing in the Route du Rhum again, she not only won, she did so in a record time.

Meticulous preparations

If MacArthur is fearsome on the water, she is arguably even more impressive off it. Support secured, she set about building the most complete shore team any sailor has ever enjoyed. She had long recognised that too many would-be record breakers, however heavily subsidised, had arrived on the starting line in a breathless panic – their preparations compromised by too little money and too little time.

When MacArthur set off to beat the single-handed round-the-world record on 28 November 2004, her preparations were faultless. Her boat wasn't just cutting edge, it had been designed with MacArthur in mind. In the words of designer Nigel Irens, it wasn't just 'the largest boat Ellen could safely sail' – and size at sea always translates into speed: put simply, the bigger the boat, the faster it will go – everything, from the headroom in the tiny cabin to the size of

Powering forward Day 15 of the journey – 3,200 km (2,000 miles) northeast of the Cape of Good Hope – MacArthur takes advantage of winds reaching 37 knots.

Fastest around the world

Direct comparisons between round-the-world voyages are rarely possible. For record purposes any such voyage must not just start and finish from the same point, but cross every degree of latitude and cross the equator. The total distance sailed must not be less than 40,000 km (21,600 nautical miles). That said, there is no agreed round-the-world course. The Vendée Globe is sailed to and from Les Sables d'Olonne in western France, for example, while the Jules Verne trophy for the fastest crewed circumnavigation specifies Ushant in northwest France as the start and finish point. This in fact was the course sailed by Joyon in 2003–2004, as well as by MacArthur the following year. Similarly, comparisons between monohulls and multihulls are not revealing. Multihulls, because they are lighter, are faster than monohulls. In the list below, only Joyon and MacArthur were on multihulls.

Year	Sailor	Country	Boat	Start/Finish	Time	Aver Speed (Knots)
1968–1969	Robin Knox-Johnston	British	*Suhaili*	Falmouth	313d	3.39
1970–1971	Chay Blyth	British	*British Steel*	Southampton	293d	3.85
1985–1986	Dodge Morgan	American	*American Promise*	Bermuda	150d	7.07
1989–1990	Titouan Lamazou	French	*Ecureuil d'Aquitaine II*	Sables d'Olonne	109d	8.23
1996–1997	Christopher Auguin	French	*Geodis*	Sables d'Olonne	105d 21h	10.2
2000–2001	Michel Desjoyeaux	French	*PRB*	Sables d'Olonne	93d 4h	11.6
2003–2004	Francis Joyon	French	*IDEC*	Ushant	72d 22h	12.42
2004–2005	Ellen MacArthur	British	*Castorama B&Q*	Ushant	71d 14h	12.66

High-tech navigation MacArthur studies the bank of computer screens and systems that plot *Castomara B&Q*'s every move. No amount of navigational wizardry compensates for the monstrous seas, gale-force winds and sleep deprivation that are a necessary evil for any round-the-world sailor.

the winches had been designed to facilitate MacArthur's sailing the boat.

Its proving voyages – from Australia, where it was built, to New Zealand and then to the Falklands, and finally with MacArthur sailing alone to the east coast of America – were as precisely graduated. MacArthur's last sail in *Castorama B&Q* before her world-record attempt was across the Atlantic. She was trying to beat the west–east single-handed record. She missed it by 75 minutes.

> **Courage is not having the energy to go on, it's going on when you don't have the energy.**
>
> Ellen MacArthur

A new record

The round-the-world time MacArthur was attempting to beat had been set less than a year before by Frenchman Francis Joyon. One of the most experienced single-handed sailors in the world, Joyon's boat, *IDEC*, was 4.5 metres (15 ft) longer than *Castorama B&Q*. At the time,

Robin Knox-Johnston said that Joyon's record could last for '10 years or more'. MacArthur thought it might take her five attempts to beat it.

Ocean racing in the 21st century is hugely dependent on technology. It is a world of computer-designed boats, travelling at high speeds, battering their way across the world's oceans with an array of electronic instruments working out courses, speeds and positions. E-mail and Internet connections are standard. Cameras mounted across the boat send live pictures anywhere in the world. Weather routing is supplied by ground-based teams.

It is also bleak and arduous. Speed is all. Weight is stripped to a minimum. Other than its high-tech navigational equipment, *Castorama B&Q*'s cupboard-sized cabin had a bunk, a sink and one gas burner. There was no

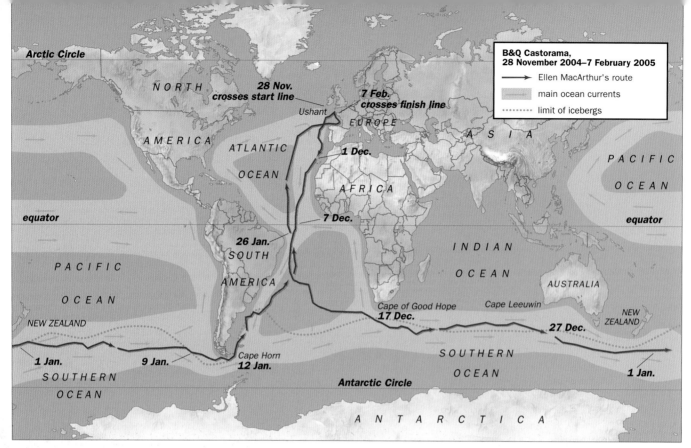

MacArthur set new records at every single major landmark during the round-the-world voyage.

lavatory. For food, MacArthur relied on energy bars, energy drinks and instant powdered foods. Her clothes consisted of wet-weather gear and T-shirts.

Sleep deprivation

Sailing the boat meant continual exhaustion. Frequently sodden, MacArthur had to simultaneously change sails, repair faltering gear and work out best courses – precisely the kind of physical and mental effort calculated to reduce even the fittest to prostration. As early as 1998, MacArthur had been consulting Dr. Claudio Stampi, a leading expert on sleep patterns at Harvard University. His advice was that snatched periods of sleep – perhaps 10 minutes, sometimes as long as 50 – were enough to keep anyone functioning efficiently, provided they didn't rely on it for too long. What 'too long' meant varied among individuals.

If she were to beat Joyon's record, MacArthur would need to be flat out from day one, averaging close to 13 knots an hour for well over two months.

However high-tech, sailing remains an essentially straightforward business: you go where the wind takes you. If it's in your favour, progress can be fast. If it's against you, there's little you can do. The wind was in MacArthur's favour from the start.

Her time to the equator – 8 days, 18 hours and 20

Overwhelming joy MacArthur has reason to celebrate. She had beaten the record set by Robin Knox-Johnston in 1969 by almost five times.

Mission accomplished MacArthur waves to the people onboard chase boats as she sails back into Falmouth on February 8, 2005. By the time she set foot ashore, she had already been made a Dame in honor of her achievement.

minutes – was a new singled-handed record. It was the first of many. She rounded the Cape of Good Hope more than 16 hours ahead of Joyon's time; she reached Cape Leeuwin in southwest Australia 1 day, 6 hours ahead. Cape Horn was reached in a new record time for a single-hander of 44 days, 23 hours and 36 minutes. She was now more than four days ahead of Joyon.

Monstrous seas

Yet as early as the third day of the voyage, MacArthur was reporting that she 'was pretty tired and stressed'. By day 16, having coped with a failure of the main generator, which saw the cabin fill with fumes, she spoke of needing 'a lot more' sleep. Her progress across the Southern Ocean – 'like sailing over mountains', as MacArthur put it – may have been fast. But it was far from simple. Monstrous seas and the ever-present threat of icebergs left her reeling with tiredness. On day 26, sailing at more than 26 knots, the boat hit something in the water, probably a whale. There was no obvious damage. Nonetheless, MacArthur reported that she was 'very, very lucky'. By the time she rounded Cape Horn, her exhaustion was reaching critical levels. She was 'mentally and emotionally zonked'.

Her progress thereafter was an endless torment. Gear failure forced her to make three climbs of the boat's mast, swaying 30 metres (100 ft) above the sea, each climb leaving her progressively more tired and bruised. Worse, ahead was a high-pressure system that no amount of weather warning could avoid. For three days she drifted in oppressive heat, her progress negligible, her lead over Joyon shrinking by the hour. It was followed by a gale from the northwest, exactly the direction she was trying to make. She would, she felt, 'be lucky to come through this without breaking something or capsizing … I'm really worried.'

Extraordinary determination

The gale was tough, but MacArthur survived it. Almost as tough were the further calms and headwinds that followed. It had been said before she left that, if necessary, MacArthur would swim over the line, dragging the boat behind her, if that was what it took to beat Joyon's record. She never quite came to that. But her commitment remains remarkable.

Ellen MacArthur encapsulates a rare combination of attributes – teeth-gritted determination combined with an understanding of the imperatives of high-tech sailing. In recognition of this she was made a Dame, even before she had stepped back on dry land.

The record man

When Frenchman Bruno Peyron and his 11-strong crew crossed the line opposite the Lizard Point in the English Channel on 6 July 2006, on their catamaran *Orange II*, they set a new record for a west–east crossing of the Atlantic under sail of 4 days, 8 hours and 23 minutes. It was a time bettered only by a handful of Atlantic liners.

Media darling Personable, articulate and persuasive, Peyron has always delivered. His appeal to sponsors and media is easily understood.

The sheer scale of Bruno Peyron's sailing records intimidates. He is a man whose life has been dedicated to the pursuit of speed at sea through the systematic application of technology. He has set three nonstop round-the-world record times – in 1993 (when he became the first man to beat 80 days), 2002 and 2005 (on this last occasion clocking an astonishing 50 days and 16 hours at an average speed of 18 knots). He has broken the record for the longest 24-hour run five times. He has set two record times across the Pacific and, sailing solo, the same number across the Atlantic, which he has crossed 35 times, 12 of them solo. But until 2006 he had never set the absolute record for the fastest Atlantic crossing.

Record breakers

Since 1980, when France's Eric Tabarly took almost two days off the existing trans-Atlantic record – set in 1905 by an American, Charlie Barr – a succession of Frenchmen progressively lowered the time. They took the record close to the kind of times a prewar luxury liner would have been pressed to make – from 10, to 8, to 7, and finally, in 1990, to 6 days and 13 hours, the time recorded by Serge Madec on *Jet Services V*.

What these record-breaking voyages had in common, other than all being achieved by Frenchmen, was that all employed evermore sophisticated technology and ever larger boats. It was a given that only multihulls were capable of the sustained high speeds necessary for the record. They are inherently faster than monohulls and

A record-breaking vessel Peyron's boat rosses the finish line at The Lizard on 6 July 2006. *Orange II* is the most formidable sailing machine ever built, capable of sustained speeds in excess of 30 knots. It is intensely demanding to sail, but no boat can match it.

much lighter because their hulls, rather than a keel, provide stability. The use of carbon fibres in sails and masts as much as hulls also meant boats that were progressively lighter, stronger and more efficient. At the same time, increasingly advanced electronics allowed instant position fixing and permanent access to continually updated weather forecasting.

Wind set fare

Any attempt on the trans-Atlantic record calls for a relatively rare set of meteorological conditions. Because the distance – 4,680 km (2,925 miles) from the Ambrose Light Tower off New York to the Lizard Point lighthouse in England – is relatively short in ocean-racing terms, record attempts can succeed only in ideal weather conditions. In practice this means riding a single weather system the whole way across, positioning yourself in front of

> ❝ It's immense joy . . . There are smiles on all the tired faces . . . It all feels a bit strange. It's as if we only set out from New York yesterday. ❞
>
> Bruno Peyron, 6 July 2006

a depression and letting it sweep you eastward. If the depression is too deep, the winds will be too strong and the sea too rough; too shallow, and there won't be enough wind. The ideal is about 30 knots of wind blowing continuously from the southwest.

Conditions this perfect are rare and unpredictable. It is not unusual for crews to wait weeks for the right weather window to open and still never find it. But it was precisely this ideal combination that American Steve Fossett encountered in October 2001. Sailing his maxi-catamaran *Playstation*, he took almost 48 hours off Madec's time, in the process ending 21 years of French supremacy. His time – 4 days, 17 hours and 23 minutes – was achieved at an average speed of 25.78 knots. This is the kind of speed at which one can comfortably water-ski; it is significantly faster than most passenger

The record breakers

Year	Sailor	Yacht	Country	Time	Aver Speed (Knots)
1905	Charlie Barr	*Atlantic*	USA	12d 4h 1m	10.02
1980	Eric Tabarly	*Paul Ricard*	FRA	10d 5h 14m	11.93
1981	Marc Pajot	*Elf Aquitaine*	FRA	9d 10h 6m	12.94
1984	Patrick Morvan	*Jet Services II*	FRA	8d 16h 33m	14.03
1986	Loïc Caradec	*Royale II*	FRA	7d 21h 5m	15.47
1987	Philippe Poupon	*Fleury Michon VIII*	FRA	7d 12h 50m	16.18
1988	Serge Madec	*Jet Services V*	FRA	7d 6h 30m	16.76
1990	Serge Madec	*Jet Services V*	FRA	6d 13h 3m	18.62
2001	Steve Fossett	*PlayStation*	USA	4d 17h 28m 6s	25.78
2006	Bruno Peyron	*Orange II*	FRA	4d 8h 23m 54s	28

ships. All this on a boat powered exclusively by wind. It was this remarkable record Peyron was determined to reclaim for France.

For France!

His boat, *Orange II*, launched in December 2003, is almost certainly the fastest oceangoing yacht ever built, a 38.6-metre (120-ft) monster, 18 metres (59 ft) wide, with a 45-metre (148-ft) mast carrying up to 1,100 square metres (11,840 sq ft) of sail. A preliminary attempt on the North Atlantic record in August 2004 failed by 31 minutes, this despite setting a new 24-hour record run of 1,130 km (706 miles).

Consolation of a sort was provided the following month when Peyron set a new record time on *Orange II* between Marseille, France, and Carthage, Tunisia, covering 848 km (458 nautical miles) in 17 hours, 56 minutes. A more substantial reward came in March the following year when Peyron beat the nonstop round-the-world record, then also held by Fossett.

But it was the Atlantic record that Peyron wanted most badly. By late June 2006, his 11 crewmen – nine Frenchmen, one Swiss and a Swede – had been flown to the United States for the final preparations. On July 1 he announced the attempt would begin at 11 the following morning. At 6 seconds past 11 on 2 July, *Orange II* crossed the start line off New York. The wind was freshening, the sea flat. Almost at once, *Orange II* was slicing through the sea at great speed.

Exceptional speed

From the beginning, Peyron's times were exceptional. Sailing faster than the wind and averaging in excess of 30 knots, speeds peaking at more than 35 knots, in the first 24 hours *Orange II* made a new record distance of 1,203 km (752 miles). On day two she covered 1,225 km (766 miles) despite meeting thick fog over the Newfoundland Grand Banks. She was already more than 320 km (200 miles) up on Fossett's *Playstation*.

It was a performance that highlighted almost the greatest hazard facing boats travelling at such speeds: a collision with a floating all-but-invisible object – typically a whale, man-made debris or ice. On the second night

Supreme seamanship Fastest around the world and fastest across the Atlantic. For Peyron, the question is simple: what next?

at sea, that is exactly what happened to *Orange II*, with the port rudder damaged seriously enough – probably after hitting ice – for Peyron to decide to slow the boat.

He could afford to. By day three Peyron's lead over Fossett was such that, barring catastrophe, a new record was almost certain. The mood on board was cautiously jubilant. There was still a final twist. Out of the mist loomed a Norwegian cargo ship making 20 knots. With *Orange II* still at 30 knots, the two were converging at close on 50 knots. They passed hardly more than 100 metres (300 ft) apart.

4

Imperialists & Adventurers

To the forbidden city

In the early 20th century Tibet exercised a hypnotic hold on Western imaginations. Sheltered high in the Himalayas, the country had successfully rebuffed almost all attempts at contact by the wider world. But lying between British India and Russia, its strategic importance impressed a British army officer-turned-explorer, Francis Younghusband. Younghusband was sent to breach the country's isolation.

Younghusband's journey to and around Tibet in 1903–1904 was 'incredible' in more ways than one. On one level it was a straightforward exercise in imperial hegemony: Britain invading and chastising a neighbouring and impoverished land that refused not only to submit to its imperial power but even to acknowledge its existence. On another, it was a simple question of practical politics. Younghusband was hardly alone in British India in believing that Russia was determined to dominate Tibet, from where it could threaten India and Britain's position there.

But what singles the journey out and gives it its special flavour is the personality of Younghusband himself. As a junior officer in India from 1882, he had found army life stultifying. His real desire, spurred by an impulsiveness bordering on recklessness, was the exploration of the vast and hardly known wastes of Central Asia. His motive in part was fame, to be known as an explorer. But these hostile regions appealed to another aspect of Younghusband: a yearning for spiritual fulfilment. The Himalayas, above all, which he referred to as 'ethereal as spirit, white and pure … insubstantial as a dream, glowing with a radiance not of earth,' were an irresistible and constant lure. And at their heart was Tibet, 'the forbidden land'.

Himalayan pioneer

Younghusband's credentials as an explorer were considerable. In 1886 he was one of three men who undertook

Younghusband in 1895 Younghusband was the English gentleman formidably erect, impeccably attired, magnificently mustachioed.

an epic eight-month unsupported tour of Manchuria in northern China. He immediately followed this by an eight-month trek across China to the northern fringes of India, travelling only with native guides. During this journey, his small party traversed the 1,920 km (1,200 miles) of the Gobi desert in only 70 days. The journey climaxed with a crossing of the 5,790-metre (19,000-ft) Mustagh Pass in the Himalayas, a difficult ridge with a near vertical ice face on its southern side. As Younghusband pointed out, he was the first European to have crossed it.

Further pioneering journeys consolidated Younghusband's reputation as one of the most intrepid travellers of the inhospitable empty spaces bordering northern India. They also cemented his role as one of the most indefatigable players of the 'Great Game', the shadowy tussle between Britain and Russia for control of these forbidding regions that lasted for most of the 19th century. In this largely self-appointed role, Younghusband was supported by Lord Curzon – a politician of legendary hauteur, formidable intellect and ruthless determination.

Younghusband first met Curzon in 1892. Both were convinced, generally on flimsy evidence, not just that Russia had designs on the region – which it did – but that its schemes for a wholesale takeover were on the verge of fulfilment – which they were not. Curzon's appointment as viceroy of India in 1899 was the opening that Younghusband had yearned for. He was not disappointed.

Mission to Tibet

In May 1903 Curzon ordered Younghusband to lead an armed mission to Tibet. Its ostensible purpose was to normalise relations. As Curzon said, it was absurd that there should be a country bordering India, 'with which it was impossible even to exchange a written communication'. Its actual purpose was to bring Tibet firmly within Britain's sphere of interest and keep the Russians out. Younghusband could hardly contain himself. It was, he wrote, 'a really magnificent business'.

He left from Siliguri, capital of the province of Sikkim, in northeast India and close to Darjeeling on 19 June 1903, at the head of a sprawling column several thousand strong and with 500 sepoys – native troops under British officers. His luggage alone required 29 trunks. On 4 July the troops were sent over the border into Tibet. On 18 July Younghusband followed. The vast majority were on foot; only the officers and high-ranking officials were on horseback. Mules were mostly used as pack animals; later they had yaks, buffalo and bullocks as

AU THIBET
Le Dalaï-Lama de Lhassa fuit la domination anglaise

Dalai Lama flees *Le Petit Journal* imaginatively illustrates the flight of the Dalai Lama in the face of Younghusband's advance.

well. They followed an established route into Tibet, crossing the border at the Kangra La, a 5,183-metre (17,000-ft) pass. These were the Himalayas, the terrain harsh and frequently frozen.

The following day, under the shadow of the Tibetans fort at Khamba Dzong, just over the border with Sikkim, Younghusband had his first encounter with a Tibetan delegation. The meeting was marked by mutual incomprehension. The Tibetans, unaware of the potential of the British mission's firepower, refused to discuss anything until Younghusband withdrew from Tibet. Younghusband was outraged. The standoff continued for two months, a flurry of cables passing between Younghusband and Curzon as they sought ways to break the deadlock. As the British advanced, they unrolled cable wire behind them; the Tibetans thought it was a device to allow them to find their way back to India.

Myth and reality

Among the numerous ironies of Younghusband's Tibetan adventure was that, far from being the trumpet blast of imperial grandeur Younghusband took it for, it was made in the face of persistent opposition from the British government. Practically no member of Prime Minister Arthur Balfour's Conservative administration in London had any desire to support what at best looked like adventurism and at worst threatened to be a potentially endless drain on public finances for the sake of a remote and barren land. Even the Russian threat, grossly overstated by Younghusband and Curzon, was discounted in a period when, faced with German expansion, Britain wanted to woo Tsarist Russia.

The government moved rapidly to renegotiate Younghusband's treaty, signed by Tibetan officials, pictured above passing soldiers with bayonets. Patrick French, Younghusband's most perceptive biographer, wrote that by 1907 'Britain's only substantive gain from the invasion of Tibet and 3,000 deaths (95 percent of them Tibetan) was the right to keep a pair of trade agents and a telegraph wire inside its borders.'

❝ [I was determined to] come to know the curious people of that secluded country [Tibet], make a great name for myself and be known ever after as a famous traveller. ❞

Sir Francis Younghusband, *Wonders of the Himalaya*, 1924

Storming Lhasa Younghusband's 2,000 troops swept aside what little resistance they met from the Tibetans, who were mainly armed with just pitchforks. Here they march into Lhasa under the West Gate. In the background the Dalai Lama's palace, the Potola, rises over the city.

were dead and 222 wounded. Twelve British troops were wounded; none was killed. A series of skirmishes followed, with an equal imbalance in the death counts. Tibetan resistance crumbled.

By early August, Lhasa, mythical capital of Tibet and seat of the Dalai Lama, had been reached. Here on 7 September – Younghusband in full-dress uniform, the Tibetans in yellow silk robes – signed the Treaty of Lhasa. The treaty was written in three languages – English, Tibetan and Chinese – and guaranteed British hegemony in Tibet. As the anonymous author of the Tibetan history, *The Annals of the All-Revealing Mirror,* wrote, Tibet 'was as helpless as if the sky had hit the earth.'

In mid-September, Younghusband did withdraw. But this was not, as the Tibetans assumed, belated recognition that Tibet was inviolate. It was because Younghusband and Curzon realised a much stronger force was needed. So in mid-December, when the temperatures were –30°C (–22°F), Younghusband led 2,000 troops, supported by more than 10,000 labourers and 20,000 pack animals, back into Tibet.

It was an obvious act of imperial aggression. Younghusband had no doubt that, as an Englishman, it was his 'duty and privilege to take over the government of inferior races … to administer, discipline and protect them.' Yet this was the same man who saw no contradiction in writing that 'in all dealings with natives, avoid assuming [an] air of superiority' and commended 'the excellence of their manners, their patience, their spirituality, their intelligence.' Earlier, he had written: 'Pitting our civilization against these poor mountain people is what I loathe most.'

March to conflict

Yet this is precisely what he did. Moving north, they reached Chumi Sengo – a small town, nondescript and impoverished – by the end of March. Here they found the Tibetan army, 2,000 strong, behind a hastily built stone wall. Most were armed with spears and swords; some had flintlock rifles. In a matter of minutes, 628

Mountain march A contemporary depiction of Younghusband's march to Tibet, bestowing the fruits of Western medicine on the poor Tibetan people.

Across the Sahara

In the European scramble for Africa at the end of the 19th century, France – whose empire eventually stretched from the Mediterranean lands of Algeria and Morocco to tropical west Africa – fared best. France's control of these territories was tenuous, particularly in the hostile wastes of the Sahara. But that it could claim them at all owed much to a series of pioneering efforts by one man, Henri Laperrine.

The Sahara is the largest desert in the world, only slightly smaller than the whole of Europe, 9,000,000 square km (3,500,000 sq miles) of arid wasteland, vast mountain ranges alternating with rocky scrubland and sand-strewn emptiness – the Great Ergs. At night, temperatures plummet; by day they soar, routinely exceeding 50°C (122°F) in summer. Survival in such extreme conditions, water permanently at a premium, is precarious.

To these natural hazards were added those of the nomadic Tuareg, slave-owning nomads who for millennia preyed on the caravans that crossed the desert. Faced with such an implacable and elusive enemy, conventional European military forces had proved helpless. Desert travel demands speed and mobility. All France could offer were ponderous, slow-moving columns of men on foot and horseback that were too large to live off the sparse resources of the desert but never large enough to carry sufficient supplies, water especially, to sustain them on campaigns that could last months.

Given the extreme hostility of the Sahara, the wonder is that the French wanted it at all. Yet the dynamics of late 19th-century colonialism were such that no European power with pretensions to greatness felt it could afford to be left behind.

Ruling the desert French *méharistes* arrive at an oasis, as depicted in this 1906 newspaper print, an image intended to highlight the exoticism of these remote lands.

Commander of the Oases

French successes in the desert were chiefly due to the single-minded Laperrine, a career military officer first posted to North Africa in 1881. Almost from the start, Laperrine had realised that to control the Sahara, France had to adopt native customs. He created a series of small isolated forts manned by lightly armed, fast-moving, camel-mounted troops able to deal out swift reprisals. The troops would be led by Frenchmen but otherwise manned by Chaamba, a people whose legendary toughness and knowledge of the desert rivalled that of their longtime enemies, the Tuareg.

As commanded by Laperrine, these *méharistes* (camel-riders) proved a formidable extension of the French army, all-but-invincible elite troops who in barely 10 years satisfied French hopes in the Sahara.

In 1904 Laperrine was made Commander of the Oases – in effect, ruler of an area three times the size of France. Laperrine led his *méharistes* on a series of tours of the region designed to underline French power and supremacy.

Journey through a waterless wasteland

On 16 March 1906, Laperrine began the most ambitious of these journeys, his destination Taoudeni far to the south, in France's colony of the Sudan. There they were to meet a small French force travelling north from the west African coast. Laperrine's party numbered 79 – 75 *méharistes* and, including himself, four French officers.

The two parties duly met – Laperrine's men after an epic of suffering that left him with hardly more than 50 camels still capable of travel from the 140 with which he had begun. On 22 May each began the long march home. Laperrine now decided on a decisive demonstration of his desert-travelling abilities. Rather than retrace his steps, he would lead his party directly home through the Erg Chech, a trackless near-waterless waste in Saharan Algeria that no European had ever crossed. It was known to contain two wells. The location of both was uncertain.

It took four days to reach the first well, at Tnihaia. The men and the few remaining animals – most had already been eaten – fell on it furiously. The water turned out to be almost undiluted chlorine, strong enough to burn clothes on contact and tasting, according to Laperrine's account, 'disgusting, like detergent'. The men

For France! Laperrine was a man almost entirely uninterested in conventional projections of personal fame. His was a life devoted to service and peculiarly French notions of *gloire*.

became bloated, swelling 'to exaggerated proportions', a thick crust of salt covering their faces.

Facing death

They were unable to leave for four days. Even the Chaamba were insensible from heat and thirst and forced to ride 'completely naked'. The next well wasn't reached for another seven days. It had been so long since it had last been visited, it took 28 hours of frantic, exhausted digging before it yielded water. When, in desperation, the last camels were then killed and eaten, the entire party, having eaten nothing but dates and couscous for several days, came down with dysentery.

Laperrine had estimated the journey could be made in 10 days. It took over a month, the ragged remnants of the party limping back to their base at Adrar only on 9 August. Given the extraordinary suffering they endured, it is incredible that only two of the party failed to make it back alive.

A time of gifts

As a boy, Patrick Leigh Fermor was described in a school report as possessing 'a dangerous mixture of sophistication and recklessness'. It was this combination that propelled him, at the age of 18, to walk from Holland to Constantinople. He wrote about his original trek across Europe in two books, *A Time of Gifts* and *Between the Woods and the Water*, providing an exhilarating portrait of interwar Central Europe.

Leigh Fermor began his walk in midwinter. He arrived in Rotterdam on 9 December 1933, having taken a small steamer across the North Sea from London. In the ensuing three and a half months he made his way across Holland, Germany, Austria and Czechoslovakia – some 1,920 km (1,200 miles).

Leigh Fermor was about to apply to Sandhurst when, in the autumn of 1933, the idea of walking across Europe 'unfolded with the speed and completeness of a Japanese paper flower unfolding in water'. In a characteristic burst of romantic enthusiasm, he saw himself as 'a pilgrim or a palmer, an errant scholar, a broken knight,' who would 'only consort with peasants and tramps,' and who would accept lifts only if 'walking became literally intolerable, and then … travel no further than a day's march.'

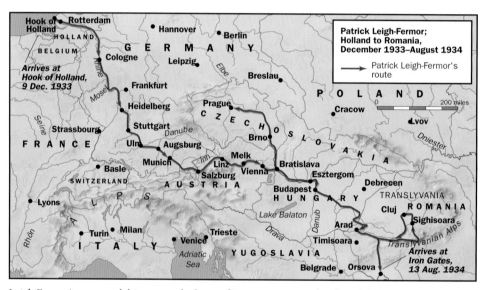

Leigh Fermor's route took him across the heart of Europe, a region of endless delights to him.

Meager funding

The one pound a week he struggled to live on in London would, he calculated, more than fund his venture and allow him to live on 'bread and cheese and apples … and an occasional mug of beer.' Every month £4 was to be forwarded to him at various points across the continent. In summer he would sleep in haystacks; in winter he would seek shelter in barns.

He pared his equipment to a minimum. Besides his clothes – an Army greatcoat, a pair of canvas shoes with rubber soles, shirts (mostly gray flannel), two ties (just in case), puttees and nailed boots – he had the *Oxford Book of English Verse* and a copy of *Horace*, given to him by his mother. He also had a series of notebooks as well as 'drawing blocks, rubbers [and] and an aluminium cylinder full of Venus and Golden Sovereign pencils.'

Leigh Fermor remained true to his determination to

A Time of Gifts Leigh Fermor's first volume, published in 1977.

complete the journey on foot – a brief spell on a barge on the Rhine and a handful of days on horseback in Hungary aside – but his hopes of sleeping in haystacks and barns frequently proved futile. This was not for lack of trying. Rather, it was that aristocrats and swineherds alike immediately warmed to his infectiously good-natured personality. Wherever he went, he found himself 'an affable tramp', as he put it, the recipient of an astonishing degree of hospitality.

This peaked during his first summer when, almost entirely by chance, he became the guest of a series of remarkable Czech, Hungarian and Romanian aristocratic families – his nights, on occasion his weeks, spent in a variety of castles, palaces and country houses. In stark and delightful contrast these periods of elegant high living alternated with nights in cowsheds and, under the stars, on mountainsides.

Leigh Fermor arrived in Germany 10 months after Hitler had come to power, and arrived, finally, in Constantinople on 1 January 1935. Within four years the Europe he described with such magnificent vigour would disappear.

Sketching for food

They may never have been alarming, but adventures studded Leigh Fermor's trek across Europe. The most unlikely came in Vienna when he fell in with a penniless schoolmaster called Konrad, who spoke English learned from reading Shakespeare. Leigh Fermor (pictured above in 1945) had arrived in the city with no money at all. Disappointingly, the £4 that he had expected from his family had not arrived.

Konrad provided the solution. 'Hark!' he announced. 'All is not lost. I have been ripening a plan. Have you your sketch-block by you?' What Konrad proposed was that Leigh Fermor should earn money by making pencil portraits, turning up at apartment blocks and offering to sketch the inhabitants. Leigh Fermor was appalled. To his astonishment the ruse proved a hit from the start. By the end of the first day, he made more than £1.

Celebrating their success that evening over the first proper meal Leigh Fermor had eaten for two days – and Konrad, he suspected, for very much longer – the older man asserted, 'You see, dear young, how boldness is always prospering?'

Across the Empty Quarter

WILFRED THESIGER   **1946–1948**

Wilfred Thesiger's epic journeys across the Rub' al Khali, the aptly named Empty Quarter of Arabia, can probably be counted the last venture of pure exploration of the 20th century. Thesiger's life was defined by a need to understand the world's most remote and hostile regions. What impelled him was not just the lure of untouched landscapes; it was their peoples and threatened ways of life.

Outside the North and South poles, there is probably nowhere more consistently hostile than the Rub' al Khali. It is the largest sand desert in the world – 650,000 square km (250,000 sq miles) of arid desolation with dunes almost 300 metres (1,000 ft) high that stretch for 160 km (100 miles) or more. The Sahara, which is the world's largest desert, consists mostly of rocky scrubland and mountains. There are two great sand deserts – the Ergs – the deserts of popular imagination, but they are relatively small compared to the whole. The Empty Quarter, by contrast, is exactly this kind of sand desert, with dunes rolling to the horizon. Across this

Thesiger (centre) with Yemen tribespeople Thesiger discovered in the harsh lives of these apparently simple peoples a dignity and a nobility that had disappeared in the pampered world of the West.

parched and unforgiving landscape, where in the summer the temperature of the sand can reach 80°C (175°F), life is barely sustained by a handful of wells containing water too bitter to drink.

When Thesiger made his journeys, these natural hazards were compounded by a nomadic population, the

Bedu, for whom any outsider was a potential source of fear and distrust – Christian infidels who threatened to despoil a way of life that had hardly changed for centuries. Thesiger began his first journey knowing the Sultan of Oman had forbidden him to enter the region at all. On his second, Ibn Saud, ruler of Saudi Arabia,

The lure of the desert Thesiger's dislike of the West never extended to one of its inventions – photography. He became not just an accomplished photographer but a key recorder of a way of life that was rapidly disappearing in the face of the seemingly unstoppable advance of Western values.

ordered he be apprehended and killed. Thesiger, unaware of the price on his head, later admitted he had survived more by luck than judgment.

A fascination with alien lands

On the other hand, it was precisely because these lands were so alien that Thesiger was attracted to them. Born to a distinctly blue-blooded English family, Thesiger had been fascinated by remote peoples and lands since childhood. He spent his early years in Addis Ababa, capital of Ethiopia, where his father was British minister and where he was born in 1910. Raised among what he called the 'barbaric splendour' of the country's imperial court, England's polite and watery charms paled in comparison to the richness – and frequent violence – of Ethiopia.

He rapidly came to 'abominate' Western civilisation, despite being a member of one of its most privileged strata, regarding Europe's colonial powers and America

> ❝ I was exhilarated by the sense of space, the silence and the clean crispness of the sand. I felt in harmony with the past. ❞
>
> Wilfred Thesiger, *The Life of My Choice*

alike with profound contempt. His education – at Eton and Oxford – saw the only extended period of his life spent in England other than in his very old age, when increasing infirmity ruled out the possibility of his continuing to live abroad.

There was more than just a streak of asceticism in his approach. He asserted famously, 'The harder the life, the finer the man.' On almost all his travels – in Africa, the Middle East, Pakistan and Afghanistan – he actively sought to ape native ways, travelling in small groups, often on foot, occasionally mounted, never using cars (an invention, with the telephone, that he dismissed). He was profoundly conservative, deeply skeptical of almost all human endeavour. 'I crave for the past,' he said in an interview at the end of his life.

His journeys across Arabia were nominally made at the behest of the United Nations' Middle East Anti-Locust League. In reality, Thesiger, never a man afraid to

The Marsh Arabs

In 1950, unable to remain in Arabia, Thesiger made a visit to southern Iraq, intending to spend a few weeks duck shooting in the marshes of the Shatt al Arab, the delta formed by the confluence of the Tigris and Euphrates. He stayed for most of the next eight years.

He discovered there a life he had 'a longing to share', living in the villages of the Madan in reed huts (pictured above) hunting duck from a 11-metre (36-ft) canoe 'accompanied by four lads who served as crew.' (At least until the numbers were threatened, Thesiger was an indefatigable hunter of animals large and small. On one trip in the Sudan in the 1930s, where he served as a political officer, he shot 70 lions.)

Again, this was a world entirely removed from modern life. It is now a world that exists only in memories. What remained of the Madan was systematically exterminated by Saddam Hussein in the aftermath of the first Gulf War in 1990–1991.

barge his way to the front of the line, tailored the United Nation's well-meaning intentions to suit his own ends. He was determined to explore the Empty Quarter and sought to exploit any means to do so.

Exploring the Empty Quarter

Thesiger was not the first European to venture into the Empty Quarter. Two other Englishmen, Bertram Thomas in 1930–1931 and Harry St. John Philby in 1932–1933, had preceded him. But Thesiger's two vast sweeps across the region, in 1946–1947 and in 1947–1948, yielded by far the most information, thanks to the extensive maps he made as well as to his sensitive accounts.

Even for the Bedu, the Empty Quarter was a place of suffering. On his first visit, Thesiger planned to cross the eastern half of the desert, a circular trip of about 2,500 km (1,600 miles), travelling north from Oman into Saudi Arabia and back again. As on his second, west to east across Saudi Arabia from the Hadhramaut to the Persian Gulf, it became clear that the fact of exploring the region was less important for Thesiger than doing so in the company of Bedu, a people for whom he developed a reverence bordering on worship, whatever their fiercely anti-Western reputation. Typically these parties consisted of five or six men. They travelled on camels and slept in the open.

'Those travels in the Empty Quarter would for me have been a pointless penance but for the comradeship of my Bedu companions,' Thesiger subsequently wrote. However materially poor – their possessions generally consisted of no more than their camels, a rifle, their clothes and rudimentary cooking utensils – they 'possessed a freedom which we, with all our craving for possessions, cannot experience ... they met every challenge, every hardship, with the proud boast: "We are Bedu".'

Realities of desert survival

The desert itself, 'where distances are measured in hours on camel-back,' provided an intense experience, despite 'almost incessant hunger and, worse still, thirst, sometimes for days on end rationing ourselves to a pint a day.' Over this empty expanse, wrote Thesiger, 'lay a

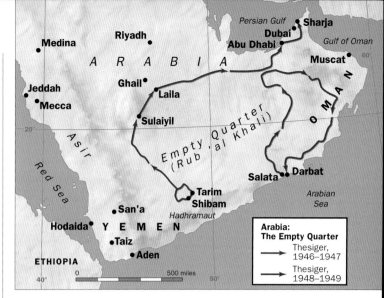

No map does justice to the reality of travel in the Empty Quarter, a land of unremitting hostility.

silence that we have now driven from our world.'

On his first crossing, his companions were forced to leave him for three days while they went in search of food. Thesiger, starving, was tormented by dreams of cars that could bring him safely out of the desert. If he could, would he have taken advantage of one? His response was wholly in character. 'No. I would rather be here starving as I was than sitting in a chair, replete with food, listening to the wireless and dependent on cars to take me through Arabia.'

> **Those travels in the Empty Quarter would for me have been a pointless penance but for the comradeship of my Bedu companions.**
>
> Wilfred Thesiger, *The Life of My Choice*

Thesiger knew that the Bedus' world was frequently brutal. While praising them for their 'open-handed generosity... their honesty ... their pride ... and their loyalty,' he also acknowleged that killings were commonplace. 'I soon acquired the same attitude,' he wrote, 'and if anyone had killed one of my companions I would unquestionably have sought to avenge him: I have no belief in the "sanctity" of life.'

A note of persistent sadness pervades Thesiger's account of his time in Arabia. It was a world on the verge of destruction. New oil wealth attracted an influx of foreigners and other changes, such as money and consumerism, that would sweep away what remained of traditional life. There was also political change in the air – the principal event being the 1958 revolution in Iraq – none of it, in Thesiger's view, for the better.

In the end, his criticisms of local rulers forced him to leave Arabia.

The *Kon-Tiki* expedition

As a young zoologist in Polynesia in 1937, the Norwegian Thor Heyerdahl was struck by the apparent similarities – physical and cultural – between aspects of Polynesian society and pre-Inca Peru. Had Peruvians settled in Polynesia 1,500 years earlier, sailing the 6,4000 km (4,000 miles) from Peru on balsa-wood rafts? Convinced they had, Heyerdahl set out to prove it by sailing the same route on a similar raft.

When Heyerdahl's raft, *Kon-Tiki*, was being built in Callao in Peru in the early spring of 1947, it attracted a stream of interested visitors. All declared the venture doomed. The raft was too small and would be swamped, they said; it was too large and, poised between waves, the unsupported centre would snap. It was variously asserted that its nine giant balsa-wood logs would become waterlogged and sink and that the hemp ropes holding them together would either chafe or bite into the soft wood and saw through it. Sailing the unwieldy craft was thought impossible. It would drift helplessly across the wastes of the Pacific until the crew starved – or went mad. Balsa rafts had been sailed on the Pacific coasts of South America for centuries, but this was dismissed as unimportant. Coastal voyaging was one thing, an ocean crossing entirely different.

There was a lot to be said for the critics. At a time when ocean sailing was presumed the exclusive preserve of large, powered craft, the idea that a vessel this primitive could make a 6,400-km (4,000-mile) crossing seemed foolhardy. Furthermore, the kind of adventuring the subsequent success of *Kon-Tiki* would set off was well in the future. There seemed ample reason to believe Heyerdahl and his five-man crew were lunatics.

Ancient evidence

Heyerdahl had arrived at his belief that the original Peruvians had made their epic voyages to the scattered

Charting a course Thor Heyerdahl (right) and Herman Watzinger, his first recruit for the expedition, in Washington, DC, December 1946.

Building *Kon-Tiki*

It was one thing to decide to build a balsa-wood raft. But as Heyerdahl discovered, it was another to find the wood itself. There was no shortage in either Peru or neighbouring Ecuador. But this was balsa intended for industrial and building purposes, ready sawed into planks. What Heyerdahl needed were complete balsa logs. They existed, above all, in the jungles of Ecuador. But this was the rainy season, and the jungle was virtually inaccessible. Heyerdahl was told to come back in six months.

Undaunted, Heyerdahl flew to Quito, 2,750 metres (9,000 ft) high in the Andes, charted a jeep and, in rain of an intensity he had never seen before, sought out one of the country's balsa kings, Don Frederico. He proved the expedition's saviour. Twelve huge trees were found and felled, each, in Polynesian style, named before it was cut down. They were then tied together in two rafts and floated downstream to Guayaquil on the coast (pictured above), from where they were shipped to Callao.

Re-creating history *Kon-Tiki*, flags bravely fluttering, is towed out to sea to begin its epic crossing of the Pacific, its uncertain crew facing the reality of a one-way voyage on a vessel everyone said would break up or simply sink.

islands of Polynesia after piecing together evidence garnered from a variety of sources. Across Polynesia, there were legends of the great god and chief Kon-Tiki, meaning 'sun' or 'fire' Tiki, who, faced by the Inca invasion in a.d. 500 in his Peruvian homeland, was said to have led his people to the coast, 'whence they finally disappeared overseas to the westward.'

Despite the immensity of Polynesia, an area four times the size of Europe, peoples as far apart as Hawaii and New Zealand all spoke variants of the same language. There were archaeological clues, too. The monumental carved stone figures of Easter Island, for example, one of the most isolated spots on the Earth, appeared clearly related to similar pre-Inca structures in Peru. Similarly, among the shorter, dark-skinned peoples of Southeast Asian origin in Polynesia, there were also taller, fair-skinned peoples, possible descendents of the 'race of white gods' Inca legend claimed had once lived in Peru.

Yet what seemed the clinching argument was geographical: the prevailing winds and currents in the central Pacific all sweep westward from South America. Given a

> ❝ Whether it was 1947 BC or AD suddenly became of no significance. We lived, and that we felt with alert intensity. ❞
>
> Thor Heyerdahl, the *Kon-Tiki Expedition*

sufficiently seaworthy vessel, anyone sailing west from Peru would inevitably arrive in Polynesia. The question was whether *Kon-Tiki* was a sufficiently seaworthy vessel. Heyerdahl's most favourable estimate was that the journey would take 97 days. Could a balsa-wood raft stay afloat this long? Equally, could Heyerdahl and his five crew, two of whom had never been to sea at all, master the lost arts of seamanship required to navigate such an improbable craft?

Early struggles

The early signs were unpromising. Heyerdahl had arranged that *Kon-Tiki* would be towed well offshore before being set adrift. The following morning, with the departure of the tug and *Kon-Tiki's* square-sail hoisted, the raft 'splashed sedately forward' as the wind freshened. On any long ocean passage, the first days at sea can be among the hardest, the crew struggling to adjust to their new world. For the crew of *Kon-Tiki*, it was especially gruelling. The cold north-flowing Humboldt current, running across the easterly tradewinds, was kicking up a confused sea, not ideal conditions for the maiden voyage of an untried Stone Age raft with a novice crew. There were positives. The raft lifted easily to the seas. And when water came aboard, it rapidly ran out through the gaps between the logs.

But there was also a major drawback. In such boisterous conditions, steering proved exhausting. Two men were required to work the 5.8-metre (19-ft) steering oar to prevent the raft from coming up into the wind and sailing smartly backwards. The first night was bad, the second worse, 'a continuous struggle against a chaos of waves', wrote Heyerdahl. It took several weeks of trial and error before the crew discovered the secret of steering *Kon-Tiki*.

By the third day they were over the worst. Though the sea remained high, conditions eased as the crew found their sea legs. There were other encouraging signs. A penknife driven into the balsa logs showed no waterlogging, the ropes binding the logs no signs of chafe.

Ocean teeming with food

One of the most distinctive features of the voyage was the teeming life surrounding the crew. Sardines, dorados, tunnies, bonitos and flying fish – the last having only to be picked off the deck – provided more food than could be eaten. At night squid would rise to the surface, their 'devilish green eyes' gazing balefully at the raft. Sharks, too, initially a cause for alarm, were frequent visitors and would eventually be caught in numbers by the crew, though they made swimming a nervous business. As many as 40 dolphins at a time would race, leaping around the raft for hours. Memorably, a 15-metre (50-ft) whale shark, 'huge and hideous', once circled *Kon-Tiki*

Westward bound Steering *Kon-Tiki* bedevilled the crew, the steering oar clumsy and unresponsive, exhausting them as they struggled to master it.

Polynesian interlude

When Heyerdahl and his crew staggered ashore, the remains of *Kon-Tiki* still on the reef, their priority was to salvage what they could from the raft. Food, water, radio and charts were all brought ashore. Their lagoon-fringed island was tiny – 180 metres (600 ft) across and no more than 1.8 metres (6 ft) high. But if Heyerdahl and his crew knew where they were, no one else did. How were they to get away?

A week or so later, help arrived in the shape of two canoes from an island 11 km (7 miles) away whose inhabitants had seen the campfires lit by *Kon-Tiki*'s crew. Heyerdahl and his team spent several weeks on this new island (pictured above), feasting and celebrating with its 127 inhabitants, who took to them with open arms and ceremoniously gave them Polynesian names. The crew's limited supplies of penicillin were used to save the life of a young boy, Haumata, who had an abscess on his head and was close to death. It was an existence, removed from time, unimaginable in the 20th century.

Eventually, a schooner from Tahiti, administrative capital of French Polynesia, picked them up, with what was left of *Kon-Tiki*, which had since floated free, in tow.

for an hour, Heyerdahl and his men watching warily.

There were whales, too, oddly comforting to the crew once they had overcome their early fears of the damage the immense creatures could do to the raft. Though they approached to within feet, none touched *Kon-Tiki*. As diverting was the 'kitchen garden' of weeds and barnacles that sprouted under the raft, home not just to hundreds of crabs but to 50 pilot fish who accompanied *Kon-Tiki* across the Pacific. Being far from shipping routes, the sense of having journeyed back in time to a more innocent age in which 'only the elements mattered' grew ever stronger.

By early July, now well over halfway, the idyll was rudely broken as a gale swept down. Though water continually thundered aboard, any anxiety was dispelled as *Kon-Tiki* 'took everything that came her way with ease and buoyancy'. But the weather remained unsettled, with frequent heavy downpours and alternating gales and calm seas.

Man overboard

On 21 July, now only 500 km (300 miles) from land, one of the crew, Knut Haugland, fell overboard. Even with the sail lowered, *Kon-Tiki* still scudded rapidly before the stiff breeze. Haugland, swimming frantically, could not keep up. The minutes before he was rescued, when a further crew member dived overboard with a rope and lifebelt, were the most anxious yet of the voyage. With Haugland safe again, the mood on board was appreciably sombre.

Increasingly, thoughts were turning to the end of the voyage. *Kon-Tiki* may have been showing signs of wear, but it was clear that she was more than capable of the last leg. But just where the raft would reach land was harder to say. To the north, and therefore effectively out of reach given the raft's limited ability to do more than sail downwind, were the Marquesas islands. To the southwest were the myriad islands of the Tuamotu group. It required only a minor change of course to head towards them.

> **❝ The whole sea was ours, and with all the gates of the horizon open real peace and freedom were wafted down from the firmament itself. ❞**
>
> Thor Heyerdahl, *The Kon-Tiki Expedition*

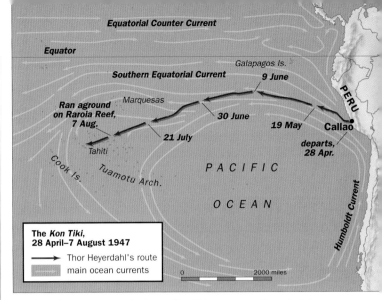

Winds and currents were the key to *Kon-Tiki*'s progress. Provided the raft remained afloat, its arrival in Polynesia was a certainty.

The Tuamotus had the advantage of being strung out over hundreds of miles, guaranteeing a landfall somewhere along their length. They had the disadvantage of sheltering behind reefs that ran their entire length and on which the Pacific rollers thundered relentlessly. Finding a way through this natural barrier would be as much a matter of luck as of skill. Failure meant the almost certain loss of *Kon-Tiki* – and quite possibly her crew.

The danger of making land

Land was sighted on 31 July. Whatever the exhilaration of having reached Polynesia, *Kon-Tiki* found herself being swept past this first island. By the following day, towering clouds in the distance indicated further land. It took until 4 August to reach, but by early afternoon *Kon-Tiki* was skirting its reef, searching for a way in. In the late afternoon the crew saw canoes heading towards them, clearly coming to guide them through the reef. In an agony of frustration and despite the best efforts of the Polynesians – who for three hours attempted to tow *Kon-Tiki* to safety – it was clear it was too late. The raft had been swept past.

Ahead now was the Raroia reef. For a further three days *Kon-Tiki* was blown inexorably toward it. At 10:00 A.M. on 7 August, it struck a series of waves 7.5 metres (25 ft) high, reducing it to a 'shattered wreck'. But however battered, the crew survived – clinging limpetlike to the disintegrating craft. They then waded across a lagoon of startling beauty toward a tiny island that 'looked like a bulging green basket of flowers', where they flung themselves on 'snow-white sand'. It was, wrote Heyerdahl, 'heaven'.

Living off the sea

As a junior doctor in postwar France, Alain Bombard was convinced that as many as 50,000 shipwrecked sailors a year might be saved if they understood that the sea contained all that was required to sustain life and, crucially, if they could resist the despair of abandonment. To prove it, he became his own experiment. He would cross the Atlantic in an open boat with no food and no water.

Bombard's contention was simple. Fish, eaten raw and supplemented by plankton, provided an adequate if sparse diet for anyone adrift at sea. In addition, between 50 and 80 percent of the weight of any fish consists of fresh water. If this could somehow be extracted – Bombard used a fruit press – the problem of drinking water was simultaneously solved. More radically, he proposed that in the absence of fish, castaways drink seawater to survive.

An extraordinary contention

It was this last assertion that did most to brand Bombard as a crank. But Bombard was right. Provided it is sipped and that no more than 1.85 litres (1½ pints) is drunk per day, seawater not only prevents dehydration, it acts as an important source of minerals.

The problem was twofold: most raw fish is all but inedible, and drinking seawater goes against the deepest human instincts. Bombard countered by arguing that with survival at stake, such niceties and taboos were unimportant. He further claimed that knowing survival was possible would in itself be vital in overcoming the worst problem facing any castaway: the horror of their predicament. Ninety percent of shipwrecked sailors die within three days. Even with no water at all, they should last longer than that.

Such unconventional views, backed by Bombard's determination to prove them by becoming his own castaway, attracted enormous interest. Most people were actively disbelieving. Nonetheless, as a result, Bombard acquired backing, including a boat. It increased the chorus of derision. It was a rubber dinghy 4.6 metres (15 ft) long and 1.8 metres (6 ft) wide. Bombard christened it

Bombard in Monaco Alain Bombard smiles for the Press just before setting out on the first leg of his improbable voyage in May 1952.

L'Hérétique. It was in this diminutive boat that Bombard intended to sail almost 10,000 km (6,000 miles) from Monte Carlo to the West Indies.

Fifteen-day purgatory

His plan was to sail with a companion, Jack Palmer, an itinerant Englishman whom he had met in the south of France. They left on 25 May, their first destination the Balearics. The journey, little more than 480 km (300 miles) on a direct course, was a 15-day storm-wracked purgatory of thirst, hunger and exhaustion. Leaving the Balearics, they had made only a few miles when they were swept onto rocks in a rising gale. After accepting a tow from a fishing boat, the dinghy capsized. Shaken yet still anxious to reach the Atlantic as fast as possible, they abandoned their planned last Mediterranean leg and had the dinghy shipped to Tangier on the Straits of Gibraltar.

Bombard sails alone

Palmer had now had enough. Whether discouraged by the thought of spending so long in close proximity to Bombard or appalled by the imminent reality of tackling the Atlantic in a 4.5-metre (15-ft) rubber boat with no food and water, he disappeared. Bombard took it in his stride. Leaving a brief note for Palmer, he set off on his own, his first stop Casablanca, 320 km (200 miles) to the southwest, from where he planned to sail to the Canaries a further 960 km (600 miles) away. He left on 13 August.

Compared to what was to come, Bombard's voyage to Casablanca and the Canaries was simple. There were fish in abundance; the weather was generally kind. The raft, meanwhile, increasingly impressed Bombard with its sea-keeping qualities. Casablanca was reached on 20 August, the Canaries on 3 September after an 11-day voyage.

Bombard's spirits were high. They became higher still with news that his wife, in Paris, had given birth to a baby girl. He dashed back to visit mother and daughter, inevitably provoking rumours that he had abandoned the trip. He hadn't. Within days he had returned to the Canaries.

His optimism didn't merely stem from the fact that he was proving the doubters wrong: it sprang from his belief that he had taught himself to navigate. Almost incredibly, when Bombard left Tangier, he had not only never used a sextant, he had only the vaguest grasp as to how. He took his success in finding Casablanca and then the Canaries as proof that he had mastered small-boat oceanic navigation. It would prove a near-fatal misapprehension.

Stormy seas and navigational errors

Bombard left the Canaries on 19 October. On the third night a wave swamped him. With no bailer, he had to use his hat to empty the boat (later, with his hat lost, he was reduced to bailing with a shoe). Two days after this, his small sail spilt in two. His only spare was then sent spinning overboard by a gust. It took a full day to repair

***L'Hérétique* in dock** Bombard (right) and Englishman Jack Palmer in Monaco. After 480 km (300 miles) of storm-wracked seas, Palmer had had enough and quit the voyage.

Sidi Ferruch and *Arakaka*

Bombard was never far from controversy. This was a question of Bombard's espousal of an apparently crackpot scheme and the result of a distinctly prickly personality. Bombard could be alarmingly quick to take offence. This talent for making enemies went far to explaining why so many sections of the press in France were so consistently critical. No two episodes gave them greater scope for attacking Bombard than his meetings at sea with two ships, both of which in different ways had helped him.

The first was in the Mediterranean with Palmer. It was a liner, *Sidi Ferruch*, which encountered *L'Hérétique* 13 days into its tortuous passage to the Balearics. Its captain gave the two men a small amount of food and water. The second was *Arakaka*, met by Bombard *in extremis* in the Atlantic (pictured above). Bombard went on board the ship, where he spent 90 minutes eating a very modest meal before clambering back into *L'Hérétique*, the British captain meanwhile imploring him to remain on board.

Given that Palmer and Bombard had subsisted for 13 days before meeting *Sidi Ferruch* and that Bombard had been at sea for 53 days before meeting *Arakaka*, his critics' gleeful claims that, in accepting outside help, Bombard had invalidated his otherwise astonishing feat of survival were sour and wide of the mark. But they make clear that Bombard was not an easy man to love.

All at sea Bombard plows on. However dazed, starving and lost, Bombard never gave up. What he was attempting seemed self-evidently absurd. The wonder is that he succeeded – even if he was never quite sure how.

the original. There were at least plenty of fish to catch.

As early as 31 October, his estimated position was almost 800 km (500 miles) out. Unaware of the error, he became convinced he would reach the West Indies no later than 30 November.

A litany of woe gradually overtook Bombard's log, stemming directly from his navigational errors. As his expectations of an early landfall were progressively dashed, he inadvertently demonstrated that despair is the castaway's greatest enemy. He took to raging against the weather: it was too cold or too hot; there was too much wind or not enough; too much rain or too little. Meanwhile, his physical state worsened. He suffered bouts of debilitating diarrhoea and developed rashes he feared would turn into boils. One by one he lost his toenails. Eventually, he became certain he would die.

On his fifty-third day at sea and in absolute despair, he met a ship, *Arakaka*. The captain confirmed Bombard's position.

He was 960 km (600 miles) farther east than he thought – at his current speed, perhaps 20 days from land. It was sickening and uplifting news. Sickening because his ordeal was still not over; uplifting because at least there was now a definite end in sight, however distant.

Weak but triumphant

Bombard reached Barbados in the West Indies 12 days later, on 22 December, 65 days after leaving the Canaries. Though desperately weak – he had lost 25 kg (55 lb.) – he was able to walk 3 km to a police station to report his arrival. It was a triumphant vindication of what, before the journey, had been widely dismissed as the ravings of a crank.

> ❝ If this goes on, the boat may arrive but they will find me in it dead. Sky still leaden, not a cloud to be seen. Am completely baffled, have no idea where I am. ❞
>
> Alain Bombard, 5 December 1952

The *Brendan* voyage

TIM SEVERIN | **May 1976–June 1977**

Scholars had long thought that the 8th-century *Navigatio Sancti Brendani Abbatis*, an account of a voyage to the Promised Land of the Saints by the 6th-century Irish monk St. Brendan in a boat made of leather, was too fantastic to be accepted literally. Tim Severin disagreed. But there was only one way to know: he would build a leather-skinned boat and sail the Atlantic from Ireland to North America.

According to the *Navigatio*, during his voyage St. Brendan had encountered a column of crystal floating in the sea; had reached an island whose inhabitants had hurled burning rocks at him and his companions; and had landed on the back of a whale, mistaking it for an island. The voyage was said to have taken seven years.

Looked at another way, these wild phenomena made sense. A column of crystal could have been an iceberg. Similarly, the burning rocks might have come from a volcano of the kind common in Iceland. Even the tale of the whale seems reasonable, given how small St. Brendan's ship would have been.

Repeating the impossible?

How could such a small vessel have made such an immense voyage? Sailing nonstop, especially for seven years, would have been impossible. But what Severin called the 'stepping-stone route' via Scotland, the Faroes and Iceland before slanting southward past Greenland to Newfoundland would not only have broken the journey into manageable stages, it would have taken St. Brendan into waters where icebergs were as common as whales. Furthermore, it would have had the advantage of the prevailing currents in the North Atlantic while avoiding the south-westerly headwinds that blow farther south.

None of which addressed two key questions. First, given that leather disintegrates in water, how could a leather boat resist prolonged immersion? Second, even if you could build it, could you sail it? It may have been true that small leather-built boats – *curraghs* – were still in use in western Ireland, but the kind of boat Severin required would have to be much larger. Was it manageable?

Tim Severin (left) and George Molony confer. The voyage would prove a striking vindication of the effectiveness of the early Medieval means.

Backbreaking work Severin (foreground) and crew heave away. *Brendan* proved an obstinately difficult boat to row, slipping sideways through the water, any gains painfully won dispiritingly lost in minutes.

Ox hide proves the saviour

The answer turned out to be ox hide. Fifty-seven would be required in all, each 6 mm (¼ inch) thick, tanned in oak bark and dressed with wool grease. It was a combination that proved water resistant and gave off a pungent foul smell. The hides were then stretched over an elaborate ash frame, itself strapped together with leather thongs, and sown with flax. The stitching – 'probably the biggest leather-working job of the century', as one expert said – proved the hardest task. If the boat was not to leak, it was essential the hides be exactly joined. It took hundreds of hours of intense work overseen by a former saddle maker to the Queen.

Early trials exceeded expectations. Not that the boat was simple to sail. It rapidly became clear that its two-masted rig, each with a square sail, was ideal for downwind sailing. Upwind sailing, however, proved impossible. The best *Brendan* could manage was to sail at right angles to the wind while slipping rapidly sideways. It was clear the boat would sail only where the wind blew it. But more important, not only was it an excellent sea boat, it

appeared not to leak at all, the leather and stitching swelling to create a watertight fit.

Beset by gales

On 17 May *Brendan* slipped into the grey Atlantic heading northwards. There were five on board, uncomfortably squeezed into its 2.4-metre (8-ft) wide, 11-metre (36-ft) length. Shelter was provided by two tiny canvas-roofed cabins, in which it was hardly possible to sit upright let alone stand. Cold and intermittent rain added to the gloom. Two of the crew were immediately prostrated with seasickness.

On 29 May a gale swept the little ship far into the Atlantic before, the weather easing, she was able to make her way to Northern Ireland. From here *Brendan* picked her way up the west coast of Scotland to the Hebrides and the start of the first major ocean passage, the 320 km (200 miles) to the Faroes.

The journey there proved easier. The little boat was funnelled though a narrow channel by a 7-knot tidal race before reaching the little harbour of Torshavn.

Severin the explorer

The success of Severin's *Brendan* voyage led him to make a further series of sea journeys in reconstructed ancient vessels. These were made to investigate the feasibility of a number of legendary voyages. In 1983, in what he called the Sinbad Voyage, he sailed an Arab dhow, sown together with coconut fibres, from the Persian Gulf to China. In 1986, in a replica Bronze Age galley, he followed the track reputedly taken by Jason and the argonauts in the 14th century 'in the finest of all ships that braved the sea with oars' across the 2,400 km (1,500 miles) from the Aegean to the Black Sea.

The following year, he reconstructed the voyage of Ulysses from Troy to Ithaca (pictured above). In 1994 he crossed the Pacific on a bamboo raft in an attempt to show that Asian sailors reached America 2,000 years ago. Three years later he navigated through the Spice Islands of the Pacific on a traditional native vessel.

He has also looked for the island where Robinson Crusoe may have been abandoned, retraced the route of Genghis Khan across central Asia and ridden from France to Jerusalem in the footsteps of an 11th-century Crusader, Godfrey de Bouillon.

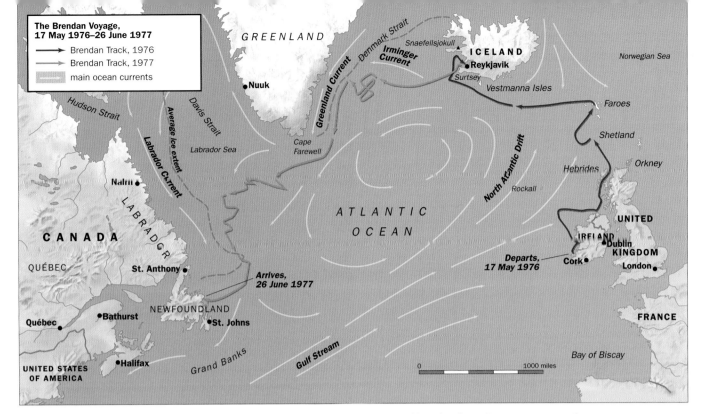

The North Atlantic is a brutally unforgiving world of frigid seas and sudden storms, problems heightened in an ancient vessel.

The ocean hopping continued, *Brendan* now sailing for Iceland, an 11-day voyage during which she recorded her two longest runs as an easterly gale swept her onwards in huge seas. These were waters teeming with life. Severin recorded a 'solid mass' of whales beneath the boat. Alarmingly, killer whales appeared, too, one bull whale surfacing only 18 metres (20 yards) from *Brendan* before swimming away.

Riding out a second gale boosted the crew's confidence. Despite the pounding and inevitable wear and tear, *Brendan* was proving a real sea boat, its hull 'flexing and shifting', its motion 'ponderous but sensitive'.

Brendan reached Iceland on 17 July, which was too late in the brief northern summer to make the final and longest leg through the ice-choked waters off Greenland and the Davis Strait to Newfoundland. *Brendan* was left in Iceland for the winter. The crew reassembled the following May, relieved to find their little ship in perfect condition.

She sailed again on 7 May. Ten days later bad weather closed in with a vengeance. It was bitterly cold, and a northwesterly gale forced *Brendan* eastwards, losing precious miles. Giant seas crashed over the boat and filled it almost to its rails, the first real crisis of the trip. A leather shield at the stern, however, deflected the worst of the waves. Fog, rain and cold reduced the crew to exhaustion. Yet, slowly, *Brendan* kept heading west.

Bitter cold and ice-choked seas

On 14 June, several hundred kilometres from Newfoundland, the ship met a 'nightmare jumble of ice'. Water poured through a hole in the hull, and the crew had to pump throughout the night to stay afloat. Daylight revealed a 8-mm (4-inch) gash. To mend it meant hanging over the side in freezing water to stitch a leather patch over the tear. He described the work as a 'miserable chore'. But the repair held. The leaking stopped.

Brendan arrived in Newfoundland on 26 June, the crew hauling her ashore on a rocky beach under a grey sky. It demonstrated the modest miracles of Dark Age technology.

> **I suspected we were beginning to appreciate what it was like to have been a medieval sailor, cast out on the seas at the mercy of wind and weather and armed only with patience and faith.**
>
> Tim Severin, The *Brendan* Voyage

By skateboard across Australia

DAVE CORNTHWAITE | **20 August 2006–22 January 2007**

Dave Cornthwaite first stepped on a skateboard in March 2005. Once introduced to the sport, the 25-year-old Englishman knew it would change his life. In his own words, he 'chucked in' his job to skateboard across Australia to raise money for charity. The distance – from Perth to Brisbane – was more than 5,800 km (3,600 miles). It proved more gruelling than he expected.

Cornthwaite warmed up for his Australian epic by skateboarding the length of Britain, from John O'Groats in Scotland to Land's End in Cornwall, exactly 1,398 km (874 miles). It took him 34 days – and it was harder than he had imagined. By day 20 there was, he said, 'a minefield under his toes'. By day 23 his right heel was so badly blistered he had to be admitted to a hospital. 'You know there is something wrong when your foot smells like death', he wrote. By now it was as much as he could do to hobble. He still made it, crossing the fin-

In high spirits Dave Cornthwaite on day two, Perth barely behind him, the vast expanse of Australia still to come. He is followed by one of the support vans and a team member on a bicycle.

The pain of long-distance boarding Almost three months in and by now the physiotherapy had become a daily constant, aching muscles screaming for treatment in the face of a relentless daily grind. Cornthwaite had full determination to see the journey through to its end.

ish line, exhausted but elated, on 2 June 2006.

Less than two months later he was in Perth, western Australia, contemplating a journey four times longer in searing summer temperatures across landscapes that were far more arduous. His backup consisted of eight unpaid volunteers driving three old camper vans. Money was so tight any delay could have derailed the project. Begging free hotel beds and campsites was crucial to success. They were rarely disappointed.

> This is brand new, this is amazing. This isn't a crazy dream, this is unusual reality and that's why it's special ... Nothing was wasted in my 2006. Despite tears and debt and arguments and strain, I don't think anyone on my team would say they've wasted 2006.
>
> Dave Cornthwaite, 30 December 2006

Crossing the Nullarbor Plain

Cornthwaite was immediately confronted by one of the world's most desolate landscapes. Perth is the most isolated major city in the world – 3,200 km (2,000 miles) from its nearest urban neighbour, Adelaide in south Australia. To reach Adelaide, Cornthwaite had to follow the immense Eyre Highway across the Nullarbor Plain, a vast expanse of near-desert scrubland. It included the '90-mile straight', the longest stretch of straight road in the world. At least it was mostly flat.

He left on 20 August. Early progress was encouraging. Cornthwaite was 'blown away' by the spectacular landscapes he was crossing as he made his way across 'this great, empty lump of land.' His target of 50 km (30 miles) a day was regularly and easily met. It took just 18 days to cross the 1,200 km (750 miles) of the Nullarbor, a distance greater than his entire trip across Britain. Even so, as early as 10 September, he was writing, 'My muscles ache, my joints ache, my back aches, my

Shoes, wheels and Elsa

Cornthwaite went through 14 pairs of shoes on his marathon journey. He was also forced to change the wheels of his skateboard five times. But the skateboard itself, the same one on which he had skated the length of Britain, survived the entire journey. He called it Elsa.

Technically it is known as a longboard. It is a high-tech carbon-fibre design specifically intended for long-distance cruising. Its most obvious feature, other than its bright yellow colour, is its low-slung design. The body of the board is only 7 cm (2.75 inches) off the ground. This means that the rider's standing leg can be kept straighter than on a conventional board, thus allowing more power to be generated by each push. In turn, to accommodate the wheels, there are distinctive wells at either end.

feet ache.' As his British trip had literally made painfully clear, the need for regular rest days was paramount. His right calf muscle was now approaching the size of 'a small grapefruit'.

On 5 October he racked up his longest day's run yet – 106 km (64 miles) – leaving his 'legs like jelly' the following morning. By 11 October he had reached Port Augusta, the first major town since Perth, now more than 2,500 km (1,500 miles) behind him. The Nullarbor was over.

Chronic fatigue and headwinds

His troubles began as he approached Adelaide. In part it was the accumulated fatigue of 40 days on the road; in part it was a new threat: consistent headwinds that left Cornthwaite on his knees. Then two of the vans broke down. In Adelaide itself he cut his left heel in a freak accident. It was the end of the day's run, and he had taken off his shoes. Posing by a signpost, he exuberantly pulled it out of the ground and leaped into the air. He landed on the metal base, slicing open his foot. It needed seven stitches and 10 days on crutches to heal. On the other hand, the enforced halt at least provided time to rest and recuperate. He still had 3,700 km (2,300 miles) to go. He wasn't even halfway.

On 5 November he crossed into the state of Victoria. The weather became wet and windy, a change reflected by the mood among the backup team, who fell victim to petty squabbles and sulks. Cornthwaite pushed on regardless, passing Melbourne, his third major city, by the middle of the month.

Long days on the road

In early December crisis loomed. To meet media demands, Cornthwaite had promised to reach Sydney by 16 December. It meant 5:00 A.M. starts and ever longer days on the road, battling the hills of southeast Australia, the Great Dividing Range. With 500 km (300 miles) to go, he was visibly on the point of collapse, reporting, 'Every part of my body is just saying "no. You just can't do this anymore."' He felt 'like an old man'.

The cumulative fatigue was such that his immune system began to break down. Alarmingly, his feet now also began to prove seriously troublesome. Both were blistered, and the relentless schedule only added to the agonies. By the time he reached Sydney, his right heel had been reduced to a 'red mulch'. Every push was sending 'a shiver of pain' through him. 'God help us,' he wrote, 'my feet are begging me for a rest!'

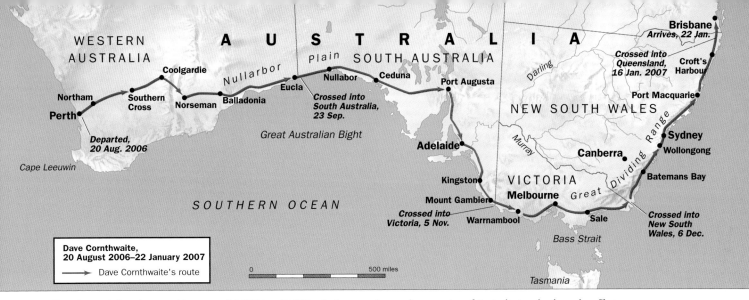

WESTERN AUSTRALIA

AUSTRALIA

SOUTH AUSTRALIA

Coolgardie

Nullarbor Plain

Nullabor

Ceduna

Port Augusta

Northam
Southern Cross
Norseman
Balladonia
Eucla

Perth

Crossed into South Australia, 23 Sep.

Departed, 20 Aug. 2006

Great Australian Bight

Cape Leeuwin

Adelaide

Kingston

VICTORIA

Melbourne

Mount Gambier

Crossed into Victoria, 5 Nov.

Warrnambool

Sale

SOUTHERN OCEAN

Brisbane
Arrives, 22 Jan.

Crossed into Queensland, 16 Jan. 2007

Croft's Harbour

Port Macquarie

NEW SOUTH WALES

Darling

Murray

Sydney

Canberra

Wollongong

Great Dividing Range

Batemans Bay

Crossed into New South Wales, 6 Dec.

Bass Strait

Tasmania

Dave Cornthwaite, 20 August 2006–22 January 2007
→ Dave Cornthwaite's route

0 ——— 500 miles

Cornthwaite's largely coastal journey of 5,823 km (3,639 miles) across the southern wastes of Australia involved much suffering.

A new record

Reaching Sydney was a shot in the arm. It meant a new world record for the longest distance ever skateboarded, beating the 4,830 km (3,018 miles) covered by American Jack Smith in 2003. Cornthwaite was reenergised. The remaining 990 km (620 miles) to Brisbane weren't easy. But the agonies of the days approaching Sydney were past. As he closed in on Brisbane – by now regularly clocking up 50-km (30-mile) daily distances – the media demands increased, taking more of his time. It may have added to the exhaustion, but it was tangible evidence that journey's end was at hand – and that his fame was spreading. As cars and trucks passed him and his mini convoy on the road, they would regularly honk their horns, the drivers calling out encouragement.

Hardly a mile outside Brisbane, he had his only serious fall of the whole trip, coming off his board at 40 km/h (25 mph) and rolling 30 metres (100 ft) down the road. He was cut and bruised, but the damage was as much to his pride as to his body.

Cornthwaite crossed the finish line in Brisbane on the morning 22 January 2007, having rolled into the city at 7:00 the previous evening. He had covered exactly 5,823 km (3,639 miles). By now the cameras were out in force.

The end Brisbane, 22 January 2007. Champagne called for, Elsa raised high, smiles all around, the satisfaction of success. The agony was less easily overlooked. It had been an epic in every sense.

5
Escapers

The rabbit-proof fence

In 1931 three mixed-race Aboriginal girls – Molly Craig, aged 14; her half-sister Daisy Kadibil, 11; and their cousin Gracie Fields, 8 – were placed in an orphanage-like institution, the Moore River Native Settlement, near Perth. They escaped almost immediately, and two of them eventually walked 1,600 km (1,000 miles) back to Jigalong. They found their way by a simple expedient: They followed the rabbit-proof fence.

The rabbit-proof fences – there were, in fact, three in all – were an audacious and pointless attempt by Australia's white settlers to impose themselves on the country's huge spaces. All the fences were built between 1901 and 1907. They were wire fences, about 1 metre (3 ft) high, supported by regularly spaced wooden poles. Together they stretched 3,256 km (2,023 miles). The main fence – officially the State-Barrier Fence of Western Australia, or the No. 1 Rabbit-Proof Fence – ran south for 1,822 km (1,139 miles) across Western Australia from Wallal to Jerdacuttup. It cost £337,841 ($1.69 million) to build them.

The rabbit-proof fence in 1926 The fence was built to precise specifications and was elaborately maintained with regular inspections from two-man camel-drawn buggies, but it was always of limited use.

The fences' purpose was to prevent the spread of rabbits across the country. Rabbits were not indigenous to Australia. Though settlers had brought them to the country in the 18th century, it was only in 1859 that they had been introduced into the wild, when Thomas Austin, an English settler in Victoria, southeast Australia, released twenty-four. He wrote, 'The introduction of a few rabbits could do little harm and might provide a touch of home, in addition to a spot of hunting.'

They did provide 'a spot of hunting', but Austin could otherwise not have been more wrong. Breeding proverbially, they spread across the country like a plague – hence the attempt to keep them out of Western Australia via a physical barrier across the country.

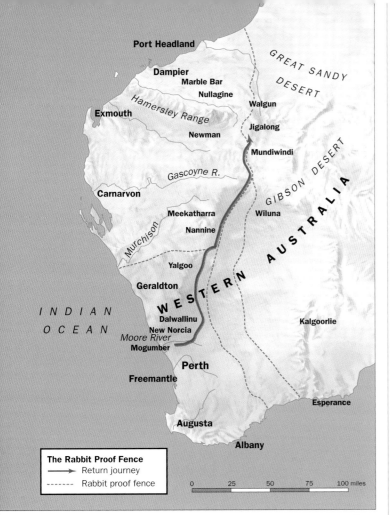

The total length of the rabbit-proof fences was 3,256 km (2,023 miles).

The Rabbit Proof Fence
→ Return journey
------- Rabbit proof fence

It was doomed before it began: the rabbits were already west of the first fence. Once built, it proved impossible to maintain, despite teams of inspectors patrolling its length on bicycles, camels and, finally, in cars.

The settlers' treatment of Australia's Aboriginal population was more controversial. Few issues have more forcibly divided Australian society. Since at least the mid-19th century, the white settlers of Australia had regarded the country's Aboriginals as an inferior race. By the early 20th century it was assumed they would disappear naturally, swept away by the unstoppable advance of white civilization. But mixed-race Aboriginals – the inevitable consequence of white population growth – were a different matter. Would they revert to their native origins in the process rejuvenating them? Or could they be assimilated into white society and thereafter be 'bred out' of their black heritage? These were the chilling terms in which the issue was discussed.

Between 1920 and 1930 more than 100,000 mixed-race Aboriginal children were taken from their mothers.

Many, as young as three, were placed in remand homes. The goal was to educate them for the settlers' world, the boys trained to become farmhands and the girls domestic servants.

Escape and evasion

The remand homes were cheerless sites of grim correctional expectations. When Molly, Daisy and Gracie arrived at the Moore River Native Settlement in August 1931, they were thrust into prison-like dormitories with barred windows. Children shivered under thin blankets on crude slatted beds and ate food not too different from Oliver Twist's workhouse gruel.

From the start Molly had made up her mind to escape. The prospects were hardly encouraging. All those who had run away before had been followed and found by Aboriginal trackers. Their punishment was severe. They were placed in solitary confinement, beaten with a strap, and had their heads shaved.

Molly and her companions made their escape on only the second day by hiding in the dormitory and then simply walking out. Each had only two simple dresses and two pairs of calico bloomers. They had no shoes. For food they had some bread. Molly, the oldest, was the leader. She knew that they had only to find the rabbit-proof fence, which was several days' walk away, and then follow it north to Jigalong through a barren landscape providing little cover.

Motion picture The story of the rabbit-proof fence shot into public awareness with the release in 2002 of a movie based on the girls' escape.

Later life

However. indomitable the girls' spirit – Molly's above all – their heroic journey had mixed consequences. Gracie, the youngest, was easily retaken once she had reached Wiluna. Her mother was not there, after all. Gracie was sent back to Moore River, in time becoming a domestic servant. She died in 1983.

Daisy's story was happier. She, too, became a housemaid – later a cook-housekeeper – but she remained in the Jigalong area for the rest of her life, married, and had four daughters.

Molly's story was curious. She, too, worked as a domestic. But in 1940, now married and with two daughters, she developed appendicitis and was taken to Perth to be operated on. Her daughters, Doris, 3, and Annabelle, 18 months, went with her. After the operation she was sent with her children to Moore River under ministerial warrant. Astonishingly, she escaped and repeated the trek she had made in 1931. But she was only able to take Annabelle. Doris remained at Moore River, where she was brought up. In 1944 Annabelle was removed from her mother and sent to a similar remand home. Mother and daughter were never reunited.

The photograph above is of Molly (left) and Daisy in Western Australia in 2002.

None had any fear of the bush. However long they would have to walk, they were confident they could live off the land. Their prime concern was not being found. This meant not just remaining in hiding – at least so far as the police and other trackers were concerned – but travelling as fast as possible. Molly hoped they could complete regular distances of almost 32 km (20 miles) a day. At the start the weather was frequently wet. This made their lives uncomfortable but had the advantage of washing away their footprints.

Life on the run

They spent their first night in a rabbit warren. On the second day, now very hungry, they were found by two Aboriginals heading in the opposite direction who gave them food and matches. That evening, they caught, cooked and ate their first rabbits. The following day, as would happen many times afterwards, they boldly approached a farmhouse. Though news of their escape had already spread, friendly white farmers fed them and gave them warmer clothes before allowing them to continue.

The police and trackers throughout the region made concerted attempts to find the three girls. This was not simply vengefulness; there was genuine concern for their welfare. Still, they evaded capture, doggedly continuing north.

By the third week in September, Gracie had had enough. She was not just exhausted – by now the other two were frequently forced to carry her – her legs had been badly cut by underbrush and were becoming infected. Learning from an Aboriginal woman that her mother had moved to a nearby settlement called Wiluna, she took a train there.

Molly and Daisy, however, were determined to continue to Jigalong. Now, without Gracie, they could travel faster, but the risks remained. Food, scavenged or hunted, remained scarce; they knew, too, they were being pursued. And now the weather – the start of the searing Australian summer – turned against them, temperatures mounting daily. Their only hope was to continue 'silently and swiftly' in the hope of remaining undetected and reaching home as fast as possible.

Author and star The movie, *Rabbit-Proof Fence*, was based on a 1996 book of the same name by Doris Pilkington, Molly's daughter. Here, the 14-year-old Everlyn Sampi, who played Molly in the film, poses with Doris Pilkington.

They reached Jigalong early in October, their marathon trek at last over after approximately two

> We followed that fence, that rabbit-proof fence, all the way home from the settlement to Jigalong. Long way, alright. We stayed in the bush hiding there for a long time.
>
> Molly, interviewed in the mid-1990s by her daughter Doris

months. Wisely, the families of both moved at once, determined that the girls should not be taken back again by the government.

By the middle of the month, the authorities called off the chase.

Escape from Devil's Island

Henri Charrière – universally known as Papillon, or 'butterfly', after a tattoo on his chest – was an assured member of the French criminal world. In 1931, at the age of 25, he was wrongly accused of killing a Parisian pimp. He was sentenced to life in the penal settlement in French Guiana. It was as good as a death sentence. But he didn't just survive, he escaped. It took him 10 years and 9 attempts.

When Papillon's autobiography was published in 1969 – it was later made into a movie starring Steve McQueen – it was met by a volatile mixture of acclaim and scepticism. Could this astonishing tale be true? Critics claimed he had taken the adventures of others and ingeniously conflated them into a single narrative, with himself centre stage, the unjustly wronged hero. Others, notably a member of the Académie Française, Francois Mauriac, poured lavish praise on the book's 'ring of truth'.

Throughout, Papillon himself – newly rich and feted – maintained his book was true. It is doubtful anyone will ever know. Papillon died in 1973.

It is true that Papillon had been in the French penal colony in South America. And it is true that the penal colony was a place of extraordinary horror, a disease-ridden hellhole presided over by sadistic wardens. Established by Napoleon III in 1852, the colony consisted of a principal camp on the mainland and three prisons 40 km (25 miles) offshore on the islands of Royale, St. Joseph and, most famously, Devil's Island,

Fact or fiction? Charrière, photographed in Paris in 1970 shortly after the publication of his book. With a robust defiance that never wavered, he battled claims that his story was largely an artful invention.

which in time gave its name to the whole complex.

The convicts, among the most hardened of France's criminals, had evolved an elaborate and corrupt society bound by Byzantine codes of loyalty enforced by their own swift and merciless justice. Violence was an every-day occurrence, killings commonplace. For those with money, almost anything – and anyone – could be bought, sold or bribed.

Papillon had money, 5,600 francs, smuggled to him when he was still in France. He was certain this substantial sum would buy his way to freedom. He kept it in what he called a 'charger', a slim metal tube inserted into his rectum. He carried it with him throughout his time in prison and on the run.

Arriving at Devil's Island

Sailings to the penal colony took place every other year. It wasn't until 2 November 1933, that Papillon arrived in French Guiana, having spent most of the previous two years in a prison in northern France. Within 25 days he made his first escape, from the hospital, which he had bribed his way into. The escape was simple. Papillon and two others – Joanes Clousiot and an 18-year-old known as Maturette – clubbed their Arab wardens to the ground and climbed over the wall. An ex-convict named Jesus, bribed in advance, hid them in the jungle for a week. Thereafter they planned to sail to safety in a dugout canoe provided by Jesus.

Things did not go smoothly. Clousiot broke his leg jumping from the wall, and the canoe proved to be rotten. Papillon procured a much sturdier boat from a leper colony that took the three men more than 1,600 km (1,000 miles) to Trinidad. There they met up with three other French fugitives and sailed to Curaçao. From Curacao they planned to sail to British Honduras in Central America.

The boat was intercepted off the coast of Colombia, and the men were thrown into jail in a town called Rio Hacha. Papillon escaped with a local smuggler, who took him to the remote peninsula of Goajira, the home of a

The 'man eater' The solitary confinement cells on the island of St. Joseph – the Réclusion or 'man eater' – photographed in 1934. By any measure these tiny cells, heavily guarded day and night by ruthless warders, amounted to a form of relentless mental torture.

Devil's Island

The three islands of the penal colony, where the most dangerous prisoners were sent, were preferable to the prison compound on the mainland. It was surrounded by mosquito-infested swamps and semijungle. The islands, swept by the trade winds, were much healthier. However, escape from the islands was much harder, since they were 40 km (25 miles) off the coast. Devil's Island was the least intimidating. It was where political prisoners were sent.

St. Joseph, site of the Réclusion (pictured above in 2000), was beastial. Royale, a teeming hotbed of criminality, was almost orderly in comparison. After his two years' solitary confinement on St. Joseph, Papillon found the island almost soothing. Nominally in charge of the cesspits, he spent most of his time fishing.

The penal settlement was shut down in 1952 in response to public outrage.

reputedly fearsome Indian tribe who lived by pearl-diving and with whom Papillon struck up an immediate rapport. He claimed to have stayed with them for seven months, entranced by the simplicity of their lives, living with a beautiful girl, Lali. When he left, taking with him 572 pearls, both Lali and her 13-year-old sister, Zoraïma, were pregnant by him.

Caught in Colombia

Crossing Colombia, he was arrested again – betrayed by a nun – and thrown into prison at Santa Marta, where for 28 days he was locked in the Black Hole, a series of underground slime-filled cells flooded to waist height twice a day by the tide. From here, reunited with Clousiot and Maturette, he was sent to a prison at Barranquilla to await his return to Devil's Island.

> **I should never have believed or imagined that a country like mine, a country like France, the mother of freedom throughout the world, a country that had brought forth the Rights of Man and of the citizen, could possibly possess an establishment of such barbarous repression as the St. Joseph solitary confinement prison.**
>
> Henri Charrière, *Papillon*

Papillon made four attempts to break out from Barranquilla. In the first, he tried to organize a riot in the chapel to cover his escape, but a fellow prisoner then alerted the guard. In the second, he drugged a sentry so he could slip over the wall. Though the guard subsequently slept for three days and four nights, he remained awake just long enough for his relief to foil Papillon. In the third attempt, he arranged for the lights to go out so that he could scale the wall. Struggling to the top, he fell 10 metres (30 ft), breaking both heels and leaving him flat-footed for life. Finally, in the fourth attempt, he blew up an outer wall with dynamite. It produced 'a shattering crash', but no hole through which to escape to the car waiting outside, for which he had spent considerable money.

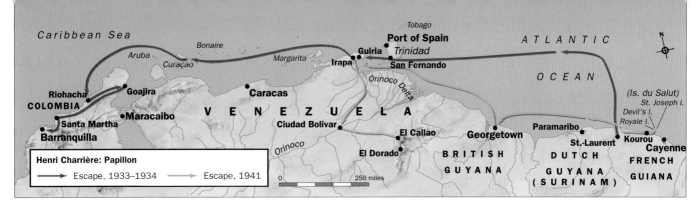

Caribbean Sea

ATLANTIC OCEAN

Henri Charrière: Papillon
→ Escape, 1933–1934   → Escape, 1941

Charrière's success in piloting a small canoe-like craft from French Guiana to Trinidad and Colombia on his first escape was remarkable.

By November 1936 he was back in French Guiana. He was given two years' solitary confinement on the island of St. Joseph in the Réclusion, known as the 'man-eater'. He was locked in a tiny cell that had many centipedes. Absolute silence was rigorously enforced. This form of extended torture caused many to go insane. Papillon survived.

On his release, he immediately set about planning his most elaborate escape so far. He bought a raft on which he and another prisoner hoped to drift to the mainland and hid it in a grave. An informer denounced him. Papillon killed the informer the next day. This time he was given eight years' solitary confinement.

He served only 19 months before the prison's doctor intervened on his behalf and got him released. In his next attempt at freedom, he feigned insanity and was admitted to the prison's lunatic asylum. From here he and an Italian, Romeo Salvidia, planned to make their getaway on two oil barrels lashed together. The makeshift raft was swept onto rocks and smashed, killing Salvidia.

In October 1941 Papillon made his ninth escape attempt. It was on an improvised raft kept afloat by coconuts. Again he had a companion, a young Frenchman named Sylvain. It took almost 48 hours to reach the mainland. Sylvain died in sight of the coast. Papillon struggled ashore and, some weeks later, in the company of two Chinese smugglers, he reached Georgetown in British Guyana. He was free.

The Papillon legend The success of Charrière's book was enhanced by the release in 1973 of an Oscar-winning film starring Steve McQueen and Dustin Hoffman. It permanently established his legend in the wider public consciousness even if the film itself was less than faithful to the book.

The Inn of Eight Happinesses

GLADYS AYLWARD | **March–April 1940**

Gladys Aylward was a parlourmaid from a modest suburb in north London when she decided that she wanted to work as a missionary in China and volunteered to help an elderly Scottish woman there. Her faith was of the simple, unshakable kind that can produce greatness. In March 1940, faced with the Japanese invasion of China, she led 94 orphans to safety in a harrowing three-week march.

Well before her journey with the orphans, Aylward had become a fierce protector of the Chinese and an implacable opponent of the Japanese. It was a role that could not have been foreseen when she first came to China in 1931 to work with missionary Jeannie Dawson in the remote town of Yungcheng in the mountains of Shanxi Province. It was a world as alien to Aylward as she, a 'foreign devil', was to its mostly peasant population. The precariousness of her position was underlined when Dawson died shortly after her arrival. Aylward was left in charge of an inn – the poetically named Inn of Eight Happinesses – that she and Dawson had just opened, hoping to convert mule drivers to Christianity, preaching to them over supper.

The Virtuous One

By 1936 Aylward could not imagine life outside China. She had become a Chinese citizen, she had a fixed position in the life of the town, she was universally revered, and she was a favourite of the local ruler, the Mandarin. She had also adopted five children. She was known as *Ai-weh-deh*, the Virtuous One.

The Japanese invasion in 1937 threw the country into chaos. China had been teetering on the abyss long before the fall of the last Manchu emperor in 1911. By the 1930s an unstable trio of Nationalists, warlords and communists were confronting each other while simultaneously struggling to contain the Japanese advance.

As the fighting intensified, Aylward found herself on the front line, treating the wounded, sheltering the homeless (including a growing number of orphans) and – increasingly – passing on information about Japanese troop movements to Nationalist leaders. The Japanese put a price on her head, branding her a spy.

By early 1940 Aylward was looking after almost 200 orphans. She managed to send just over half to an orphanage in the Nationalist-controlled city of Sian (Xi'an),

The Lord's work Aylward was genuinely dedicated to spreading the Gospel and was determined to do whatever she could to help the Chinese.

Happier times Aylward (far left) with some of the Chinese children shortly before their epic journey across the mountains to Sian.

160 km (100 miles) away; she hoped to send the others later, but when the Japanese advanced again and the Nationalists were forced to retreat, she was pressed into action. In March she escorted the remaining 94 children – a few between the ages of 11 and 15, the majority between 4 and 8 – on foot, over the mountains to Sian.

Aylward estimated that the first leg of the journey to the Yellow River might take 12 days. There was only enough food for two days. She hoped they would find shelter at night. The first night was spent in a rat-infested Buddhist monastery, the succeeding nights in the open. The elder children scavenged for what food they could find, but the party was almost always hungry and thirsty, frequently frozen, and increasingly exhausted.

When they reached the Yellow River, there were no boats. They waited for three days; a chance encounter with Nationalist troops procured a small boat on which the children could be ferried across. Aylward was now seriously ill, and the remainder of the journey was for her a painful blur. Sometimes they travelled by slow, uncertain trains; at other times they walked, again crossing mountains and sleeping outside, scavenging for food. At journey's end Aylward could only guess how long they had travelled: 'About a month', she thought. But she and all the children reached Sian, still holding hands, still singing hymns.

> ❝ My heart is full of praise that one so insignificant, uneducated and ordinary in every way could be used to His glory for the blessing of His people in poor persecuted China. ❞
>
> Gladys Aylward

The Inn of the Sixth Happiness

When Aylward reached Sian, she was suffering from a combination of typhus and pneumonia exacerbated by malnutrition. She spent several months in a hospital. But she refused to leave China, until in 1949 the new communist government expelled her. In England, again working as a missionary, a chance encounter with a BBC journalist, Alan Burgess, lead to a book on her life, *The Small Woman*.

In 1958 a movie based on the book was made starring Ingrid Bergman as Aylward (pictured above); the Inn of Eight Happinesses mutated into the film's title, *The Inn of the Sixth Happiness*. Though sympathetic to Aylward, the film distressed her greatly. This was partly because Aylward was a modest woman with no desire for personal fame, but mostly because of its many inaccuracies, not least of which was its portrayal of Aylward's relationship with a nationalist soldier, Colonel Linnan, a Hollywood love interest Aylward found embarrassing.

The wolf girl

In 1941 Misha Defonseca's parents were arrested by the Nazis in Belgium for being Jews. Misha was 6 years old. She was spared because her parents had already arranged for her to be hidden and given a new identity. She didn't understand. Knowing only that her parents had been taken to 'the East', she ran away to find them. For four years she walked alone across war-ravaged Europe searching in vain.

The fate of Defonseca's parents was commonplace in Nazi-occupied Europe. Her mother was Russian, her father German. Driven out of Germany after the rise of Hitler, they had settled in Brussels.

With the German invasion of Belgium in May 1940, they were forced into hiding, living in a small apartment, increasingly impoverished. Misha was forbidden even to go onto the small balcony. But they were a family. For Misha it was all she knew, and it was security. At night, sleeping between her parents, she was, she wrote, many years later in *Surviving With Wolves*, 'safe from everything, cradled by love, cocooned by the lily of the valley fragrance of Maman's [her mother's] hair. … She was my home.'

Misha went to school only occasionally. She later realized she was sent to the school so she could be hidden when her parents – in contact with the Belgian Resistance – believed they were particularly threatened. She was at school on the day her parents were rounded up. Misha was collected by an unknown woman who took her to a strange house. It was presided over by a 'mauve-haired woman', sour-faced and mean-spirited, who had agreed to take in the bewildered little girl only because she had been paid.

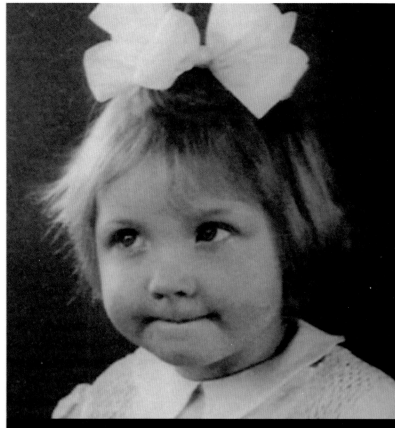

Childhood suffering Defonseca, aged 7, photographed in Brussels. Although she didn't know it, her world had been shattered.

Saved from the Nazis

Misha was one of perhaps 5,000 Belgian children rescued in this way by the Resistance, given new identities – often those of children whose deaths had not been offi-

cially recorded – and settled with other families. She was now to be called Monique. Equally disturbing for her, she was told she was now 4 years old, born in 1937 and not, as she knew, in 1934. She was forbidden to talk about her parents.

The only rays of light in the 'gaping hole' caused by this upheaval were the uncle of her mean-spirited new 'mother', a man she knew simply as Grandpère, and his wife, Marthe. They lived on a nearby farm. It was Grandpère – 'gruff, warm-hearted and alive' – who explained that her parents had been arrested and taken to 'the East' by the 'filthy *Boches*', as the Germans were contemptuously known. And it was Grandpère who brought her a simple atlas, revealing where and what 'the East' was: Germany, Poland and, beyond them, Russia. He also gave her a tiny compass as a gift.

The journey 'east'

In the autumn of 1941, with the *Boches* becoming more active, she was forced to give up visiting Grandpère. Separation from this lifeline only increased her 'desperate need' to be with her mother. Apart from anything else, she now knew where 'the East' was. It hardly seemed any distance in her atlas. If her parents couldn't come to her, she would go to them. She ran away.

She left at night, taking with her a small knapsack in which she had two apples, some bread, a knife, and the compass. She slept wherever she could: by the road, in trees, in farm buildings, once in the belly of a dead horse. She also became an accomplished thief, stealing clothes and food whenever the opportunity arose. But hunger, even more than cold, was constant. When she could find no food, she ate

Ray of light Marthe and Misha Defonseca in Brussels in 1941. Marthe had just bought her a doll. It was the first and last new toy she ever had. She 'cradled it like a baby'.

'worms, grass, leaves and berries.' Later, animal carcasses, often 'putrid', always identified by crows circling overhead, provided food. In desperation, she chewed bark; in

Aftermath

The girl who arrived back in Brussels in 1945 was an outcast from the world. She was covered in scabs and scars, her feet permanently damaged, the toes bent forward like claws. More sadly, she found contact with the everyday world nearly impossible. Her years of solitude and suffering had left her incapable of normal speech, suspicious and sullen. She was prone to sudden and terrifying rages. 'I have lived with the wolves,' she wrote, 'and become a wolf myself in body and spirit.'

For almost a year she lived with a gang of adolescent thieves in a ruined house on the outskirts of Brussels, their days spent in petty pilfering. When eventually she was picked up by the police, she resisted all attempts to be reintegrated into everyday life.

Two spinsters, kindhearted but unworldly, took her on, struggling to tame her. She hated the clothes they made her wear; she refused to use their bathroom, climbing out her window at night to urinate in their small garden. Once, they read *Little Red Riding Hood* to her. In a rage she 'flung the book across the room', claiming a wolf would never eat a child.

Even today, happily married for many years and living in America, Defonseca yearns to escape 'the noise and violence of human life'. 'My memory,' she has written, 'belongs to my parents ... unknown victims of the Holocaust.'

> **‘** I didn't need anyone. All I needed were my legs for walking and a few provisions. My compass and my determination to see Maman would guide me. I was strong, I had sturdy legs, I was tough and I was daring. **’**
>
> Misha Defonseca, *Surviving With Wolves*

her darkest moments she ate earth. Water came from streams and puddles.

She forced herself onwards, refusing to acknowledge pain, talking incessantly to herself 'in a state of delirium brought on by starvation and … complete isolation.' She naturally favoured woods and forests over open country, seeking out the shelter they provided. At all times she avoided humans, reasoning that it was humans who had stolen her parents and who would therefore steal her. She was determined not to be caught.

Misha had no fear of the dark or of animals. In 1942, by now in Poland, she was surprised while raiding a farm. As she ran off, her pursuer threw a stone that hit her in the back, probably cracking a vertebra. In 'excruciating pain', she hauled herself into some woods and passed out.

Joining the wolf pack

When she came to, a wolf was watching her. Gradually the bond between girl and animal strengthened; the wolf – Maman Rita to Misha – became almost a surrogate mother, protecting her, even bringing her food. She felt a genuine loss when the wolf was shot by a hunter. 'My mother had been taken away from me for a second time,' she wrote. For Misha, starving, alone and terrified, it was 'mankind' who was now 'the universal enemy'.

Later she fell in with a wolf pack in the Ukraine. Again they provided a refuge from the savagery of the war closing in around her. Theirs seemed a world more reasonable than that of humanity's. She had already spent some days in the Warsaw ghetto, believing that if Jews were gathered there, this was where she would find her parents. She found instead only what she called 'the stink of death'. Earlier, she had been taken up by Polish partisans, bent on brutal reprisals against the occupying Nazis. Everywhere she went now, she was surrounded by death.

A loving family Misha in 1987 with her husband Maurice and their son, Morris. They have helped her readjustment to the human world.

It was in the Ukraine, too, that Misha killed a German soldier, stabbing him repeatedly after he had found her in a hedge from where she had seen him rape and then kill a girl, casually shooting her in the head. But there was kindness, too: an old woman who fed Misha; Russian underground fighters who looked after her for much of one winter. 'The time I spent with them', she wrote, 'renewed my desire to be cherished and loved.'

A tormented childhood

She knew now that she had to go home, not because she had accepted that her parents were dead, but because she had convinced herself they were back in Belgium looking for her. This, too, was a journey made on foot, across Romania and Yugoslavia, then north through Italy and France. She was now 11. 'I already felt 100 years old,' she wrote. Hers had been a childhood summarily stripped away.

The jungle of death

Stephen Brookes was 11 years old when the Japanese invaded Burma in 1941. It was an event that demolished British colonial rule there. The Brookes family were forced to flee, mostly on foot, more than 640 km (400 miles) to India. Thousands of refugees died, struggling over mountains and through jungles – disease, malnutrition and exhaustion taking their grim toll.

In one sense the Brookes clan were a model colonial family in British India, of which Burma was a part. Stephen Brookes's father was a professional soldier, an army doctor, born in India in 1873 and posted to Burma in 1910. Their life in a hill station called Maymyo in the centre of the country was a near idyll: stable, prosperous and secure. Their house, Lindfield, was 'large and rambling' and sat in a four-acre plot. For Stephen Brookes, as recounted years later in *Through the Jungle of Death*, it was a 'paradise … filled with relatives, friends and servants.'

Yet in one respect their family was unusual. Stephen's mother, his father's second wife, was not just 22 years younger than her husband – he was 38 when

Halcyon days Lindfield, the Brookes's house, in 1924. Stephen's mother is seated to the left, his father, trilby-hatted, standing to the right, servants strategically placed to the far left and far right. These were, Stephen later wrote, 'Halcyon days … brim-full of wonders.'

Helpless refugees The Japanese advance through Burma was swift, complete and ruthless. The British empire forces, whatever their apparent superiority, were brushed aside. Here Burmese natives sit guarded by Japanese forces, the officers mounted, with soldiers on foot, in the south of the country.

they married, she 16 – she was Burmese. In a world as sensitive to social nicety and as racist as British India, it instantly put the Brookes family outside of society.

Not that any of this mattered to the 11-year-old Stephen. It was no more than the natural order of things, just as it was that the British army – whose ethos permeated Stephen's childhood – was unconquerable. But this natural order was smashed in December 1941 when the Japanese rapidly advanced in neighbouring British Malaya as well as in Burma, with British troops seemingly brushed aside at will.

The Brookes family was ignorant of the threat. Even the fall of Rangoon, the capital, in early March failed to

jolt them from their complacency. But reality hit in April 1942. First, one of Stephen's brothers, Richard, a junior army officer, was killed in an air attack. Then Maymyo

> ❝ I was a child, yet on this trek I had also become a man, wise beyond my years, for circumstances had made me so. Gradually in my dull head, thudding with confusion and misery, a tiny flame flickered, "I will not die," said the man/child. "I WILL NOT DIE. I WILL ... NOT ... DIE." ❞
>
> Stephen Brookes, *Through the Jungle of Death*

itself was bombed. The bombers were the first planes Stephen had ever seen.

The Brookes family made urgent plans to leave for China, approximately 240 km (150 miles) away. Early

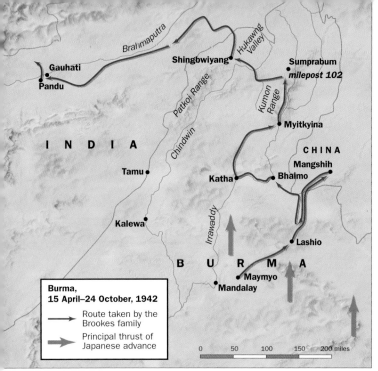

Thick jungle, muddy rivers and mountains made Burma exceptionally impenetrable for the thousands of refugees fleeing the invasion.

on 15 April, Stephen's parents and their three youngest children – Maisie, George and Stephen himself – left in a hastily commandeered army truck. They never saw Lindfield again. Stephen was still wearing his school uniform.

The horrors of reaching India

However last-minute and traumatic, the first part of their journey was straightforward – at least compared with the horrors to come. They may have been jolted about in the back of their canvas-roofed truck, but they were travelling fast enough to outdistance their Japanese pursuers. They had money and food, and they could count on safe places to sleep at night. Stephen's father, his uniform still crisp, sat in the front, barking out orders. A semblance of normality prevailed.

It rapidly ran out. Having reached China, from where the children and their mother at least could have flown to safety in India, they turned around and headed back to Burma, toward the advancing Japanese. As Stephen subsequently discovered, the reason for this baffling decision was his father's determination to stay in China, treating the wounded. His mother, however, refused to leave him. Faced with her intransigence, he agreed they should all return in the hope of catching one of the last flights to India. Reaching the small town of Bhamo on 1 May, they were forced to abandon their truck, instead taking a dan-

Playing soldiers Stephen, in an oversized pith helmet, air-gun at the ready, with dreams of martial glory before the Japanese invasion.

gerously crowded riverboat west to Katna, from where they caught an equally crowded train north to Myitkyina.

Here, with a wave of Japanese bombers sweeping overhead, their hopes of flying to India were ended. There were at most two or three flights, which hundreds fought to board. So the Brookes were forced north again, this time on another truck. By now the monsoon had begun, the rain falling in sheets, turning the ground to a 'treacherous skating-rink of churned-up brown slush' over which the truck could at best inch forward.

They struggled to what was known as Milepost 102, in effect the most northerly point of the country reachable by conventional transport. And then they began to walk. They were still 480 km (300 miles) from India. In the weeks that followed, they struggled over the Kumon range, outliers of the Himalayas, climbing peak after peak through the most dense jungle in Burma, lucky to make even 16 km (10 miles) a day. The mud was so thick, they all lost their shoes. Their slow barefoot progress summed up the desperation they had reached.

Then, from early June, they crossed the Hukawng Valley, known as the Valley of Death. It meant 400 km (250 miles) across a 'vast cauldron of steaming vegetation'. By now almost every veneer of civilisation had been stripped off. Shoeless, starving, shuffling painfully forwards, they had been reduced to the lowest common denominator of humanity. Survival was all that counted. They were no better and no worse than the other wretched refugees who accompanied them. Twice they were attacked by gangs of Chinese soldiers.

Surrounded by suffering

Death was commonplace. Where once a corpse was a source of revulsion and horror, now the bodies littering the track through the jungle were scarcely a matter for comment. It has been estimated that, of the 50,000 refugees making the journey, half died.

Yet the final indignity awaited. On 19 June they reached Shingbwiyang, a small village still 190 km (120 miles) from India. Here housed what remained of the country's colonial administration, which refused to allow them to continue. Instead, for more than three months they lived in a foul-smelling native longhouse surrounded by the dead and the dying.

For Stephen, starving like the rest but buoyed by youthful zest and a capacity to adapt, the sense of adventure persisted. For his mother it meant only a grim acceptance of their misery. For his father it was, simply, more than he could bear. At the moment of crisis, the certainties that had governed his life had proved worthless. It was an impossible burden. His death from blackwater fever was a release.

The Brookes family were allowed to continue their journey only in early October 1942. It proved almost an anticlimax. Porters were provided to carry food and those too sick to walk, including the children's mother. With the monsoon now at last over, travel conditions were easier. They crossed the border into India on 24 October 1942.

India and beyond

In India, Stephen, his brother, sister and mother spent 'several depressing weeks feeling disorientated and vulnerable in various refugee camps' before being reunited with those members of his family already in the country. After the horrors of the longhouse at Shingbwiyang, it was an inevitably emotional period.

But the journey itself had broken the family in ways they were unable to admit even to themselves. It was more than a matter of the complete destruction of what had once been a settled way of life, more even than the loss of their money and their house. They never spoke about the journey, never acknowledged it. Worse, with the end of the war, Stephen's mother returned to Burma with Maisie and George, leaving him in India. He never returned to Burma, and in 1951 he settled in England. Stephen never saw his mother again. She remarried and lived until 1971. George died in 1969. He was only 42.

The photograph above shows (left to right) Maisie, Stephen, George and their mother in Jhansi, India.

The man on the plateau

When Norway fell to the Germans in 1940, Britain backed every effort at Norwegian resistance. In March 1943 Jan Baalsrud was one of a four-man Norwegian team who landed in northern Norway from Britain to harass the Germans and organise resistance movements. They were intercepted almost at once. Only Baalsrud escaped, sparking an extraordinary two months on the run.

Northern Norway is a land of fjords, mountains and snow guarded by many islands. It is among the most desolate regions of Europe, almost entirely cut off from the cities of the south. In the 1940s its sparse population made a meagre living from fishing and small homesteads. Inland, there were – and are – only snow-fields, most unmapped, all unpopulated, on a plateau 915 metres (3,000 ft) high.

It was on this icy coast that a 23-metre (75-ft) fishing boat, *Brattholm*, made its landfall on 29 March, having sailed from Scotland 1,600 km (1,000 miles) to the south-west. On board were the four Norwegian resistance men – Baalsrud; Sigurd Eskeland; the leader, Per Blindheim; and a radio operator named Salvesen. That night, Eskeland went ashore, seeking a shopkeeper he had been told would help them. It turned out to be a different man who, terrified, telephoned a local official early the next morning. He, in turn, called the Gestapo.

In pursuit

The following afternoon a German gunboat steamed into the bay where the Norwegian team had anchored. There was just time for the crew to lay a time-delayed charge before attempting to row ashore. Two, possibly three, of the crew were shot as they scrambled up the rocky shoreline. Baalsrud, drenched but alive, was suddenly on his own.

By now German soldiers had landed. The only way out for Baalsrud was up a snow gully 60 metres (200 ft) high. At its foot, where four Germans lurked, was a small mound.

Against all odds Jan Baalsrud pictured after the war. His survival owed much to luck. But it owed much, too, to extraordinary fortitude.

Baalsrud gambled that the Germans would circle it to their left. They did. He went right. For a moment he was out of sight. He began scrambling up the gully, taking shelter behind the first boulder he saw.

From here Baalsrud shot and killed one of the Germans and wounded a second. The other two fled. He continued up, shots thudding into the snow behind him. At the summit he hid behind a boulder. He already knew he had lost his right boot. Only now did he see that half the big toe on that foot had been shot off.

Freezing waters

For the next few hours he struggled across the little island until he reached a beach on its southern tip. There was a rock 45 metres (150 ft) offshore. Baalsrud swam to it. The respite was temporary. He was dangerously tired and cold. If he stayed on the rock, he knew he would never survive.

To the east was another island, Hersöy. Baalsrud could reach it only by swimming. The distance was hardly 200

Here Baalsrud shot X the German Officer

The drama begins Tottefjord from an annotated photograph, showing the snow gully where Baalsrud killed one of his German pursuers. It was the start of an extraordinary two months on the run.

> ❝ After five days, he could only believe that Gronvöld and everyone who knew he was there had been arrested and shot ... and that he was condemned to lie in the desolate hut until the poisoning killed him or till he wasted away through starvation. ❞
>
> Account later related by Jan Baalsrud to author David Howarth, quoted in *We Die Alone*

yards, but it proved a dismal purgatory in freezing waters. Following the swim, it was as much as he could do to drag himself ashore. As he did so, two small girls, wide-eyed and silent, confronted his slumped form. Their mother, Fru Pedersen, confirmed to Baalsrud the fate of his compatriots. With a neighbour, Fru Idrupsen, she took him to her small house. At first light they rowed Baalsrud to a

new and much larger island, Ringvassöy. He never forgot the women's kindness.

This behaviour, all the more heroic knowing the savage reprisals they would face if the Germans discovered they had assisted him, turned out to be typical of the help Baalsrud encountered. Over the next six days he was passed from house to house, all the time making south for the mainland, where he planned to continue to neutral Sweden, a distance he estimated at 80 km (50 miles). How he would cross the plateau itself he didn't know. For the moment it was enough that he was still on the move.

He reached the mainland on 5 April. He had been given a pair of skis so he could travel faster. His immediate goal was Lyngenfjord, a fjord to the east. To reach it meant crossing the Lyngen Alps 900 metres (3,000 ft) high. En route the weather closed in. Baalsrud became hopelessly lost. For four days he stumbled helplessly, mostly in circles. Frostbitten, hallucinating wildly and in the end blind from snow glare, he entered a nightmare world hardly discernable from death. He continued to stumble onwards only because he knew that if he stopped, he would die.

Marius Grönvold A farmer and part-time journalist, Grönvold was the man who, more than anyone, was responsible for saving Baalsrud's life.

Unknowingly he found a tiny settlement, Furuflaten. He sensed rather than saw a door. He pushed it open and fell through it. It was a real door leading to a real house. Inside, there was a woman with two children. They leaped to their feet as this bizarre apparition, frozen almost solid, crashed to the ground. Baalsrud had found the house belonging to the sister of a man named Marius Grönvold.

For four days Marius Grönvold nursed Baalsrud to a semblance of health. It was clear that Grönvold would do whatever he could to help Baalsrud; it was equally clear that Baalsrud would not be travelling anywhere on his own for a long time, but it was far too dangerous for him to stay in Furuflaten.

The hidden hut

On 12 April, smuggling Baalsrud at night on a stretcher under the windows of the German garrison, Gronvöld took him to a tiny hut on the other side of the fjord at a place called Revdal. At first the hut, unknown to the Germans, provided a glorious interlude for Baalsrud, a place of solitude and sleep. When Grönvold visited him two days later, Baalsrud's spirits and health had improved. Grönvold believed that as soon as Baalsrud was well enough to walk, the inhabitants of a neighbouring settlement, Mandal, would escort him across the plateau to Sweden, a distance of only 40 km (25 miles). For a fit man all that lay between Revdal and the 900-metre (3,000-ft) -high plateau was a stiff but far from intimidating climb.

A further storm meant that Grönvold was unable to return to the hut for a week. During this time Baalsrud's health declined alarmingly; he suffered appalling pains in his feet and was convinced they would have to be amputated. His toes turned black and, as reported later in *We Die Alone*, started 'oozing a foul-smelling liquid'. He began to slip in and out of consciousness.

Gronvöld found him in this semidelirious state on 21 April. It was obvious that Baalsrud could now never climb to the plateau and would have to be taken to a hospital as soon as possible – and that could only mean getting him to Sweden.

Mountain hideaway The tiny hut at Revdal where Baalsrud was hidden for more than a fortnight. His health deteriorated rapidly in that time, and he slipped in and out of consciousness.

The snow tomb

When Baalsrud was first left on the plateau, he was placed at the foot of a boulder in the hope it would offer some shelter. A snow wall was built on his exposed side. He had a small amount of food and some brandy. He was still on the sled and was wrapped in two blankets in a canvas sleeping bag. His memories were of hunger, cold and loneliness; later, of despair.

Ironically, the snowfalls that prevented the men from Mandal from first climbing to the plateau and then, once there, from finding him, were what kept Baalsrud alive. As the snow settled over him, gradually covering him entirely, it protected him from the worst of the weather and ensured that the temperature in his tomblike enclosure never dropped more than a few degrees below freezing. Because the snow was fresh, there was never a problem breathing. But Baalsrud knew that if it thawed, the snow would become compacted. And then he would suffocate. He was buried like this, defying death, for four or five days. He was never sure which.

In the above photograph, taken in the early 1950s, Alvin Larsen, who helped carry Baalsrud to the plateau, points out the snow hole where Baalsrud was buried.

> **He still had his pocket knife and he still had some brandy. With the brandy as anaesthetic and the knife as a scalpel ... he began carefully to dissect them [his toes] one by one.**
>
> Account later related by Jan Baalsrud to author
> David Howarth, quoted in *We Die Alone*

Four days later Grönvold and three others began the laborious business of dragging the semidelirious Baalsrud on a sled to the plateau where they had arranged to hand him to a party from Mandal. It proved a very hard climb. When they finally arrived at the meeting point, there was no one there.

It was impossible for Grönvold and the others to know what had happened. They could only assume the worst. It was clear they could never take Baalsrud back down to the hut. The only option was to leave him on the plateau. They found a raised boulder, enough to provide limited shelter (*see* box p. 199), and placed him there with some basic rations. It seemed as good as signing his death warrant.

Nazis closing in

The reason the men from Mandal had not been at the plateau was that that morning, for the first time in the war, German troops arrived in the tiny settlement. No rea-son was given, but it seemed impossible to imagine it was coincidence. To risk the climb to the plateau was out of the question. Heavy snowfalls then made it impossible to make the climb for two more days. When they did reach it, they could find no sign of Baalsrud. The snow had obliterated all trace of him.

It wasn't until 1 May, a week after Baalsrud had been left, that Grönvold, accompanied by Agnethe Lanes, the sister of one of the men who had carried Baalsrud to the plateau, was able to return. Certain he had found the right place, he began to dig. He was confronted by a 'ghastly waxen face'. 'He's dead', he said to Agnethe. 'I'm not dead, damn you,' came the reply.

Immediate efforts were made to take Baalsrud to Sweden. On 2 May and 9 May parties from Mandal hauled him towards the frontier. On both occasions they were defeated by the terrain and weather. Again he had to be left on the plateau. He was at least receiving regular visits from helpers in Mandal now, which meant more food. During this period he summoned the strength to amputate all but one of his toes with a pocket knife, smearing the stubs with castor oil. But he was weakening.

The final days

On 22 May he was brought down to Mandal and placed in a cave for four days. He improved. Word was then received that a party of Lapps had agreed, after painful negotiations, to take him to Sweden. He was hauled back to the plateau to meet with them. The Lapps weren't there. Baalsrud spent four days waiting. Now he was sure he would die.

He woke on 31 May to find a Lapp staring silently at him. He then became aware that he was surrounded by hundreds of reindeer. He was picked up, bundled in furs, and strapped to a sled. The following evening he was in Sweden.

Sweden ... and afterwards

Baalsrud and his Lapp rescuers, accompanied by their huge herd of reindeer, reached the Swedish border before the end of the second day. The Lapps added to the surreal mood by becoming very drunk on the brandy they had been given by the Norwegians as payment when they camped overnight.

At some point on the second day – Baalsrud had lost track of time by now – the convoy stopped, and the Lapps volubly tried to explain something to the Norwegian. Eventually he grasped that they had reached Lake Kilpisjarvi and that the land on the far side was Sweden. He also understood that the Lapps were saying that the ice on the lake was unsafe to cross. It rapidly became academic. A German ski patrol appeared and opened fire. Lapps, reindeer and sled took off, careering wildly over the 'groaning' ice.

Baalsrud spent three months in a Swedish hospital. His feet were saved. That autumn he returned to England, from where he was eventually able to return to Norway to work behind the lines. He survived the war and lived in Oslo with his American wife, Evie, until he died in 1988. In the photograph above, Baalsrud is introduced to the Norwegian king, Haakon VII, after the war.

Three years to freedom

CLEMENS FORELL	October 1949–November 1952

The fate of many German soldiers trapped within the Soviet Union at the end of World War II was grim; those found guilty of 'antisocialist activities' would be treated as slave labour. Clemens Forell was one. He was condemned to 25 years in a lead mine in the most remote corner of northeast Siberia. After several desperate attempts he finally escaped, only to begin a harrowing 13,400-km trek back to his homeland.

In 1954, two years after his return to Germany, Forell was questioned by a would-be publisher, scenting a sensational book, as to whether his extraordinary story of escape and survival could be true. Forell told his story slowly, often reluctantly, carefully fleshing out the details. What emerged was a tale of survival – *As Far As My Feet Will Carry Me* – that defied credibility. Yet the more Forell spoke, the more it became clear he was telling the truth.

Forell was captured by the Russians in 1944 after he had been dropped behind the Ural mountains. He was held as a normal POW until 1945, when he was accused and convicted of being a war criminal. He was one of more than 20,000 Germans effectively sentenced to life imprisonment in Siberia. These Germans became forgotten men, victims of Stalin's implacable vengeance.

The remoteness of Cape East, their place of imprisonment, just south of the Arctic Circle, was

The horrors of Cape East That the Germans, in invading the Soviet Union in 1941, had murdered millions of its people was only part of Stalin's motive in confining German POWs to incarceration in Siberia after the war.

Raging river Clemens Forell (left) during his three-year journey to freedom, as depicted in the German movie *As Far As My Feet Will Carry Me* (2001). Forell's incredible journey was also the subject of a German miniseries in 1959.

underlined by their journey to it. They left Moscow in October 1945. They didn't arrive for almost a year, travelling first by train in cattle trucks, then by horse-drawn sleds and finally by dogsleds. Three thousand men began the journey; only 1,236 survived it.

Life at Cape East

They were housed underground in lead mines, caves lit by a single lamp. They were let out perhaps once a week for an hour. Bread, potatoes and barley gruel were the men's only food. They worked 12 hours a day.

If they could resist the exhaustion, they faced the cer-tainty of lead poisoning. The prospects of escape were almost none. The men were not merely emaciated and starving, they were surrounded by a wilderness of frozen tundra. It was a life beyond hope.

Forell made his first escape attempt almost at once. He was recaptured 11 days later. To compound his humil-iation, he was forced to run between a line of fellow pris-oners who beat him nearly to death. Since his escape, their rations had been cut to almost nothing. They knew Forell was the reason for their near starvation, and they were accordingly determined to punish him. Such were the crude subtleties of a Soviet slave camp.

The Siberian wastes However much Forell, taught by native peoples, adapted to the harsh environment confronting him, his survival in so vast and alien a land remains a remarkable testament to the resilience of the human spirit.

It was three years before Forell could make a second attempt. The camp doctor, a fellow German, had been determined to escape himself using his privileged position in the camp hospital to lay in supplies: a map, food, money, clothing, even skis and a gun. He then discovered he had cancer. He chose Forell as his surrogate, asking only that Forell one day make contact with his wife in Germany.

Avoiding capture

Forell made his escape from the hospital with the help of the doctor who distracted the guards. It was 30 October 1949. He had just one thought: to go west as far and as fast as he could. He estimated he would need to be at least 320 km (200 miles) from the camp before the guards would give up the attempt to hunt him down.

Thereafter, he hoped to head south to Manchuria.

From the start he was like a hunted animal. Desperate to escape what he knew would be the

> ❝ He had lived too long as a hunted animal to project his thoughts far ahead or to let tomorrow's dangers disturb tonight's sleep. Once again, he was content not to know where he was or what the future would bring, so long as he could find a sheltered spot to sleep in and accept the truce that twilight offered to his sufferings. ❞
>
> *As Far As My Feet Will Carry Me*, Josef M. Bauer, 1955

inevitable pursuit, he pushed himself inhumanly. He covered 32, even 48 km (20 and 30 miles) a day, obsessively counting his steps to measure his progress, never daring to light a fire, eking out what little food he had, all the while heading west.

The wilderness both intimidated and protected him, its very emptiness a form of safety. It was people Forell feared. After a month of his solitary existence, he was discovered by two nomadic reindeer herdsmen. Forell assumed they would either kill him or turn him in. They did neither, instead taking him back to their camp, where remarkably he stayed for almost three months. Forell not only struck up a curious rapport with the herdsmen, they taught him the rudiments of survival in the Siberian winter: where to fish and hunt, how to make a fire from moss, how to build a makeshift tent. Above all, they taught him that to survive, he needed to absolutely depend on such contacts. He could never hope to endure so hostile an environment on his own. Whether he could expect others to protect him in the same way remained unknown.

Panning for gold

By April, Forell had fallen in with another group of herdsmen. They, too, took to their fugitive visitor. He stayed with them for two months before encountering a third and, in most respects, even more improbable group of protectors. They were three Russians, 'villainous-looking scoundrels', escaped prisoners who scraped a precarious existence in the Siberian wilderness. In the summer they prospected for gold; in the winter they hunted.

Forell, now calling himself Pyotr Jakubovitsch, stayed with them for almost a year. From June to October they panned for gold, working 12 hours a day, eventually ending up with a small pile of gold dust they meticulously split four ways. With the onset of winter, having stolen six reindeer as pack animals for their sleds, they returned to the wilderness, ending with a substantial heap of furs.

They then had a falling out. One of the men – he called himself Grigori – had been hiding a gold nugget in his pack, stolen when he was working as a prisoner in a

Friends and companions Forell was sustained by relations with those he encountered, whether fellow prisoners, the camp doctor – Stauffer – or those he met on the run. Yet perhaps his most enduring source of companionship was provided by a husky, Willem, more wolf than pet, given to him by a native Yakute.

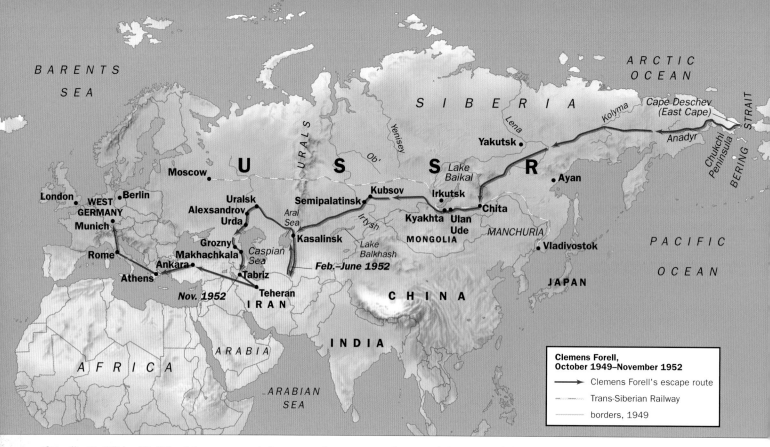

If Forell's 13,400-km (8,400-mile) route can only be tentatively reconstructed, it nonetheless covered almost the entire width of the USSR.

gold mine. The other two found it. In the inevitable reprisals, two were shot and killed. Forell now found himself alone with the apparently insane Grigori. Five days later Grigori pushed Forell off a cliff, leaving him for dead after having stolen his gold, too, and his pistol.

Forell was picked up, near death, several days later by yet another group of nomadic herdsmen. Again, they took care of him before sending him on his way. They gave him a dog – a husky – as a parting gift. Forell called the dog Willem.

Twenty months on the run

It was now the summer of 1951. Forell had been on the run for 20 months. Though he was still almost 1,280 km (800 miles) from Manchuria, the outposts of civilisation were getting nearer. And at least he now had a reasonable cover story. He claimed to be a Latvian, hence his poor Russian, who had finished an eight-year term in a labour camp

Death train On the grim train journey that made up the first leg to the prison camp, the death rate was predictably high – from exhaustion, malnutrition or dysentry; others simply froze to death.

and who had been ordered to report to Chita, close to the Manchurian border.

It was a good enough story to convince a gang of woodcutters, met by chance. They suggested Forell be sent to Chita by train as escort for a timber consignment. Better still, they gave him a travel permit. At Chita, he simply stayed on the train until it reached the end of the line at Ulan Ude, where a drunk Chinese truck driver unsuspectingly gave him a lift to the border itself.

It was heavily fortified and guarded. Crossing it was out of the question. Willem, his dog, was then shot by a guard. Forell was forced to flee for his life. He now became a kind of 'professional vagabond', stealing food, hiding by day, travelling at night, stealing rides on trains, occasionally hitchhiking.

By chance he next crossed paths with a group of forestry workers. One of them was the son of an Austrian baker, captured by the Russians in 1914, who immediately realized Forell was a German. He told him to make for Abakan, 960 km (600 miles) to the west, where his father now worked. The father, appalled by the obvious risks Forell was taking, suggested only that Forell try for the Iranian border. By his best estimate the distance was about 2,400 km (1,500 miles).

Then, early in 1952, in Novo-Kasalinsk, just east of the Aral Sea, he met an Armenian Jew – a member of a shadowy underground movement called the Kulaki – who recognised that Forell was German. He could, he claimed, smuggle Forell out of the country, though it would mean travelling north around the Caspian Sea and from there making for Iran via the Caucasus. Forell didn't trust him, instead going south straight for the border. Five months later, 'a skeleton', he was back in Novo-Kasalinsk. This time he did go north, passed from safe house to safe house by members of the organization until, in November, he reached the Caucasus.

Iran and freedom

The risks were increasing rapidly. Forell was now in heavily populated regions, the empty spaces of Siberia and central Asia long behind him. The danger of being picked up by the police grew greater all the time. He also remained suspicious of his protectors, particularly when he learned that a group of smugglers were to escort him over the frontier. Even when they told him he had crossed the border, an icy river, he suspected a trap. But they were as good as their word. Forell was in Iran. He was free.

The final leg

It took Forell three days to travel from the frontier to the nearest town, Tabriz. He went straight to the police. Predictably, they refused to believe him, assuming he must be a Soviet spy. They arrested him. He was taken to Tehran, where for several weeks he was interrogated almost daily. Again he was not believed. By now he was ill, suffering from renal colic.

In desperation he asked that his uncle, who had moved to Turkey before the war, be brought to Iran to identify him. A week later his uncle appeared. He didn't recognise Forell. He had, however, brought a photograph album that had belonged to Forell's mother. Forell clinched his argument when he claimed that on the back of a picture of his mother he had written the date of her birthday, the day he had given her the picture. The picture was found, the back duly examined. On it was written, 'October 18, 1939.'

Forell and his uncle flew to Ankara, capital of Turkey; from there Forell continued, via Athens and Rome, to Munich. He reached home on 22 December 1952.

6
Survivors

The great Antarctic rescue

ERNEST SHACKLETON | **1914–1916**

Ernest Shackleton's Imperial Trans-Antarctic Expedition ranks as one of the most heroic ventures ever completed. His aim was to cross Antarctica via the South Pole, from the Weddell Sea to the Ross Sea – a distance of 2,880 km (1,800 miles). But he never even reached Antarctica. His ship was trapped in ice and crushed en route, leaving him and 27 crew members adrift on pack ice.

From the outset the expedition suffered problems. Shackleton's preparations were rushed, his finances shaky. He left London on *Endurance* on 1 August 1914. Three days later, Britain and Germany were at war. When he cabled the Admiralty in London to ask if he should cancel the expedition, he received the reply, 'Proceed'.

On 5 November *Endurance* arrived at her last port of call before the Antarctic – the mountainous island of South Georgia in the South Atlantic, site of an isolated Norwegian whaling station. Ominously, the whalers reported that the pack ice (ice floes driven together in large masses) was farther north than usual.

Ocean camp This camp was established on 1 November 1915, after the abandonment of *Endurance* and was left on 23 December in a further abortive attempt to reach the known land to the west. Shackleton is on the extreme left, his second-in-command, Frank Wild, standing alongside him.

Endurance in pack ice On 16 March 1915, Shackleton ordered the ship's boilers to be blown down. The cairns running from the ships, ropes strung between them, were intended to act as a marked trail in the event of blizzards during the long polar nights.

The Weddell Sea was among the least-known regions of Antarctica. Only three ships, all exploration vessels, had visited it before. The first, the Scottish *Scotia*, in 1902 had scarcely been able to penetrate the ice and turned back. The second, Norwegian *Antarctic*, was caught in the ice and sank in 1903. The third, German *Deutschland*, was also trapped in the ice – between 1911 and 1912 – and drifted more than 960 km (600 miles) before being freed nine months later.

Beset in pack ice

Shackleton continued on course, undeterred. On 8 December *Endurance* had her first encounter with pack ice. Over the following seven weeks the ship plowed her way south, sometimes finding open water, more often having to push her way past loose ice, and occasionally trapped between ice floes. On 10 January the first land was sighted, but a little more than a week later the ship was solidly caught in the pack ice. By the middle of February, Shackleton became resigned to spending the winter in the pack ice and abandoned attempts to free the ship. The pack drifted northwards with *Endurance* its prisoner.

Drifting towards disaster

By the beginning of June, the total darkness of the Antarctic winter had set in. *Endurance* had been trapped for four and a half months and had drifted 1,040 km (650 miles). If their luck held and the ship wasn't crushed, the northwards drift of the ice into warmer waters would eventually allow *Endurance*'s release. By July the ice was becoming unstable. On 1 August the ship was suddenly rolled to starboard and then to port as thousands of tons of pressure from the ice were applied to the hull. By the end of September, the pressure from ice was increasing again. On 17 October the ship was thrown violently onto her starboard beam. She developed leaks so severe that 24-hour pumping proved useless. On 27 October she was 'bent like a bow' while 'the whole time there was an incessant creaking and groaning of timbers.' Shackleton ordered the crew out of the ship and onto the ice.

Earlier, Shackleton had the ship's three lifeboats and most of the stores unloaded in anticipation of the ship's loss. His original plan was to march west, dragging two of the ship's lifeboats to the nearest known land, Snow

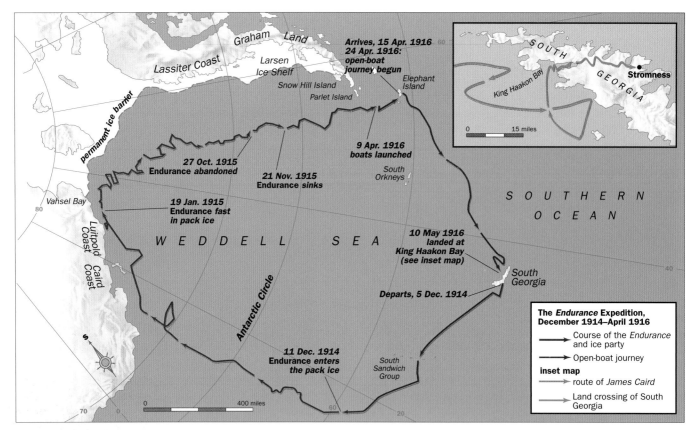

Endurance drifted 2,080 km (1,300 miles) in 10 months before being crushed; over the following six months Shackleton and his men drifted a further 1,120 km (700 miles) before meeting open water.

Hill Island. The distance was 499 km (312 miles). From there, he expected to lead a small party 208 km (130 miles) to Wilhelmina Bay, which whalers were known to visit periodically. All nonessential equipment was dumped. No one was allowed more than 0.9 kg (2 lb.) of personal gear.

Abandoning ship

Marching proved onerous. On the first day, October 30, they covered only 1.6 km (1 mile); on the next day, scarcely more. On 1 November Shackleton made the decision to abandon the attempt. He announced that the party would stay where it was, on a 'floating lump of ice about a mile square'. There they stayed for two months, drifting north at about 5 km (3 miles) a day. With the shattered remains of the ship kept afloat only by the pressure of the ice gripping it, Shackleton ordered his crew to salvage the remaining lifeboat and as many stores as could be carried. The men christened their new home Ocean Camp.

Their last link with civilisation came on 21 November when Endurance, still only a few miles distant, finally sank. 'At 5 P.M. she went down by the head,' Shackleton recorded in his diary. 'I cannot write about it.'

Ominously, their icy refuge began to drift to the east. The implications were clear: If they were taken too far east, they would be carried away from the known land to

Heading for South Georgia The launch of James Caird, April 24, 1916, from Elephant Island. Overloaded and underpowered, the little boat was unsuitable for such an epic voyage.

the west. As the ice broke up, they would then be deposited in the South Atlantic with no prospect of survival. On 23 December Shackleton ordered the crew to decamp. Once again, after days of backbreaking labour dragging boats and stores over a shattered landscape of ice, they had made heartbreakingly little progress. Finally, on 1 January, Shackleton ordered a halt.

The new outpost was christened Patience Camp. Here they waited once more. The moment of crisis was approaching – the breakup of the ice. Where the pack ice and the open sea met was a treacherous half world that was neither sea nor ice. It was no place to navigate three small open boats overloaded with stores and men. On 9 March they could feel their own floe beginning to move on the swell.

On 23 March they sighted land, perhaps 64 km (40 miles) to the west. It was already apparent that they were being carried too far north. Snow Hill Island had long since been abandoned as a possible destination in favor of Paulet Island, about 80 km (50 miles) north of Snow Hill Island. Now the goal had to be shifted north again to Elephant Island. Beyond Elephant Island was only sea.

> ❝ We watched them until they were out of sight, which was not long, for such a tiny boat was soon lost to sight on that great heaving ocean. ❞
>
> Thomas Orde-Lees, expedition member, on the departure of James Caird from Elephant Island, 24 April 1916

Elephant Island

On 9 April the party took to the lifeboats. They had been adrift on the pack ice for fourteen and a half months – first in *Endurance*, then for more than five months in makeshift camps on ice floes – and had covered 3,200 km (2,000 miles).

The voyage to Elephant Island took six days. The first two nights were spent on ice floes, both of which split, the first depositing one of the sleeping crew in the water before being rescued. Thereafter, the little fleet was continuously at sea. Nights were a misery, as icy seas broke over the boats, drenching the sodden and shivering men. All were at the limit of their endurance.

By 15 April they had reached their bleak destination; Shackleton was gaunt and haggard and scarcely able to speak above a whisper. 'Most of us hardly knew whether to

The forgotten *Aurora*

Shackleton's heroic rescue of his *Endurance* men has always overshadowed the exploits of a second party of men who were part of the expedition. This group sailed on *Aurora*, from Tasmania to McMurdo Sound, on the other side of the continent, to drop off supplies on the Ross Ice Shelf.

Very much against the odds, the McMurdo party succeeded in depositing the supplies. It was the expedition's sole success. The tragedy was, of course, that it was pointless. Shackleton, desperately struggling to save his own men on the opposite side of Antarctica, would never need the supplies.

Three of the seven-man *Aurora* party died. One, an Anglican clergyman named Spencer-Smith, succumbed to scurvy on the return leg of the supply trip a day before the party reached safety on the Ross Ice Shelf. The other two, including the expedition's leader, were lost two months later during an attempt to cross the sea ice to reach the expedition's base at Cape Evans, on Ross Island. A sudden gale blew up, breaking up the ice. Their bodies were never found.

Shackleton, now subsidised by an unenthusiastic New Zealand government, reached and rescued the remaining four members of the party (pictured above with Shackleton fourth fom left) on 7 January 1917.

Rescue from Elephant Island

Once safely at Stromness, Shackleton's immediate priority was to rescue the three men on the island's south coast. Within 48 hours Norwegian whalers had picked up all three without incident. Rescuing the men on Elephant Island was a much more difficult operation.

Shackleton made four attempts to reach them. The first, arranged almost at once from South Georgia, was on *Southern Sky*, a steel whaler, which Shackleton simply requisitioned. It got to within 110 km (70 miles) of Elephant Island before being forced back by the pack ice. Shackleton travelled to the Falklands, then persuaded the Uruguayan government to lend him a trawler, *Instituto de Pesca*. He sailed on 10 June. The trawler met impenetrable pack ice 30 km (20 miles) short of Elephant Island. The third attempt was made on a 40-year-old schooner, *Emma*, on which Shackleton left Punta Arenas in Patagonia on 12 July, towed by a tug, *Yelcho*, lent by the Chilean government, who were keen to help. (*Emma*, all that was available, could not make the entire voyage under its own power.) Once again, the pack ice proved impenetrable. The closest *Emma* came to Elephant Island was 160 km (100 miles).

Shackleton's anxiety had now given way to frenzy. The men on Elephant Island had been there almost four months. Their prospects of survival were shrinking by the day. He implored the Chilean government to lend him *Yelcho*. It agreed, and the ship sailed from Punta Arenas on 25 August. The season was improving, but the chances of reaching Elephant Island remained slim. For once, however, the weather – and the ice – relented. *Yelcho* reached Elephant Island on 30 August (pictured above). The 22 men, 'just at the end of their resources', were taken off within an hour. The only casualty was Percy Blackborrow, a stowaway on *Endurance* who had been made a steward. He had had five frostbitten toes amputated while waiting for rescue.

laugh or cry,' he wrote. 'We had stepped on no land since 5 December 1914.'

They could scarcely have found themselves in a more desolate spot. Shackleton proposed to leave all but six of them on the island while he and five others sailed to South Georgia, about 1,000 km (700 miles) away to fetch help.

The voyage to South Georgia

He took the largest and most seaworthy of the lifeboats, the 6.5-metre (22-ft) -long *James Caird*. It was crudely decked over, with canvas stretched across a frame of packing cases and sled runners. This provided protection of a kind but made the space below extremely cramped.

The voyage took 16 days, during which Frank Worsley, the navigator, managed only four sights. For two days they were hove-to in gales, waking on the second day to discover the boat labouring under the weight of ice almost a foot thick, which they soon chopped off. On the twelfth day they discovered that the second of their two water casks had been contaminated with seawater, adding acute thirst to their privations. With their landfall on 8 May came a gale that rose to hurricane strength and threatened to dash the boat against the island's immense ice-studded cliffs. For more than a day they were forced to claw offshore. Worsley held out no hope for their survival. When finally, late on 10 May, they stumbled ashore, they had had nothing to drink for 48 hours.

The respite was brief. They had landed on the south coast of South Georgia, and they knew that the Norwegian whaling station was on the north coast at Stromness. Three of the six men were too incapacitated to undertake further travel. A three-man party consisting of Shackleton, Worsley and Tom Crean would have to walk across the island to fetch help. The distance was only 32 km (20 miles). But between them and safety lay an unknown

Extreme survival Twenty-two men were left on Elephant Island. They stayed there for 128 days, living in a cramped makeshift hut made from the two upturned lifeboats, subsisting on a dwindling supply of seal meat.

mountain range. They had no specialised mountaineering equipment and took with them only a coil of rope, an adze (for use as an ice ax), three days' food, a small cooking stove and 48 matches. Worsley also had two compasses and an outline map of the island. Their clothes were threadbare. In Shackleton's words, they were 'a trio of scarecrows'.

Hallucinations

During the crossing, which took 38 hours, Shackleton had no sleep and Worsley and Crean slept for only five minutes.

> **We looked at each other with cheerful foolish grins of joy. The feelings uppermost were 'We've done it.'**
>
> Frank Worsley, *The Great Antarctic Escape*, on sighting South Georgia, 8 May 1916

(Shackleton, kicking them awake, told them they had been asleep for 30 minutes.) During the trek all three at different times were convinced there was a fourth member of their party padding quietly beside them.

Five hours after they reached the whaling station at Stromness, another gale set in. Worsley wrote, 'Had we been crossing [the island] that night nothing could have saved us.' The first question Shackleton put to the manager of the whaling station was, 'Tell me, when was the war over?' It was 20 May 1916.

70 days in a lifeboat

On August 21, 1940, the German merchant raider *Widder* sank a British tramp steamer, *Anglo Saxon*, 800 miles (1,280 km) southwest of the Canary Islands. Seven of *Anglo Saxon*'s 41-member crew escaped in an 18-foot (5.5-m) open boat. Nineteen days later only two were still alive. They survived a further 51 days before being washed up, near death, on a beach in the Bahamas.

Widder looked like an ordinary merchant ship, but she was actually a heavily armed raider sailing under false colours. She was one of nine such German ships that in 1940 sank almost 1,000,000 tons of Allied shipping. In general, their tactic was simple: to converge with their quarry and fire a shot across its bows. The crew would then be ordered into their lifeboats and picked up as prisoners of war.

Widder, under Capt. Helmut von Ruckteschell, adopted a different approach. In part, this was because *Widder* was slow and unable to hunt down faster-moving ships. More particularly, von Ruckteschell, a submarine commander in World War I, seems to have been an aggressive officer.

Targets, spotted during the day, were tracked from over the horizon. At nightfall *Widder* would close at her best speed, aiming to overwhelm its victims with a devastating close-range attack. Survivors were not expected.

Calm waters The SS *Anglo Saxon*, shown here in Liverpool, shortly before the war. The jolly boat can be seen just below the ship's bridge. She was carrying a cargo of coal to Argentina when she was sunk by *Widder* in August 1940.

The jolly boat Robert Tapscott (right) and Roy Widdicombe back in the jolly boat posing for photographs, several months after their ordeal, now fit and well . The crew cut notches in the gunwhale of the boat to mark the first 24 days at sea. Tapscott and Widdicombe survived for another 46 days.

This was the fate of *Anglo Saxon*, attacked without warning soon after nightfall. The ship was battered by *Widder*'s main armament and her decks raked with small-arms fire. Many of the 41-strong crew were killed when a shell hit the forward upper deck. Another hit the gun platform at the rear of the ship, setting its ammunition on fire. Another shell hit the engine room, bursting the main boiler. The wireless room was largely destroyed. As the remaining crew attempted to launch the two lifeboats, more were killed and the boats badly damaged. The captain, Paddy Flynn, was killed while throwing the ship's papers overboard.

On the far side of *Anglo Saxon*, unseen by *Widder*, the first mate, Barry Denny, and a sailor launched the remaining boat, a gig – or jolly boat – and slid down the ship into it. A third man followed. Four sailors on the deck below also scrambled aboard. As they floated away, they saw lights on two life rafts, which had also been launched. The Germans saw them, too, and

> ❝ Trusting to make a landfall in vicinity of Leeward Islands, with God's will and British determination. 10:30 P.M. wind freshening from eastward skimming along fine at about 5 knots. ❞
>
> Barry Denny, log of the jolly boat, 26 August 1940

opened fire, killing them all. At much the same time, after being hit by a torpedo, *Anglo Saxon* sank, stern first. *Widder* sailed away.

Escaped but in grave danger

Of the seven men on the jolly boat, now under the command of the 31-year-old Denny, three were wounded.

The most seriously hurt was Roy Pilcher, a 21-year-old radio operator who had been shot in the left foot. Francis Penny, a 44-year-old Royal Marine gunner, had been shot in the right arm and right leg. Leslie Morgan, 21, the ship's assistant cook, had been shot in the right foot. The other three crew members were Lionel Hawks (an engineer) and able seamen Robert Tapscott, 19, and Roy Widdicombe, 21.

As dawn broke, Denny took stock. The jolly boat, never intended to be used as a lifeboat, carried few supplies. For navigation there was a compass, a lug sail and

What happened next

Tapscott (right) and Widdicombe (left), pictured above during a visit from the Duke of Windsor and his wife, made remarkably rapid recoveries given the extremity of their ordeal. However, in February 1941, having travelled to New York, Widdicombe sailed for England on *Siamese Prince*, a merchant ship. A day from her destination, Liverpool, she was torpedoed. She went down with the loss of all hands.

After leaving the hospital, Tapscott joined the Canadian Army but in March 1943 signed on with the Merchant Navy again. Perhaps his ordeal in 1940 took too much from him. He died in 1963 at the age of 42.

Helmut von Ruckteschell, the captain of *Widder*, was the only captain in Germany's Hilfskreuzer (merchant raiders) to be tried for war crimes. Machine-gunning the crew of *Anglo Saxon* on their life rafts was the chief charge against him. In May 1947 a British court sentenced him to 10 years in prison. There he died, in 1949, from a heart attack. He was 58.

six pairs of oars. Food consisted of one box of ships' biscuits, 11 tins of condensed milk and 8 kilos (18 lb.) of tinned mutton. There were 18 litres (4 gallons) of water. They also had an ax, a canvas cover, some flares, a handful of matches and a rudimentary medical kit.

The Canaries may have been the nearest land, but they were directly upwind. Denny headed west. His hope was to reach the Caribbean almost 2,560 km (1,600 miles) away, a distance he thought could be made in 16 days. The food and water was rationed accordingly. Each man would have 0.14 litres (4 ounces) of water a day and half a biscuit, with the mutton and condensed milk held in reserve.

The first man died on the eleventh day, 1 September. It was Pilcher, the radio operator, his foot rotten with gangrene. On 4 September Penny, the gunner, died. The following day Lionel Hawks – the third engineer – and Denny himself died. Four days later Leslie Morgan died. There were now two left alive – Tapscott and Widdicombe.

Death on record

The initial fate of the boat party is poignantly revealed by the log, first kept by Denny, later by Widdicombe. Courses, wind direction and sea conditions are all recorded, as well as Denny's best estimates of their position and the state of the crew. On 25 August Denny recorded, 'Morale is splendid. No sign of giving up hope.' The following day he described the crew as being 'in good spirits and very cheerful.' By 29 August the lack of water was becoming serious, 'but no one is complaining,' he added.

Yet by 2 September, the day after Pilcher's death, as well as lamenting their lack of supplies, Denny was commenting, 'Crew now feeling rather low.' It was his last log entry. The few remaining entries in the tattered book were made by Widdicombe. On 3 September, 'Things going from bad to worse. 1st mate going fast.' Penny's death the following day was briefly recorded, as were Denny's and Hawks's the next day. The next entry was made on 9 September. '2nd cook goes mad, dies. Two of us left.'

Widdicombe made three more entries, the last on 24 September, 'All water and biscuits gone but still hoping to make land.'

Tapscott and Widdicombe's remaining 36 days were spent drifting erratically through the Sargasso Sea. They ate minute crabs and sucked seaweed. Widdicombe tried to eat his shoes, breaking his front teeth in the process.

Safe at last The morning after their rescue, Tapscott, too ill to walk, is carried, while he and Widdicombe (behind) prepare to board a plane to Nassau.

When a flying fish flopped aboard, it was devoured. Though occasional showers provided just enough water to keep them alive, they suffered appallingly from thirst. In their desperation they smashed the compass to drink the distilled water and alcohol it contained. Both, skeletal and burned black by the sun, were conscious of slipping closer to insanity. Tapscott lay near comatose in the bottom of the boat.

On 28 October, their 68th day adrift, Widdicombe saw a seagull. Two days later, they reached Eleuthera in the Bahamas. They were found, collapsed on the sand, by a farmer.

Death of a ship

At 12:14 A.M. on 29 July 1945, USS *Indianapolis* was hit by two torpedoes from a Japanese submarine. The ship sank in 12 minutes. There were 1,196 men on board. About 300 went down with the ship, leaving 900 men in the water. They were not rescued for five days. Only 317 men survived. It was the worst disaster in the history of the US Navy.

The sinking of *Indianapolis* continues to exercise a peculiar and terrible fascination. This is more than a matter of lost lives, horrifying though this was. It is more even than the fact that it was *Indianapolis*, flagship of the US Pacific Fifth Fleet. Only three days before, in conditions of absolute secrecy, it had arrived in the Philippines after a high-speed trip across the Pacific from San Francisco carrying the raw materials for the atomic bomb that would be dropped on Hiroshima on 6 August. Rather, it is that it was so clearly unnecessary.

A senseless waste

No satisfactory reason has ever been given as to why a ship with no antisubmarine capacity was sailing without a destroyer escort in waters where an enemy submarine was known to be active. Similarly, the ship's failure to arrive at Leyte – her destination in the Philippines – on the morning of 29 July triggered no alarm. There was no search-and-rescue operation when *Indianapolis* became overdue; nothing was done to look for the ship. When the survivors were eventually found, it was chance.

In addition, there has long been indignation at the treatment of her captain, Charles Butler McVay III, who survived the sinking. He later became the sole American naval commander in World War II to be court-martialed for the loss of his ship. He was made a scapegoat for the faults of others (*see* box p. 223). But it is the fate of the men in the water that commands most attention. It is miraculous that any survived at all.

An all-out attack

The first torpedo to hit *Indianapolis* blew about 50 ft (15 metres) off the bow of the ship. It killed all the men in it and, with the ship still steaming forward, caused her to rapidly fill with water and list steeply to starboard. The second torpedo hit amidships, starting a fire and knocking out all electrical power. In the ensuing confusion only a handful of life rafts ended up in the water – although they were designed to deploy automatically if the ship sank.

With the ship on her side, the men scrambled into the water; those who could grabbed life jackets. But perhaps as many as a third of the men in the water didn't have one.

Commission day Members of the crew of *Indianapolis* on 15 November 1952, the day the heavy cruiser was commissioned into the US Navy.

Sendoff The prestige of *Indianapolis* was made evident when she was chosen as the ship from which President Roosevelt reviewed the US fleet off New York on 31 May 1934. Here she leaves her dock.

Initially, most attempted to swim as far from the ship as they could to avoid being sucked down with it. As the ship sank nosefirst, propellers continued to turn and men still leaped from her. A number of survivors reported then feeling a series of massive underwater explosions.

Initially, there was terrible confusion. Many men were wounded, mostly with burns. The majority of the survivors were not on rafts and were coated with oil, which covered the sea's surface to a depth of 5–7.5 cm (2 to 3 inches). Most were vomiting because it was impossible to avoid swallowing the oil and seawater.

Hundreds of men dead or dying

Daylight brought greater order. As the ship had still been moving forward almost until the moment it sank, the survivors were scattered over a wide area, perhaps as much as 32 square km (20 sq miles). There were two large groups of men. The largest, which had no life rafts, had 366 men. It would later be known as the Hayes Group because of the presence in it of one of the ship's doctors,

Lewis Hayes. All but 95 of the men died. The other group, effectively under the command of a junior officer, Harlan Twible, had 325 men. They at least had a number of rafts, onto which the more seriously wounded were placed. As a result, the survival rate was higher – 171 of the men made it.

The remaining 200 or so men were in smaller groups. Giles McCoy of the Marines, for example, was in a group of 17 clinging to a fragment of a raft. Only five survived. Less typical was the fate of Capt. Charles McVay, who found himself in a flotilla of four rafts and a floater net holding a total of 10, all of whom survived. They were well to the north of the main groups of survivors and, though they could see another raft with perhaps 20 more men, they assumed there were no other survivors.

For the first 48 hours, though many of the wounded died, hopes remained high that they would be picked up once they had failed to arrive at Leyte. But by the third day, still with no sign of rescue, a grim despair had settled over the men. At night they froze, longing for the sun, but

The lucky ones Survivors of the sinking are carried ashore in Guam. All were hospitalised, some for several months. Many lives were lost in the disaster due to the lack of a prompt rescue mission.

with daybreak the heat became unbearable. Men began to hallucinate, claiming to have seen islands or that the ship was just underneath them and all you had to do was swim down to get water. All by now were suffering agonies of thirst; for many the temptation to drink seawater was irresistible. Sharks, seen permanently circling below them, increased in numbers. But most of those who died simply gave up. 'It was much easier to die than it was to fight and stay alive,' as McCoy put it. Lewis Hayes, still attempting to treat his men, recalled how he had become little more than a coroner.

A chance rescue

On the fourth day at 11:25 A.M., when the men had been in the water for 80 hours, they were spotted by a PB Ventura antisubmarine plane. In fact, numerous planes had flown over the men without seeing them. It was a coincidence that they were seen now, the pilot having opened his bomb bay in an attempt to free a jammed aerial, through which he glanced at the sea. In fact, he saw

> ❝ The worst part was giving up my life, accepting that I was going to die – it wasn't the sharks, and it wasn't seeing your buddies die. And we were young men, healthy men. All of a sudden, there's no chance, we can't make it. They've forgotten us. We can't last out here forever – we're gonna die. ❞
>
> Private Giles McCoy, 2001

the oil, not the men. Assuming it had come from a Japanese submarine, he prepared to bomb it. Only when he was making his final approach were the men seen. He at once radioed, 'Many men seen in water.' Now at last a major operation – with seven ships and many more planes – was launched, but it took a further 30 hours before the last of the men had been rescued. They had been in the water for 113 hours.

The fate of Captain Charles Butler McVay III

Almost from the moment the survivors were safe, the US Navy began a campaign to limit the public relations damage of the sinking. News of the sinking was delayed until August 14, the day Japan surrendered, guaranteeing minimum coverage. Simultaneously, a board of inquiry was set up that, despite objections from several senior officers, recommended Captain McVay (pictured above at his trial) be court-martialled. The authorities in Washington, D.C., accepted the recommendation and the trial began on 3 December 1945.

The charges were announced only four days before the trial, giving McVay and his defence counsel – an officer who had never appeared in a trial before – minimum time to prepare. Two charges were brought: that McVay had failed to issue the order to abandon ship 'in a timely fashion' and that he had been 'hazarding his ship by failing to zigzag in good visibility.'

Intelligence intercepts showing that an enemy submarine was in the area *Indianapolis* would cross was deemed classified and withheld from the court, as was the fact that McVay was not told of the submarine. McVay was cleared of the first charge but found guilty of the second, despite eyewitness accounts that the visibility was poor – information also not made available to the court – and testimony from the captain of the submarine, Mochitura Hashmoto, that it would have made no difference if *Indianapolis* had been zigzagging or not.

Though the sentence was subsequently remitted, his military record still contained the conviction. In 1968 McVay shot himself. In October 2000, after a sustained campaign by survivors, the US Congress passed a bill exonerating him.

Apollo 13: the successful failure

JIM LOVELL, FRED HAISE AND JACK SWIGERT | 11–17 April 1970

NASA's senior management had always been acutely aware of the risks posed by the Apollo moon-landing programme. But after the successes of *Apollo 11* and *Apollo 12*, no one else seemed to be worried. Spaceflight looked to have become routine, and when *Apollo 13* took off in April 1970, it was seen as just another mission. It was anything but.

Two days, 7 hours and 54 minutes into *Apollo 13*'s flight to the Moon and approximately 320,000 km (200,000 miles) from the Earth, Jack Swigert, pilot of the command module, was asked by mission control in Houston, Texas, to perform a routine stir of the craft's oxygen and hydrogen tanks. The supercold fluids these contained, the ships' only sources of oxygen and electricity, tended to stratify, making it hard to measure them. The simple solution was a fan in each tank. A 'cryo stir' was a regular feature of all *Apollo* flights.

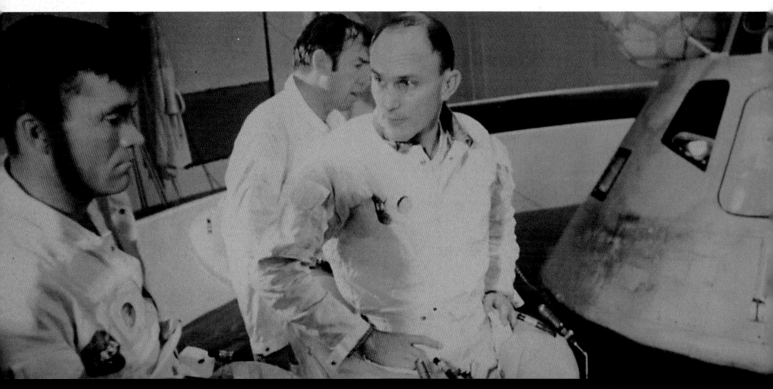

Final preparations Ken Mattingly (right) talks to Fred Haise (left), with Jim Lovell in the background, during testing in the days prior to takeoff. Ultimately, Mattingly was pulled from the crew at the last moment due to a risk of ill health and replaced by Jack Swigert.

Sixteen seconds later one of the two oxygen tanks exploded. The blast critically damaged the other tank and slammed shut the valves on the hydrogen tanks. It took more than an hour for ground controllers and the three astronauts to realise the severity of the situation. In effect, *Apollo 13* was now a dead ship. It was losing its oxygen supplies and all its power.

Confronted by an array of warning lights, the astronauts were at a loss. According to their instruments, fuel cells and oxygen tanks that were full one moment were empty the next before registering full again. In Houston it was widely assumed it was the readings that were wrong, products of an outbreak of rogue data produced by faulty instrumentation.

Losing oxygen

But for the astronauts there was another alarming event – not only had there been a 'loud, dull bang' just moments before the warning lights lit up, the ship had since been gyrating. Thirteen minutes after the explosion the mission commander, Jim Lovell, looked out one of the ship's windows.

'It looks to me that we are venting something,' he radioed. 'We're venting something out into space. It's a gas of some sort.' What this gas was, as Lovell instantly realised, was oxygen. And what that meant was the crew of *Apollo 13*, far from landing on the Moon, would be lucky to make it back home at all.

An Apollo spacecraft consisted of three basic components – the conical command module (or

Liftoff *Apollo 13* lifted off at 2.13 P.M. on 11 April 1970. Five minutes into the flight the centre engine of the second stage cut out 132 seconds early. It was the first of many problems.

Unlucky 13?

Jim Lovell always vigorously decried the notion that *Apollo 13* was an unlucky flight, doomed even before it was launched merely by virtue of its number. 'Thirteen,' he said, 'is just a number. It comes after twelve and before fourteen.' Nonetheless, as even Lovell later admitted, the flight had more than its share of bad luck.

The most obvious came two days before launch when the command module pilot, Ken Mattingly (pictured above), was pulled off the flight after it was thought he might have been exposed to German measles. The likelihood of his becoming ill during the flight was near zero. But ever mindful of the press fallout in the improbable event that Mattingly did become ill in space, this was a risk Houston deemed unacceptable.

Lovell, deeply disturbed by this decision, had no choice but to accept a backup. In theory all Apollo crews were interchangeable. In practice no one could predict how individual crew members would react together.

CM), in which the three-man crew travelled to and from the Moon; the service module (SM), which powered the command module and contained the engine that put the ship into orbit around the Moon and brought it back to the Earth; and the lunar module (LM), the improbably frail ship in which two of the crew would land on the Moon and then take off to rejoin the command module.

With the service module now irrecoverably damaged, the command module – code-named *Odyssey* – was fast on its way towards becoming inoperable. All that would then be left was the lunar module, code-named *Aquarius*. It had become the crew's lifeboat.

> ❝ Okay Houston. We've had a problem. ❞
>
> James Lovell, moments after the explosion, 13 April 1970

Lunar module – the only hope

Ninety minutes after the explosion, Houston tentatively radioed: 'We're starting to think about the LM lifeboat.' The third member of the crew, Fred Haise, who probably knew more about the LM than any other astronaut on NASA's roster, immediately made his way through the narrow tunnel connecting *Odyssey* and *Aquarius*.

The situation facing the crew was stark. *Odyssey* now had perhaps 15 minutes of power left. To power up the LM normally took 2 hours. Haise, joined by Lovell, had to condense this exacting programme into these 15 minutes. This was more than just a matter of a complex series of switch throwing. It meant transferring the navigational data from *Odyssey*'s computer to *Aquarius*'s. Without this the crew would have no means of orienting the ship to get back to Earth.

The LM was designed to support two men for 48 hours. It would now have to sustain three men for perhaps 100 hours. *Apollo 13* was not only still speeding away from Earth, it was on what NASA called a hybrid trajectory. This meant that unless it changed to an Earthbound free-return trajectory, it would speed Earthwards once slung by gravity around the Moon. However, it would miss Earth by 77,000 km (48,000 miles) before, as inevitably impelled by gravity, being sent back to the Moon. *Apollo 13* risked becoming 'a permanent monument to the space programme', endlessly orbiting the Moon and Earth with its dead crew.

There was concern about the command module. Even if the LM could bring the astronauts back to Earth, they could only reenter the Earth's atmosphere in the command module, because only the command module could withstand the huge temperatures of reentry. *Odyssey* still had a limited reserve – about 45 minutes – of battery power and oxygen for reentry. But it had now been completely powered down. Within three days NASA had to devise a programme to power it back up using no more than its limited battery power. It was a programme that might normally take three months to devise. There were concerns that the explosion might have also damaged the heat shield, without which *Odyssey*, powered up or not, could never survive reentry.

Firing the motor

But for now the short term dominated. Could the LM's motor be fired to place *Apollo 13* on a free-return trajectory? The immediate answer was yes. Five and a half hours after the explosion, *Aquarius*'s descent engine was lit. It burned for no more than 35 seconds. But when it was shut down, the crew at least knew they would now be heading back to the Earth once they had rounded the Moon.

No sooner was one imperative dealt with than others, equally urgent, presented themselves. Could *Aquarius*'s limited 'consumables' – its electricity and oxygen – be eked out long enough to bring the crew home? Would its water supplies hold out? This wasn't a question of whether there would be enough water for the crew to drink. It was a question of whether there would be enough to cool the ship's easily overheated electrical systems.

In the meantime, with *Apollo 13* still hurtling towards the Moon, Houston had decided on a further major burn of the LM's motor, one that would bring the ship back to Earth almost a whole day faster. It was called the PC+2 burn (or pericynthian plus two). But it would work only if Houston and the crew were sure the LM's navigational computer was accurate. To test it, they asked it to sight on the Sun.

Plummeting temperatures

When Lovell, his voice cracking with fatigue, called, 'We got it!' crew and ship had passed perhaps their most demanding test yet. Two hours after circling the Moon, the descent engine on the LM was fired again.

Apollo 13 may have been heading home, but in many ways the worst was to come. The crew had not slept for almost two days. Temperatures in both *Odyssey* and *Aquarius* – the former frozen and tomblike, the latter cramped and dark – were plummeting. Water was strictly rationed, the only food frozen. To save power, Houston

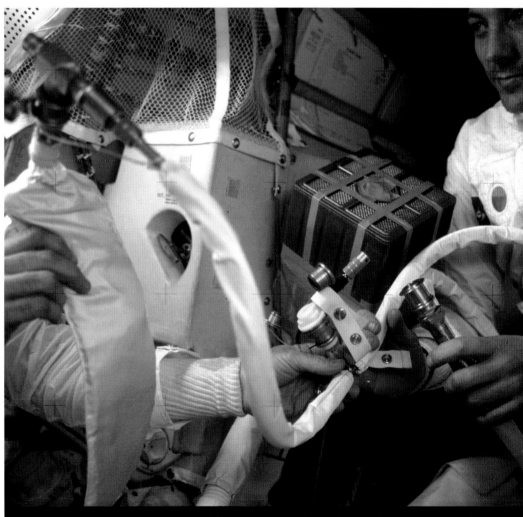

Lifesaver Jack Swigert with an improvised filtration canister, a low-tech triumph in a high-tech world. Without this unlikely solution, the crew would have suffocated on their own breath.

Oxygen tank 2

The explosion of *Apollo 13*'s oxygen tank 2 classically demonstrated how major disasters are almost invariably the result of a series of minor errors, by themselves seemingly insignificant, cumulatively often fatal. The tank, built in 1967 by the Beech Aircraft Company, was initially installed in *Apollo 10*. Then, it was intended to be run off the spacecraft's own electricity supply of 28 volts. NASA subsequently changed the specification so that the tanks could also be run on the 65-volt current used by the ground engineers at the Kennedy Space Center.

The tank was modified. It was then removed from *Apollo 10* for further modifications but, in the process, dropped, knocking the tube used to fill and empty the tank out of shape. It hardly seemed a problem. The tank was subsequently installed on *Apollo 13*.

However, a month before *Apollo 13* launched, a routine test ran up against the problem of the out-of-shape filler line. Having been filled, the tank now could not be emptied. The engineers decided the simple answer was to boil the liquid oxygen out of the tank. On the face of it there was no risk. The tank's thermostat would automatically cut in once the temperatures reached 26°C (80°F). Unfortunately, the thermostat was the only part of the tank that had not been upgraded to run on 65 volts. It was an oversight.

The thermostat fused almost instantly. Temperatures in the tank rose to 1000°F (538°C), burning the plastic coating off the internal wiring. When Jack Swigert conscientiously 'stirred the tanks' on the evening of 15 April 1970, a series of naked wires in an oxygen-soaked tank were suddenly pulsing with electricity. The consequences of the ensuing spark were unstoppable. The damage it caused to the subsequently jettisoned command module is pictured above.

NASA watches in awe Mission control, Houston, Texas, after the successful splashdown, the air already thick with cigar smoke. For flight director Gene Kranz, in particular, it was a remarkable triumph in the face of apparently inevitable disaster.

had ordered the crew not to dump urine overboard. Plastic bags bulging with urine littered the ship. Haise, dehydrated and exhausted, fell ill, his temperature soaring. All the crew would lose weight during the flight.

Worse still, they were also slowly suffocating. Like the command module, the lunar lander had lithium hydroxide canisters to filter the carbon dioxide exhaled by the crew. These were slowly being overwhelmed as the LM's environmental control system struggled to cope with the extra demands placed on it. There was no shortage of these canisters in the command module, but they were square, while those on the lunar lander were round. Following instructions from Houston, the command module's canisters were hastily modified using duct tape, plastic bags, and hoses from space suits, with socks used to plug leaks.

'Farewell, *Aquarius*'

Less than 12 hours before splashdown, Houston radioed up the checklist to reactivate the command module. It took Swigert more than 2 hours to copy it down. The only question was whether it would work. Every surface of the command module was now sodden, the result of cold and condensation. It was clear to the crew that there must be water behind the control panels as well as on them. There was a real risk of a fatal shorting out.

As he threw the switches, Swigert saw the ship hum miraculously back to life. By now the command module had already been cast off, the crew crowding the windows to see it spin into space. What they saw exceeded anything they could have imagined. Lovell, on the radio to Houston, captured the crew's astonishment, 'There's one whole side of that spacecraft missing! Look out there, would you!'

> ❝ Okay, let's everybody keep cool. Let's make sure we don't do anything that's going to blow our electrical power or cause us to lose fuel cell number two. Let's solve the problem but let's not make it any worse by guessing. ❞
>
> Flight director Gene Kranz, mission control, Houston

Then the lunar module was jettisoned. In Houston capsule communicator (Capcom) Joe Kerwin precisely summed up the mood, 'Farewell, *Aquarius*, and we thank you.'

Splashdown

Apollo 13 splashed down safely in the South Pacific at 1:07 P.M. on 17 April 1970. On paper the flight had wholly failed. There had been no Moon landing; if the crew had survived, it had been by the slimmest of margins. But in some respects this had been NASA's finest moment – an astonishing tale of survival against overwhelming odds.

Flight 571

The Old Christians, a rugby club from Montevideo, chartered Uruguayan Air Force Flight 571. They were en route to Santiago, Chile, for a match when the plane crashed in the Andes. Ten days later rescue efforts ceased as the plane could not be located. But of the 45 on board, 33 had survived. Sixteen were eventually saved. They lived because they accepted reality: they ate those who had died.

Flight 571 crashed 4,000 metres (13,000 ft) up in the Andes. The pilots had failed to allow for headwinds and, thinking they had already crossed the Andes, had begun their descent. As they came through the clouds, they found themselves trapped by mountains. Their desperate attempts to gain height failed. The right wing hit a rock and sheared off, slicing away the tail and leaving a gaping hole at the rear of the plane, through which five passengers and two crew disappeared. The remaining wing was then torn off before the fuselage sped downhill and slammed to a halt.

The immediate aftermath

The deceleration was so violent that the seats were wrenched off their mountings, crushing five people, including one of the pilots, at the front. Four died from injuries that night. The following day the 50-year-old mother of one of the players, Fernando Parrado, died. Among the survivors were 19-year-old Alvaro Mangino, who had a broken leg, and 22-year-old Arturo Nogueiro, who had two broken legs; 22-year-old Rafael Echavarren had a serious injury to the calf muscle on his right leg; a 15-cm (6-inch) steel tube had speared the abdomen of 22-year-old Enrique Platero. Others suffered concussions; almost all the passengers had cuts and bruises. Two 19-year-old medical students, Roberto Canessa and Gustavo Zerbino, themselves

Sheer devastation Given the enormity of damage to the aeroplane – this section of the fuselage was the only part to remain largely intact – it is surprising that 33 passengers survived the impact.

Waiting and hoping The survivors used the remnants of the aeroplane for shelter and scoured the debris for whatever clothes, food and other rations they could find. Eventually, as hope of rescue grew unlikely, the dwindling survivors had little option but to resort to cannibalism.

both dazed, provided the only medical care available.

For the survivors the situation was desperate. At these heights the cold was fearsome, at night dropping to –33°C (–30°F). Because it was still early spring, the snow was waist deep, ruling out walking to safety. Rescue was a faint hope. The only clothes they had were those they wore or could salvage from suitcases. Certainly, there was no survival gear. The food supply consisted of a handful of chocolate, some nougat, a few crackers, a little jam and some nuts. There were also a few bottles of wine.

On the third day Parrado was given his final ration: a single chocolate-covered nut. He made it last three days. On the first day he sucked off the chocolate; on the second he ate half the nut; on the third the other half.

> Finally, I slipped the flesh into my mouth. It had no taste. I chewed, once or twice, then forced myself to swallow. I felt no guilt. I understood the magnitude of the taboo we had just broken, but if I felt any strong emotion, it was resentment that fate had forced us to choose between this horror and the horror of certain death. Now it was up to luck.
>
> Nando Parrado, *Miracle in the Andes*

The shattered fuselage at least provided some shelter. The worst of the weather was kept at bay with suitcases jammed in the jagged hole in its rear, the gaps filled with snow. Yet even huddled together for warmth, the survivors could feel themselves freezing. In desperation they burned all the paper money they had, some $7,500. It produced a pitifully brief amount of warmth.

They had water from melted snow. A transistor radio

The impulse for life: cannibalism

From the moment the gaunt survivors of Flight 571 were rescued, the question of cannibalism was raised. There were, inevitably, attempts to sensationalise it but the stark facts of the case and the obvious integrity of the survivors put an end to ugly speculation.

Those who survived had been in an environment in which even the barest essentials of life did not exist. In extreme circumstances survival is simple. Parrado put it eloquently, 'When the brain senses an onset of starvation, it sets off an adrenaline surge as powerful as the impulse that compels an animal to flee an attacking predator.' In his own case it was agreed that the bodies of his mother and sister would not be eaten. The others, however, were eaten, even the newly dead bodies of those killed in the avalanche when, after three days incarcerated in the aeroplane, those still alive were desperate for anything to eat.

They all understood the line they had crossed, but none of them regretted it.

proved to be a mixed blessing – not just because it worked intermittently, but because it was how they learned, on 23 October, that the rescue efforts to find them had been halted. Two days earlier Parrado's 19-year-old sister, Susy, had died, cradled in her brother's arms, bringing the death toll to 18.

They began to starve. In Parrado's words, 'We were obsessed by the search for food.' They rummaged in the clothes of the dead; they cut leather strips from suitcases to suck; they tore open the seat covers hoping to find straw (and found only foam padding).

Feeding on the dead
The decision to eat the bodies of the dead was inevitable. There was nothing else. All of them eventually ate the grim offerings. It is a measure of the humility and dignity of the survivors that they never sought to hide what they had done. They knew what it meant.

Hope gradually revived with their feebly increasing strength. It was nearly extinguished on the night of 29 October, when an avalanche swept over the plane, bursting through the opening at the rear. Parrado, pinned rigid by the snow, wrote, 'I felt as if my body were encased in concrete. ... Snow packed into my mouth and nostrils and I began to suffocate.' Eight survivors were killed. With the plane buried under tons of snow, those still alive were unable to escape for three days. It took eight days to clear the rock-hard snow from the interior.

Survival lay in their own hands. On 15 and 18 November, two more survivors died. Parrado pushed for an all-out effort by a party of the strongest to head westwards to raise help. Like the others, he took hope from the last words of the copilot, who died on the first day, that they had been well to the west of the Andes when they crashed. If they could surmount the mountains immediately to their west, salvation was surely at hand.

Hero of the hour Fernando Parrado sipping water inside the plane's tail. It was Parrado's decision to trek westwards on 10 December that led to the rescue of the remaining 16 survivors.

The trek westwards
The copilot was wrong. But on 10 December Parrado, Canessa and Antonio Vizintín – equipped with little more than borrowed shirts, jerseys, and an improvised sleeping bag sewn with copper wire – set off.

After three days of intense slogging, they reached the summit of what they assumed was the last peak confronting them, confident the Andean lowlands would be spread out below. They saw instead a limitless series of snowcapped mountains. It was the moment of crisis.

Vizintín, who was struggling, was sent back; Parrado and Canessa continued. It was now march or die. It took seven days of stupefying work before they reached a river. On the other side, they saw a man on horseback. Parrado and Canessa were able to catch his attention. The next day he returned, having raised the alarm. Two days later all the remaining survivors were rescued by helicopter. It was a deliverance none could have expected.

The marathon of hope

Terry Fox was 18 when his cancerous right leg was amputated. He then decided to run across Canada to raise money to fight cancer. In 143 days he covered 5,342 km (3,339 miles). The cancer came back, this time in his lungs. Fox didn't survive, but his spirit endures. The Terry Fox Run has been held every year since then, not just in Canada but across the globe.

For a sports-mad 18-year-old, it is impossible to imagine the trauma of losing a leg. Sports, especially basketball, had dominated Terry Fox's life. He was only in his first year at Simon Fraser University in British Columbia, Canada, where he had already secured a place on the junior varsity basketball team, when what he thought was maybe a ligament or cartilage problem in his right knee was diagnosed as a malignant tumor. That was just one week after the problem first surfaced. Four days later the leg had been amputated. At the time, it was the only treatment known. His doctors estimated that his prospects of a full recovery were 50 to 70 percent.

Fox spent 16 months in the hospital. It was not just his own experience that changed him. It was the experiences of the other patients there. He saw suffering of a kind he hadn't realised existed. He saw hope; he saw despair. And he saw death. And he knew he wanted to make a difference.

'I like challenges. I don't give up.'

Thanks to Rick Hansen (*see* p. 242), Fox was already involved in sports again after joining a wheelchair basketball team. It reinforced an idea he had had since the day before the operation, when his high school basketball coach had shown him a magazine article about an amputee who had taken part in the New York City Marathon. He would run across Canada.

His rationale was simple, 'I like challenges. I don't give up. When I decided to do it, I knew I was going to go all

Welcome break Fox chats to a friend and supporter during a rare break. He set himself a punishing daily schedule while on the road.

Long road home By June 1980 Fox was regularly running in temperatures approaching 40°C (100°F), conditions that left him near prostrate. But they never stopped him. On 7 June he recorded his greatest single day's distance: 48 km (30 miles). In his words, 'I flew!'

out. There was no in-between.' He trained for 15 months, at first running in the dark so that no one would see him, gradually increasing the distances he was covering until, by the end, he was regularly running more than 30 km a day. The distance he covered – more than 5,000 km (5,000 miles) – was extraordinary. In the months leading up to Christmas in 1979, he trained for 101 days in a row, stopping for Christmas Day only because his mother begged him to take a break.

213 consecutive marathons

What he was planning would have been daunting for an able-bodied professional athlete. To run a single 41-km (26-mile) marathon is draining enough. Fox was going to

run the equivalent of 213 marathons. Quite apart from the cumulative exhaustion, there was the certainty of injury. But he had become immune to pain. He had trained until his stump was raw. And still he kept running. Blisters, too, he accepted with a shrug. 'I've seen people in so much pain,' he said. 'The little bit of pain I am going through is nothing.'

There was also the question of who would finance the run. Fox was not trying to make money for himself. His goal was to raise 23 million Canadian dollars for cancer research, one dollar for every Canadian. Yet he struggled from the start. The Canadian Cancer Society believed he couldn't raise even C$1 million. In the end, lack of money made Fox's entourage very small – a truck driven by long-

The legacy

Fox's forced conclusion of his run only intensified the fund-raising efforts. The
Canadian broadcasting network CTV arranged a telethon that raised C$10 million in
48 hours. The provinces of British Columbia and Ontario both pledged C$1 million.
Individuals across Canada continued to make donations large and small. By February
1981 Fox's goal of one dollar for every Canadian had been reached. C$24.17 million
had been raised.

More lastingly, the Terry Fox Run was established. Fox knew about it before he
died, even if he didn't live to see the first run in the autumn of 1981. Three hundred
thousand took part and raised C$3.5 million. The Terry Fox Run continues in many
countries. By 2007 C$400 million had been raised to fight cancer.

time friend Doug Alward to shepherd Fox and act as an all-around mobile headquarters cum home, along with Fox himself, running ever onwards.

At 2:45 P.M. on 12 April 1980, at St. John's, Newfoundland, on Canada's east coast, Fox symbolically dipped his artificial leg in the Atlantic and then set off on his 7,500-km (4,500-mile) road race. When he arrived home in Vancouver more than 200 days later, he planned to dip his leg in the Pacific.

A national phenomenon

Fox's first days were low key. Media interest was sporadic at best. Few people knew what he was attempting; fewer still seemed interested in the unknown curly-haired 21-year-old with the artificial leg, part loping, part hopping, part running his way along deserted roads.

Yet just nine days into the run at Gander, Newfoundland, things started to turn around. For the first time people lined the streets, clapping and cheering him on, pressing money into his hand. On 6 May he ran through Port-aux-Basques, the last Newfoundland town on his route. Its population of 10,000 had raised C$10,000 for his cause.

From obscurity Fox had suddenly become the biggest story in Canada. As he headed westwards, the crowds grew. 'He makes you believe in the human race again,' said one woman. Schools regularly shut when Fox passed through, the children not just lining the streets but running with him. The president of a hotel chain gave C$10,000 and then asked that 999 other Canadian companies do the same.

Not that it was ever easy. On narrow roads Fox found himself being run off the road by cars. In Quebec headwinds slowed progress to a crawl and left Fox drained. The wind 'zaps it right out of your body and head', he said. And there was the pain, 'the usual torture,' as Fox called it. On the other hand, the rewards were immense. Not just the money flooding in, but for Fox something more intangible. 'People thought I was going through hell. Maybe I was partly, but still I was doing what I wanted and a dream was coming true and that, above everything else, made it all worthwhile to me.'

A tragic finale

On 4 August in Ontario, Fox reached the halfway mark. He had now run 4,905 km (3,066 miles). Less than a month later, on 1 September, the Marathon of Hope came to an abrupt end. Fox ran 29 km (18 miles) and was approaching the town of Thunder Bay on the 143rd day of his run when he began coughing and felt a 'choking pain' in his neck and chest. He continued for a further 5 km (3 miles) before wearily climbing into the truck and asking Alward to take him to a hospital.

The diagnosis was swift; the cancer had returned. If an immediate return to Vancouver was inevitable, Fox still hoped he might finish his run. He didn't. On 28 June 1981, he slipped into a coma and died. A country mourned.

Terry Fox:
The Marathon of Hope,
12 April–1 September 1980

→ Terry Fox's route

LABRADOR

CANADA

ONTARIO

QUÉBEC

NEWFOUNDLAND
Gander
21 Apr.
(215 m/346 km)
Port-aux-Basques
St. John's
12 Apr.
start

1 Sep.
(3,331 m/
5,373 km)

18 Aug.
(3,038 m/
4,901 km)

15 June
(1,651 m/2,663 km)

20 May
(1,071 m/1,728 km)

Charlottestown
NEW
BRUNSWICK
PRINCE EDWARD I.
NOVA SCOTIA

4 Aug.
(2,747 m/
4,430 km)
Québec City

Thunder
Bay
Wawa

Sault Ste Marie
12 Aug.
(2,898 m/4,675 km)
Sudbury

Montréal

St John
31 May
(1,215 m/1,959 km)

Dartmouth
20 May
(851 m/1,373 km)

St. Lawrence

Gravenhurst
28 July
(2,575 m/4,153 km)

Ottawa

23 June
(1,809 m/2,917 km)

Atlantic Ocean

UNITED STATES
OF AMERICA

London
17 July
(2,353 m/3,795 km)

Toronto
11 July
(2,184 m/3,523 km)

1 July
(1,936 m/3,123 km)

New York

0   500 miles

The scale of what Fox attempted is frightening – to run across the world's second-largest country in a series of back-to-back marathons.

I don't feel that this is unfair. That's the thing about cancer. I'm not the only one, it happens all the time to people. I'm not special. This just intensifies what I did. It gives it more meaning. It'll inspire more people. I just wish people would realize that anything's possible if you try.

Terry Fox speaking to the press, Thunder Bay, Ontario, September 1, 1980

Touching the void: man versus mountain

JOE SIMPSON | **3–10 June 1985**

In May 1985 two English mountaineers, Joe Simpson and Simon Yates, set out to climb the unconquered west face of the 6,400-metre (21,000-ft) Siula Grande in the Peruvian Andes. They were cocky, young and brash (Simpson was 25, Yates 21). However, they were serious climbers, experienced beyond their years.

Simpson and Yates planned to tackle the mountain Alpine-style, climbing fast and hard, carrying their supplies with them. At their base camp they left the third member of the party, Richard Hawking, who had never climbed before. They found the climb much harder than they had anticipated, treacherously steep and icy. As they neared the 'spectacularly unsafe' summit, they encountered huge overhangs of powdery snow that threatened imminent collapse. It took almost a full day longer to reach the top than they had planned, forcing them to spend an extra night on the mountain, stretching already limited supplies.

If anything, the initial descent was more dangerous still, an intensely demanding narrow and unstable snow ridge running north from Siula Grande with precipitous falls to either side. Progress was slow. Another unscheduled night had to be spent near the summit. Nonetheless, once across the ridge, there was a relatively simple 915-metre (3,000-ft) descent to the glacier at the foot of the mountain.

Crippling pain

Struggling through snow sometimes up to their necks, they inched their way toward the head of the snowfield that swept to the glacier below. Simpson, leading, found the

Preparing for the climb At a height of 4,750 metres (10,000 ft) in the Andes under Siula Grande. Joe Simpson and Simon Yates spent two weeks here acclimatising and making reconnaissance trips before their attempt on the summit itself.

Falling to certain death? The moment in the movie *Touching the Void*, when Joe plummets down the ice cliff. Unable to hold on to his stricken friend any longer, and certain Simpson could not be saved, Simon Yates cuts the rope.

way blocked by a last obstacle, an ice cliff 7.5 metres (25 ft) high. He edged down it, anchoring himself with an ice axe. With a 'sharp cracking sound' the axe came loose. Simpson fell to the base of the cliff. His right tibia was forced up through his knee joint, and his ankle and heel were shattered.

The situation could hardly have been more clear-cut. Not only were the two climbers still almost 7,000 metres (20,000 ft) high, Simpson had fallen down the east side of the mountain, away from the slope leading to the glacier that held their base camp. To reach it meant an agonizing traverse back up the mountain, followed by a 180-metre (600-ft) descent to the snow slope itself. In mountaineering terms, the logic of the situation was unarguable – Simpson would die.

Nevertheless, not only did the two make it to the head of the snowfield through sheer guts, Yates then proposed

to lower Simpson the 915 metres (3,000 ft) to the glacier. The technique was simple – a series of bucket seats dug into the snow to support Yates as he lowered Simpson down the mountain with two 45-metre (150-ft) ropes tied together. Nine times they repeated the manoeuvre. Astonishingly, despite worsening weather, frostbite and Simpson's repeated terrifying spasms of pain as his leg snagged in the snow, Yates, though tiring rapidly, lowered his stricken companion almost to the glacier.

As night fell, Yates, unable either to see or hear Simpson at the end of the rope, inadvertently lowered him over an ice cliff. Pulling him back up was out of the question. All Yates could do was hang on as Simpson swung helplessly back and forth. For almost an hour Yates clung to the rope, his strength ebbing, the snow seat disintegrating. Then, exhausted and certain nothing could save Simpson, he cut the rope.

Crawled to camp Simpson was so weak he was unable to sit up. Yates (standing) insisted they leave at once to get to a hospital. Simpson had lost 19 kg (42 lb.).

Cheating death

Neither had known there was a crevasse directly below the cliff, though for Yates it scarcely mattered – Simpson was surely dead the moment the rope was cut. Instead, Simpson had plummeted to the ground and fell directly into the crevasse. Yates, haunted by guilt yet desperately rationalising his decision, made camp before continuing his descent the following morning.

Simpson spent the night 'weeping and cursing in impotent rage.' With the dawn the full horror of his predicament was clear. He had fallen 30 metres (100 ft), landing on a precarious snow bridge inside the crevasse. Above him he could see the crevasse mouth; below him there was only a 'pitch-black void'. Even fully fit, he could never have climbed out of the crevasse. As he put it later, 'You've got to keep on making decisions, even if they are the wrong decisions.' He decided to continue downwards, lowering himself on the rope into the void. He found himself in a huge ice cavern. He also found a way out, a snow cone 39 metres (130 ft) high leading to the roof of the cavern and the glacier above. Uninjured, it might have taken 10 minutes to climb. Now it took him 5 hours.

Simpson was numb with pain and severely dehydrated. He also had no food. Nonetheless, over the next two and a half days, he dragged himself – sometimes hopping, repeatedly falling in excruciat-

ing pain, mostly merely crawling – more than 9.6 km (6 miles) across the crevasse-studded glacier, down a further ice cliff and over boulder-strewn rubble toward the two small tents that constituted the base camp. As his struggles increased, his mind wandered. Interspersed with hallucinations, an absurd disco background accompanied him. Round and round, Boney M's *Brown Girl in the Ring* repeated itself in his head. As he neared the camp, he was increasingly tormented by the thought that Yates and Hawking already left. What, after all, was there to keep them there when it was clear that he was dead?

> ❝ He [Yates] knew logically that he did the only thing possible, but guilt is not logical. He actually said to me, "Jesus, if I'd just walked back for a couple of hours I'd have found you." And I remember saying to him, "Why would you do that? I was dead" ❞
>
> Joe Simpson, interview for the film *Touching the Void*

Struggling to camp

Two lakes marked the final stretch. From the lower the camp was normally a 10-minute walk. It took Simpson 5 hours to cover the distance, until long after midnight. By now he was perhaps as close to death as it is possible to be and still live. He realised, dimly, that he had reached the camp when he found himself sitting in human excrement. It was the crude latrine, hidden behind a rock, that he, Yates and Hawking used. It was now as much as he could do to howl into the night, pleading for help.

A light came on in the tent, glowing red and green, as Hawking and Yates struggled awake. In his delirium Simpson took it for a spaceship. Utter hallucinatory exhaustion, combined with overwhelming relief when he realised that the others were still there, reduced him to a state of continuous sobbing hysteria.

Simpson has never been an easy man. He readily admits to an 'anarchic, aggressive and abrasive streak.' Many years later he wrote of 'the sense of invincibility' that drove him in his youth. It was precisely this stubbornness that saw him live on Siula Grande when, by all mountaineering logic, his death was a certainty.

Return to civilisation

Getting Simpson to a hospital was vital. This was easier said than done. Simpson was so weak he was unable even to sit up. He later discovered he had lost 19 kg (42 lb.). He had also had only three hours' sleep since arriving at the camp. He pleaded to be allowed to stay. Yates, who had seen the extent of Simpson's injuries, was adamant they leave at once.

It was two days to the nearest town. Simpson riding on a mule, the others walking (pictured above) the journey 'a blur of exhaustion and pain'. From there it was a jolting 128 km (80 miles) in a hired truck with a drunken driver to Lima. 'I no longer had the strength or desperation to cope with this added torment', wrote Simpson.

Once in the hospital it took two days – during which he was given no food, painkillers or antibiotics – to confirm Simpson's insurance was valid before the hospital would agree to treat him.

Simpson later wrote a prizewinning book about his experience, *Touching the Void*, subsequently made into a movie. Today he is a motivational speaker and environmental campaigner.

Man in motion

Canadian Rick Hansen was 15 in 1972 when he broke his back. It left him paralysed from the waist down. His response was remarkable – to make himself one of the world's leading disabled athletes. In 1985 his goal became more audacious – to travel around the world in a wheelchair to raise money for spinal-injury research. The 40,000-km (25,000-mile) trip took him more than two years.

Between 1979 and 1984 Rick Hansen won 19 international wheelchair marathons and 19 gold medals in track meets for the disabled across the world. In 1983 he was cowinner – with Wayne Gretzky – of Canada's Outstanding Athlete of the Year award.

The following year, he represented Canada at the Los Angeles Olympics. By any measure, he was a world-class athlete.

These achievements placed Hansen at the forefront of the growth in sports for the disabled, a movement designed to show that disability was no barrier to sports, more particularly that the disabled could have dreams as great as those of any able-bodied athlete. But it wasn't enough for Hansen. Partly inspired by fellow Canadian Terry Fox (*see* p. 234), in part determined to raise awareness of spinal injuries, Hansen set his sights higher – to circle the globe.

Wheeling around the world

From the beginning, there were problems. It wasn't just the physical challenge – as his physiotherapist (and later wife), Amanda Reid, put it: 'Upper arms are not meant to be your prime form of motion.' The logistical hurdles were many and expensive. Hansen began an exhausting round of fundraising.

But he needed backup. He assembled a small team who lived in a motor home crammed with spare equipment. Their job was to look after Hansen, check the route, liaise with authorities and organise promotional events.

The start in Vancouver was unpromising. Everyone was tired, media interest was lukewarm and money was still short. The first leg lasted until June and covered 7,665 km (4,764 miles) south to California, then east to Florida. The two greatest difficulties were obvious –

A disastrous departure Not long into the journey the team drove the motor home into a low tunnel, smashing the box containing Hansen's only spare wheelchair.

The tour in figures During the course of the tour – which lasted 2 years, 2 months and 2 days – Rick visited 34 countries and spent 470 days wheeling at an average daily distance of 85 km (53 miles). During this time he suffered 126 flat tyres and wore out 94 gloves.

extreme weather and injury, the inevitable result of wheeling eight hours a day.

The problems were compounded on the second leg, across Europe, by bad weather and a virus that left Hansen drained. But like the weather, his spirits revived, and in five months he covered 9,525 km (5,920 miles), visiting 20 countries. Nonetheless, by early December, in Greece, he had to be admitted to a hospital for extreme exhaustion.

After a brief tour of the Middle East, the team flew to New Zealand. They spent three months there and in Australia, covering 4,670 km (2,902 miles). They then flew to China, where Hansen wheeled along the Great Wall. The Asian leg ended in Japan on 16 June.

The team now returned to the United States, heading north up the East Coast from Florida and returning to Canada on 24 August.

Hansen had planned that the total length of his journey would be 40,075 km (24,901 miles) – the circumference of the globe – so the final Canadian leg was artificially extended. Despite bitterly cold midwinter weather in

> ❝ The goal you set must be challenging. At the same time, it should be realistic and attainable, not impossible to reach. It should be challenging enough to make you stretch, but not so far that you break. ❞
>
> Nick Hansen

central Canada, Hansen's fame began to grow rapidly. When he reached Vancouver on 23 May, he was not just the most famous person in Canada or even the most admired. He was the most loved.

Left for dead

On 10 May 1996, four expeditions were attempting to reach the summit of Mount Everest. During a period of 36 hours, eight climbers died, victims of a sudden storm. The figure should have been nine. But a 49-year-old Texan, Beck Weathers, severely frostbitten and rendered near blind by the altitude, not only survived 39 hours with no shelter, but made his way back to camp unaided.

The 12 deaths on Mount Everest in May 1996 – in addition to the eight who died on 10 and 11 May, four other climbers died in accidents – sparked a debate about the wisdom of letting unprecedented numbers of climbers tackle the mountain. Not only were the climbers turning a pristine wilderness into 'the world's highest junkyard', but it seemed very risky to allow enthusiastic but inexperienced climbers to be escorted to the top by professional guides.

Dangerous business

Everest is hazardous enough for experienced climbers with guides. Novices, no matter how much they are willing to pay their guides, present serious risks to their party and the guides. The price for tackling Everest in 1996 was as high as $65,000. Paying that kind of money, climbers might well feel they have a right to the summit even if they don't have the skills or fitness to achieve it.

These criticisms are hard to refute. But Rob Hall, a 35-year-old New Zealander, felt differently in 1996. His company, Adventure Consultants, prided itself on its professionalism and its commitment to safety. Hall's record was excellent. He had made eight trips to Everest, four times reaching the summit. Moreover, between 1990 and 1995, he had guided 39 people to the top – and brought them all down safely.

And it was with Hall that Beck Weathers had signed up. Weathers, a doctor from Dallas, Texas, was not inexperienced. Climbing gave purpose to his life and helped him deal with a lifelong depression. The tougher the challenge, the better Weathers coped with his inner angst. By the time he came to tackle Everest in 1996, he

Caught on film Filmmakers were in the process of shooting a documentary, *Everest*, when they encountered some of the stricken climbers and came to their aid. This is a still from the film.

Hall and Fischer

Both Rob Hall (front-row centre) and Scott Fischer (to Hall's right) were among those who died on Everest in May 1996. Uncertainty still surrounds their deaths. Hall in particular made it an absolute rule that no climber – Sherpa or client – should continue up to the summit after 2:00 P.M., the last possible turnaround time if they were to make it down again before nightfall. As he put it himself, 'With enough determination, any bloody idiot can get up this hill. The trick is to get back down alive.' Yet at 3:00 P.M. on 10 May, Hall was still at the summit with a client, a Seattle postal worker named Doug Hansen, who would also die.

The death of Fischer is equally curious. On 10 May 1996, for the first time, he appeared unable to cope with the severe oxygen deprivation met during any attempt on Everest. When Jon Krakauer, descending, passed Fischer still plodding summit-wards at about 2:00 P.M., he was struck by how lethargic Fischer seemed. Fischer's attempt to laugh it off – 'Just dragging ass a little today for some reason. No big deal' – did not convince. Ironically, all six of his clients not only reached the summit, they all survived the trip down as well.

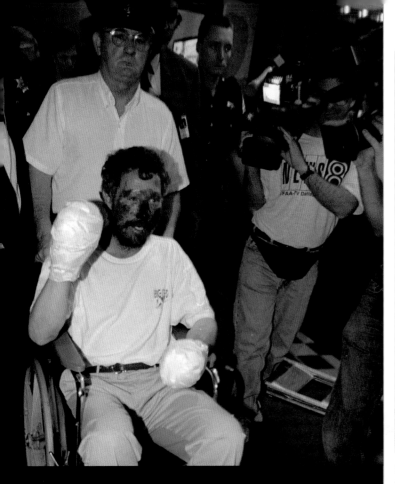

Aftermath

When Weathers arrived at Camp 4, it was assumed that his death was inevitable. Though he was put in a tent with a hot-water bottle, no one expected him to emerge from it alive. He was then effectively abandoned – again. The first person to visit him the following day expected to find a corpse. In fact, for nearly three hours Weathers had been desperately calling for help, his feeble cries drowned by the noise of the wind.

It seems callous, but in the extreme conditions of high-altitude mountaineering, it is understandable. Even the strongest members of the party were at the limit of their endurance. Later, doctors at the base camp said that Weathers had the worst case of frostbite any had seen. His right hand, subsequently amputated, had frozen solid. His left hand, all but the thumb of which was also amputated, was almost as bad. He also lost almost his whole nose. Weathers is pictured above arriving back in Texas on 16 May.

Death mountain The front cover of the May 1996 issue of *Time* magazine says it all.

had climbed all but two of the so-called Seven Summits, the highest peaks in each of the world's continents.

Early on 8 May Hall's party – three professional guides, four Sherpas or native guides and eight clients – reached Camp 3, which is 7,315 metres (24,000 ft) high. Also at Camp 3 was an American party of three professional guides, five Sherpas and six clients led by Scott Fischer, an experienced 40-year-old, and a small party from Taiwan. Early that morning, one of the Taiwanese climbers fell headfirst into a crevasse. He was

❝ I was lying on my back in the ice. It was colder than anything you can believe. I figured I had three or four hours to live. All I knew was that, so long as my legs would run and I could stand up, I was going to keep moving toward the camp. ❞

Beck Weathers, from his book, *Left for Dead*

taken back down the mountain, apparently unharmed. That afternoon, however, he died.

Tragedy after Camp 4

The same evening, the climbers had reached Camp 4 on the snowfield known as the South Col, 7,925 metres (26,000 ft) up. By midnight they began their final attempts on the summit. Weathers knew almost at once he wouldn't make it. The extreme altitude had seriously exacerbated an existing eye condition, and he could see no more than 1 metre (3 or 4 ft) in front of him. Nonetheless, he continued upwards to the Balcony, an isolated snow ridge 8,380 metres (27,500 ft) high. There, reluctantly, he told Hall what had happened.

Hall wanted to send him back to Camp 4 at once with a Sherpa. Weathers argued that with daylight his vision might improve. Hall agreed to wait half an hour. After that time, Weathers's eyes were no better, and it was agreed that he was to stay at the Balcony and join the rest of the party as they made their way down. It was to be a long wait.

'Shivering violently'

It wasn't until about 4:00 P.M. that the first of Hall's party reached Weathers. It was Jon Krakauer, a journalist, who had reached the summit shortly after 1:00 P.M. By now Weathers had been waiting almost 10 hours. Krakauer reported him as 'shivering violently'. But rather than going back with Krakauer, Weathers waited until the first of Hall's guides reached him. This was an Australian, Mike Groom, helping another of Hall's clients, a Japanese woman named Yasuko Namba, who was rapidly getting weaker.

They were met by six members of Scott's party – a guide, Neal Beidleman, and five clients, all of whom had reached the summit. Travelling together, they continued towards Camp 4.

The weather that day had been flawless. Now it was rapidly worsening. By nightfall the wind was gusting at 110 km/h (70 mph) and the temperature plummeting. With visibility reduced to feet only, the party became hopelessly lost. They more or less bumped into two Sherpas, equally lost. By 10:00 P.M. they had no option but to stop, huddling together, oxygen exhausted, all fading alarmingly. They didn't know it, but they were only 320 metres (350 yards) from the camp.

At midnight the weather had cleared enough for the guides, the Sherpas and two of the clients to try again to

Fateful end Among Everest's casualties in May 1996 were three Indian climbers. 'Green Boot', as he is brutally known, was among them.

find the camp. Of the others, four – including Namba and Weathers – were prostrate, unable to continue, apparently near death. It was obvious they would have to be left behind, and the remaining climber, Tim Madsen, volunteered to stay with them.

Left on the mountain

The descending party found the camp and immediately collapsed into their tents. Meanwhile, an extraordinary solo rescue of three of the stranded climbers was made by another of Fischer's guides, Anatoli Boukreev. He didn't bother with Namba, assuming she was dead, and he claims never even to have seen Weathers.

At first light Canadian doctor Stuart Hutchison and four Sherpas returned to Namba and Weathers. Incredibly, Hutchison found them alive, but it was clear they could not live much longer. The safety of the rest of the party dictated that these patients be left on the mountain. As Krakauer wrote, 'Nobody doubted it was the correct thing to do.' It was the logic of survival at high altitudes.

At 4:30 P.M. a figure stumbled into the camp, right arm held stiffly in front of him. It was Weathers. His completely unexpected survival he ascribes to a 'vision' of his family in Texas, one 'powerful enough to rewire my mind'. Yasuko Namba never made it.

Race for survival

On Christmas Day 1996 the 18-metre (60-ft) yacht *Algimouss* was a waterlogged hulk deep in the Southern Ocean. Harnessed to what was left of its mast was a 28-year-old French sailor, Raphael Dinelli. He was taking part in the Vendée Globe, a nonstop round-the-world race for single-handers. In an astonishing feat of seamanship, he was rescued two days later by a fellow competitor, Briton Pete Goss.

Raphael Dinelli shouldn't really have been in the Vendée Globe at all. All the competitors had to complete a 3,200-km (2,000-mile) proving voyage. Dinelli, short of money, rushing to get his boat ready, never had time. Not that this deterred him. When the 15-strong fleet left France in early November 1996, Dinelli was among them – an unofficial sixteenth competitor, affectionately dubbed the Little Pirate by the French media.

Predictably, as the frontrunners stretched away, Dinelli found himself towards the rear of the fleet. Deep in the Southern Ocean, 2,400 km (1,500 miles) southwest of Australia, disaster struck. A gale – savage even by the standards of this desolate region, the wind gusting at 130 km/h (80 mph), the seas over 18 metres (60 ft) – built up. It was survival sailing.

Algimouss was catapulted off a giant wave and flung upside down. It remained inverted for more than three hours, filling with water after the boom shattered a window and the mast punched a table-sized hole in the deck. The mast was then wrenched off, breaking a few feet from its base. Slowly the boat righted itself. It was as much as Dinelli

End of the ordeal Moments after docking at the end of the race on 23 February 1997, Goss poses (second right) with his wife, Tracey, and to his right, Dinelli and his fiancée, Virginie.

could manage to clamber outside and strap himself to the shattered remains of the mast.

Out of communication

All the boats in the race carried a satellite communication system that automatically broadcast a Mayday call and gave its precise position. It was a major step forward in safety at sea. But knowing where a boat was didn't mean being able to reach it. In Dinelli's case hundreds of miles from the nearest shipping lanes and just as far beyond the reach of conventional rescue services, his only potential rescuers were his fellow competitors.

The nearest, Belgian Patrick de Radiques, was 96 km (60 miles) away. With his electricity out, he never even heard the Mayday. That left Pete Goss on his 15-metre (50-ft) *Aqua Quorum*, 260 km (160 miles) to the east. Goss had been severely battered by the same storm. His boat had been knocked over several times; there was 30 cm (1 ft) of water in the cabin. Even with only a scrap of sail set, he was swooping down waves at nearly 30 knots, teetering on the verge of disaster. Now he had to turn around and sail against a hurricane-force wind to find Dinelli.

> ❝ It was that simple; the decision had been made for me a long time ago by a tradition of the sea. When someone is in trouble you help. ❞
>
> Pete Goss, from his book *Close to the Wind*

Help at hand

It took him almost two days, during which *Aqua Quorum* received a battering violent enough to break two of the mounts holding the generator. Its designers, anxiously following events in Europe, were certain the boat would break up. At the height of the storm, Goss estimated that at times *Aqua Quorum* was being pushed sideways at 10 knots.

Dinelli, meanwhile, had reconciled himself to death. When Goss reached him, the Frenchman – hypothermic, partly frostbitten and tormented by thirst – was probably just hours from dying. Once Goss had heaved him from the mast he used as a life raft, the Frenchman was unable to move. Goss had to drag him heels first into the cockpit and then wrestle him down below. He was, said Goss, 'The best Christmas present I have ever had.'

Triumph – and disaster

Dinelli was not the only competitor in the 1996–1997 Vendée Globe to lose his boat. On 4 January 1997, veteran British sailor Tony Bullimore and Frenchman Thierry Dubois (pictured above) were battling the same hurricane-force storm, sailing within 64 km (40 miles) of each other. Then the keel dropped off Bullimore's boat, *Exide Challenge*, which immediately flipped over. Dubois's yacht, *Pour Amnesty International*, was rolled through 360 degrees, breaking the mast. The boat then rolled over again, leaving the Frenchman clinging to the hull, wedged against the rudder. Bullimore and Dubois were both picked up by Australian rescue services – Bullimore after five days, during which one of his fingers had been crushed, forcing him to amputate what remained of it with a penknife. The fee, borne jointly by the Australian navy and air force, was estimated at several million Australian dollars.

On 7 January, at the head of the fleet, *PRB*, sailed by Frenchwoman Isabelle Autissier – one of only two women in the race – was knocked down six times. In the same storm Canadian Gerry Roufs, an experienced sailor, disappeared probably after falling overboard. Several months later his boat, *Groupe LG2*, was washed up on the coast of Chile.

Index

Picture credits